P9-EDF-630

Of Blood and Hope

Of Blood and Hope

SAMUEL PISAR

LITTLE, BROWN AND COMPANY BOSTON TORONTO

COPYRIGHT © 1979 BY SAMUEL PISAR
ENGLISH-LANGUAGE VERSION COPYRIGHT © 1980 BY AUCTOR PUBLISHING B.V.
ALL RIGHTS RESERVED. NO PART OF THIS BOOK MAY BE REPRODUCED IN ANY FORM OR BY ANY ELECTRONIC OR MECHANICAL MEANS INCLUDING INFORMATION STORAGE AND RETRIEVAL SYSTEMS WITHOUT PERMISSION IN WRITING FROM THE PUBLISHER, EXCEPT BY A REVIEWER WHO MAY QUOTE BRIEF PASSAGES IN A REVIEW.

LIBRARY OF CONGRESS CATALOG CARD NO. 80-10696

FIRST ENGLISH-LANGUAGE EDITION

Second Printing

The author is grateful to Yevgeni Yevtushenko and E. P. Dutton for permission to quote lines from "Babi Yar" by Yevgeni Yevtushenko, as translated by Samuel Pisar.

Photograph of the author with daughter Leah and Servan-Schreiber by Franklin Servan-Schreiber; with Henry Kissinger by Patricia Vincente Alisau, *The News;* with wife Judith, and with daughters Helaina and Alexandra by Claude Azoulay, *Paris-Match;* with Giscard d'Estaing and Gierek by Bernard Charlon, *L'Express*.

MV

Published simulanteously in Canada
by Little, Brown & Company (Canada) Limited

PRINTED IN THE UNITED STATES OF AMERICA

For my mother and father

Mine is yesterday, I know tomorrow.

—Papyrus, Ptolemaic Dynasty

Contents

Illustrations

Prologue
Fire from the Ashes

Who among us can dwell with the devouring fire.
— Isaiah

STANDING frozen like a statue before the stilled assemblage of presidents, ministers, generals, ambassadors, and other dignitaries, I feel as though my wounds are opening again. It takes the sight of my wife, Judith — her composure, her beauty in these hideous surroundings — to break the trance and reassure me that I am well and free, with a loving family and an unthreatened hold on life.

The President of France, at my right, speaks slowly, hesitantly: "Here, in this peaceful landscape, the ship of mankind went under. . . . We must teach the youth of the world the horror of that horror."

On my left, the leader of Poland stands stiffly at attention. For a brief moment, democrats and communists, we are united by the same mute pain.

"Let us not forget that it was in these death camps that East and West first met. The same struggle enabled the Soviet army to liberate Auschwitz as the American army liberated Dachau."

Yes, I see it again: a huge tank with a strange white star lumbering across a clearing, a scared kid jumping out of his hiding place, running through machine-gun fire toward the cannon pointed at his chest; yelling at the top of his wasted lungs the few words of English his mother had taught him: "*God Bless America*"; and a tall, black, helmeted savior pulling him down the hatch to safety and to freedom. Yes, I want to shout it out, in a forest near Dachau, after Auschwitz, after Maidanek, after hell, the American army liberated *me*.

The barracks, the chimneys, the barbed wire — it's all still here, preserved, unchanged. But is it really me standing here today, am I really among friends? Was it really me, that skeletal youngster with shaved head and sunken eyes, trying to hold on, in this godforsaken place, to a weak flicker of life? Could this strange odyssey have taken only one lifetime?

"As one of the youngest survivors of Auschwitz, who is here with us today, has said, 'Building bridges across the gulf that divides us is a difficult task. But our common interest in survival requires that the process go on.' "

I recognize the words, for they are mine. With a start I realize that the President has finished. A heavy silence presses down upon us. But the hypnotic trance that overpowered me a moment earlier catches me again. In the pale sunlight, hazy images dance before my eyes. The dark business suits blur into the prison garb that once covered me and my comrades behind this gate with its obscene slogan: WORK BRINGS FREEDOM. The crowd of dignitaries around me is a gathering of skeletons in skin. We are on the central square, lined up by our guards for the ritual head count, back in the camps and the gulags.

I must get hold of myself. Because of all those television cameras, millions are watching. In my hand I clutch a brief address written in French. My lips move silently to the cadence of the Kaddish, the Hebrews' ancient prayer for the dead.

"To return at your side, Mr. President, to this altar of the Holocaust, where as a boy I died so many deaths and lived so many tortures and humiliations — where all I ever loved was reduced to cinders — is an experience that wrenches the soul. But it is also a journey from tragedy to triumph.

"From here we speak to generations, to nations, to creeds, to black and white, to rich and poor, to young and old. For the spot on which we stand is the deepest wound ever inflicted upon human civilization, the place where grim reality eclipsed Dante's vision of hell. On this I bear you the testimony of a rare survivor, perhaps the youngest survivor of all."

Can I go on? Unspeakable reminiscences flood my mind in these strangely familiar surroundings. But one heartbreaking image stands out. That is the only one about which I must force myself to say a word.

"Near those machine-gun towers, there once sat and played a most remarkable symphony orchestra. It was made up of virtuosos from Warsaw and Paris, from Kiev and Oslo, from Budapest and Rome.

The precious violins they brought along on their last journey were signed by Stradivari and Guarneri and Amati. To accompany the daily hangings and shootings, while the furnaces over there belched fire and smoke, these gentle musicians were ordered to play Mozart, the Mozart you and I adore.

"If such horrors seem relevant today, it is because we dare not forget that the past can also be prologue, that amidst the ashes of Auschwitz we can discern a specter of doomsday, a warning to mankind of what might still lie ahead. It is to this barbed-wire fence, therefore, that man must come, in emulation of your example, to bow his head and meditate on peace, on justice, on tolerance, on human rights, on new moral values that can reclaim the world's alienated youth.

"Mr. President, in this cursed and sacred place you face your greatest audience. Here you stand in the presence of millions of innocent souls. In their name, and with the authority of the number engraved on my arm, I say to you that if they could speak, they would cry out: 'Never again!' "

It is over. But I feel drained, dissatisfied. I have been unable to convey in words the full force of my fear that the irrational, the madness I lived in my body and soul as a teenager on this bloodiest killing ground of the century, is creeping back upon us in many irresistible, insidious forms and pushing us toward untold holocausts on a world scale.

❖ ❖ ❖

When in the summer of 1975 Giscard d'Estaing, with whom I had enjoyed a long relationship, invited me to accompany him on a pilgrimage to Auschwitz, I was shaken. In our conversations no allusion was ever made to the gruesome events of my childhood, nor to the fact that his father-in-law had perished at Buchenwald. After I became a free man, at the age of sixteen, and began my slow and difficult climb back to life, I turned away from all that. A normal, healthy, creative existence — this would be my vengeance, my victory over the past.

I had always refused to return to those places where I saw my world, my people, my family, my school friends, my identity, systematically destroyed, where I myself barely escaped physical obliteration as one of the subhumans of the Third Reich. Just a short time earlier when I arrived in Warsaw as the American chairman of an international conference on economic cooperation, the Polish government suggested that I lay a wreath at the Auschwitz memorial. Respectfully, but without hesitation, I declined, asking instead to be taken to a concert at Chopin's birthplace.

Yet as I observed shock wave after shock wave thrusting mankind toward new disasters, America herself falling into disarray, her white star that gave me freedom soiled in a senseless war, her youth in rebellion, her institutions vulnerable, her economy fragile; as I observed a President assassinated, another unable to govern, a third chased from office, confidence in political leadership undermined; as I observed this theater of the absurd, the feeling mounted within me that the past was again becoming present.

Increasingly, I found myself drawing on that past for insights into why my world had once collapsed, into how my children's world could be preserved.

Somehow it became more and more difficult for me to nurse the comforting illusion that Hitler was a mere aberration, an accident of history; that Germany had gone momentarily mad. The truth was more chilling. Hitler had come to power through the normal democratic process. One of the most enlightened nations on earth, the nation that gave the world Gutenberg, Goethe, and Beethoven, willingly had laid at his feet an unlimited mandate to govern. He was the progeny of economic depression, of deep unemployment, and of rampant inflation. Auschwitz was the logical outcome of these upheavals and of the venomous hatreds they inevitably engender.

Suddenly, I understood that I had to revisit my nightmare, to come to terms with it, so I could draw its poison and learn to use it as a warning and a cure. And that meant that a reincarnated Samuel Pisar, clothed snugly in his respectable attire of international lawyer, scholar, American citizen, had to step into the light and avow that once, not so long ago, he had crawled in the pain, the filth, and the degradation of the factories of death.

It was hard, but it had to be done. So I went to confront my horror-filled past. I realize now that I was in search of something to help me, and others, to understand the present and, more important, the grave dangers ahead.

It is curious how a connection, once made, can develop imperceptibly in your psyche, until one day you stop and wonder how it was that you had never understood what you see so clearly now. Since that pilgrimage, my perception of the ominous problems that assail the world today has been sharpened by long-suppressed memories of what I experienced as a youth. The nature of these problems, which, without promise of solution, threaten to doom us all, are no different from what I faced and managed to survive.

The fear, the despair, the suffering, the mounting anger at the root of the international issues that are debated so bloodlessly and impersonally by myriad diplomats, economists, and politicians, and that endanger what remains of our freedom and of peace — I feel them in my bones. All of them were present in the ugly microcosm into which I was thrown.

The energy crisis? An alarming economic reality, to be sure, but is it not primarily a drama for the rich? The inability of the Western consumer to control his insatiable appetite for oil at a level his country can afford — an adjustment that would do little more than cut down on traffic jams and lower the temperature in overheated apartments — is seen and felt differently by one who had to live through winter after bitter winter without light, without heat, with hardly any coverings or clothes.

Terrorism? The methods of its current practitioners scarcely differ from the ground rules that prevailed in the ghettos and the camps, where hostages were taken and shot routinely for no other reason than to sow panic and fear. To our hangmen, the slightest deviance, the smallest gesture that departed from routine, seemed a threat to the established order and had to be punished by death. Among the prisoners themselves, the reign of terror could be just as pitiless — whether a product of pure sadism, or somehow justified by the need to hang on.

Hunger? The gnawing starvation that sucks the will out of two-thirds of mankind and subjects whole continents to political and social convulsions is no abstraction to one who, like me, had to grasp at morsels in a frenzy to endure. How to convey to people whose garbage cans are filled with edible food the constant, obsessive, hallucinating search for something to eat, that extinguishes the senses and the mind?

Unemployment? Sending people to camps was a logical and effective way to solve this problem. When we were not worked to exhaustion and death, like an expendable raw material, we performed for hours, before members of the Master Race, an elaborate "caps off" exercise; we marched in place to test the durability of their army boots and our aching feet; falling out of step meant a blow that could crack open one's skull.

Pollution? Health care? For years, every day and every night we lived in filth, promiscuity, and stench, packed into crowded barracks with other extenuated human beings, like cattle waiting our turn to be processed in the slaughterhouse. Without hygiene, without drugs, without doctors, our sole contact with the world of medicine was the prospect of becoming guinea pigs for Dr. Josef Mengele, the "Angel of Death," and the other "scientists" who experimented on helpless victims.

Human rights? I witnessed innocents by the thousand condemned to execution on the spot; families dismembered; girls raped; women, children, and old people sent to the ovens; able-bodied men placed in bondage, their death merely deferred. Habeas corpus, trial by jury, the right of appeal, and all the other guarantees of our Constitution and our laws are like sacred talismans to me. Every act of arbitrary injustice conjures up in my mind the road back to the abyss.

The Third World? The conviction that we must come to see the peoples of the underprivileged countries as brothers to be succored in the name of common humanity, not as faceless masses best left to founder in their own misery; the conviction that only through such a new vision, translated into bolder policies of trade and assistance, can the great democracies survive the coming era of global shortages without fatal political damage to themselves — such convictions come easily to a man who himself was once among the disinherited and the despised.

Prosperity? After several centuries of economic domination, we in the West are faced with a bitter new truth. We are no longer masters, sahibs, the lords of this earth. Other peoples, long regarded as inferior, are beginning to surpass us. The millions of Asia, and increasingly of other continents, are proving themselves more industrious, more inventive, more productive, and far less vulnerable to need and privation. Will the wheel of fortune that turns slowly and inexorably through time soon transform us into the "underdeveloped" nations of the future?

Dictatorship? Militarism? From continent to continent I recognize the clatter of the boots. Fate saw fit to subject me, at the most tender age, not to one, but two tyrants, Hitler and Stalin, as their armies trampled through my hometown, back and forth. I came to know — with my family — exile, martial law, daily curfews, and the dreaded midnight knock on the door. The only freedoms of assembly, association, and free speech I enjoyed were the macabre roll call at dawn and at dusk, and the right to shout "Present."

Democracy? Does it still have the will to survive or does it merely throw off a few more brilliant sparks, like a dead star flaring up briefly at the end of its journey? The shocks that buffet our societies and threaten to dislocate our economies into careening inflation or bottomless depression once again could tempt well-meaning but desperate majorities to surrender political power to totalitarian leaders. We might then be governed by the same brand of despotic "law and order" that the mayor of Moscow, a city surely "peaceful," described to me with undisguised pride at a private dinner at his sumptuous home.

And peace? I know how peace could come to be viewed as a less than desirable condition. War can reshuffle the cards, sweep away the whole mess of unbearable, seemingly insoluble problems; it can freeze all claims, all debts, all disputes. When the war is over one can make a fresh start: a new vitality can be injected into the economic system; shattered towns and industries can be rebuilt and modernized; and entrepreneurs with energy and daring will always manage to start new careers and generate new wealth.

A society does not have to go mad for its representatives to adopt policies of madness. A new flood of events, unexpected, alarming, and badly understood, can sweep open the doors of power to men and forces whose true nature is not recognized in time. Once installed, the new rulers generate a momentum for paranoia too great for the country to withstand; soon they are in control. That is what happened to Germany with Hitler. Can it conceivably happen in America?

I could go on. At every turn, the essence of these dangers is clarified for me by insights drawn from personal experience, by visions seen through the prism of my peculiar life.

And the most overwhelming danger is the one that has the most direct link with what I barely managed to survive — the arms race. The insensate competition among the major powers in the endless sale of weapons to emerging countries and the insane upward spiral of the nuclear and conventional arsenal of the Soviet Union together loom before my eyes as gigantic gas chambers of the future.

Auschwitz was a monument to logic, once the Nazi imperative to clear the world of Jews and other "inferior" peoples was accepted as a rational aim. So is the growing stockpile of weapons on land, in space, and under the sea, once one accepts the view, in the West or the East, that the leaders of the other side are reckless and foolhardy men ready to gamble on national suicide for the prize of world domination. I do not accept that view; the wisest Americans and Russians I know don't accept it; yet the feverish arms race, stimulated at each phase by new technological breakthroughs, goes on and on.

We stand poised for destruction. Within hours the smallest conflict can turn into a massive conflagration that will take the lives of millions. As if to insure that we have adequate means for "a final solution," we are busy developing the science of chemical warfare, as well. The Nazis engaged in intensive research to find the gas most deadly and least costly per human being. Today we have resumed their work, except this time the madness is called "deterrence."

In Treblinka, Maidanek, and Auschwitz the innocent victims who were herded into the gas chambers — I saw it with my own eyes — had but three minutes to live once the doors were locked. Somehow they found sufficient time and strength to dig their fingernails into the walls and scratch the words "Never forget!"

Have we already forgotten?

Inevitably, my intuitive fear that this irrational state of affairs will carry us to new disasters is fed by the demented horror of what I knew and lived firsthand.

Perhaps a man who cheated death the way I did, and learned to savor the intoxicating luxury of freedom, is fated to live his days minus an outer skin. But sometimes, at moments of dark premonition, I see in the images of political helplessness, hysterical mobs, religious fanaticism, refugee boats, and mushroom clouds the vision of a global Auschwitz. At such times, against my profound commitment to calm reason, against my love of life, against my confidence in man, I feel as though in that indescribable period when a man-made typhoon shattered my world, my existence, and my mind, and took me lower than the slaves of ancient Egypt and Babylon, I experienced what is yet to come.

Having lived through a pilot project for the destruction of humanity, I know that the unthinkable is possible, and that it is at least as realistic to expect of man the worst as it is to expect the best. I have no packaged program of remedies, but I have an enhanced perception of perils. Must everyone have an Auschwitz first? Or can those who have experienced only normal life also understand that the sacrifices required to cope with some of the world's problems are much less than they suppose; but that the dangers involved in ignoring any of them are infinitely greater than they imagine.

Can one transmit — can I? — the true meanings of these dangers, their dreadful immediacy, for our world? And what it takes — the attitude of mind and effort of will — to adapt, and to overcome?

As I write these lines in the blessed countryside of New England, where democracy and prosperity have been taken so long for granted, where I was once reborn and remade to think and to love — as I relive the time when history chewed me up and spat me out at the most violent crossroads of this century, I feel my once highly developed instincts coming back to life, instincts that are part of the eternal struggle for survival.

I have never had the slightest wish to lick the long-healed wounds of my youth. If I have decided now to let my memory speak, to describe the blood, the tears, the pain, the joys of friendship and knowledge that have nourished my faith in mankind's ability to endure and create, it is because our idealistic and confused youth of today need to know. They need to arm themselves against the tragedies, the hypocrisies, the false gods of history.

It is our children that I have in mind as I write this book, a book that is not about the past, but about the future, a future that belongs to them.

I

Collapse of a World

Man is a pliable animal, a being who gets accustomed to everything.
— Dostoevski

1

WE were ecstatic, my classmates and I, when we heard in 1938 that the black boxer Joe Louis had knocked out the Nazi Max Schmeling for the heavyweight championship of the world. So much for the "Master Race!"

Although only eight or nine, we already saw things in political terms, with a precociousness born of the troubled times in which we lived and the special nature of our native city.

Bialystok, before the war, with its 120,000 inhabitants, was the same vibrant center of Jewish cultural life it had been for almost three centuries and, as the second biggest textile supplier in Poland, a bustling commercial crossroads. Political movements, associated with reform socialism, Zionism, and revolutionary labor, mingled and vied with the teaching of the Torah in the city's communal life. The predominantly Jewish population lived more or less peacefully with the fifty thousand Poles, Russians, and Ukrainians in their midst. The political winds that had unfurled the swastika over Nazi Germany were felt more keenly among us than in most of the great world outside.

At school, we repeated debates heard in our homes, as though such preoccupations were normal at our age. In geography class we talked about Asia and the endless border battles between the Chinese and the Japanese, and about Africa and the courage of Emperor Haile Selassie in resisting Mussolini's invasion of Abyssinia. We talked about local heroes who had volunteered to fight fascism in Spain and about the older boys and girls from our school who emigrated to Palestine to live and till the earth on a kibbutz.

At the movies we stared in disbelief at newsreels showing helmeted

Nazi soldiers goose-stepping into the Ruhr, then Vienna, then Prague, and masses of seemingly grown-up people in the stadium of the Berlin Olympic games or at political rallies in Nuremberg standing with outthrust arms, shouting "Heil Hitler, Heil Hitler, Heil Hitler!"

❖ ❖ ❖

My mother wanted us to leave Europe while there was still time. Her brothers, Nachman and Lazar, who had emigrated to Australia, urged us to join them there. Better still, there was America, where relatives on both sides of the family from earlier waves of emigration were ready to welcome us. With determination typical of her, my mother threw herself into the study of English. At bedtime she would read aloud from *Huckleberry Finn* and *David Copperfield,* translating passages into Yiddish or Polish; I recall once crying uncontrollably at a particularly poignant scene from *Uncle Tom's Cabin*. She would talk about the life that awaited us in the New World as if she were sure that one day we would get there, and the phrase "God Bless America" was often on her lips.

Mother was a handsome, vivacious, and modern woman, with dark biblical features. She was, for one thing, a crack shot with a rifle and I remember seeing her hit a matchbox with devastating precision at what seemed an incredible distance. She thought I had talent for music and wanted me to be a violinst when I grew up. I loved to hear her sing Russian lullabies to my little sister, Frieda, and songs from the sound tracks of films that starred Jeannette MacDonald and Nelson Eddy. These melodies ring in my ears even today and are an indelible link to my happy childhood.

My father did not want to hear about leaving Poland. The prospect of becoming a refugee in some foreign land went against his grain. Bialystok had been his family's home for generations. His own father, Leon Pisar (an exceptional man by accounts I read after the war in the New York Jewish press), had been considered something of a local sage and a pillar of the community.

In the bloody pogrom of 1906, when the city was still a part of the czarist empire, he was credited with saving many Jews through his friendship with the prelate of the local Russian Orthodox church. He had died when I was too young to remember, but I heard many stories about him from the caretaker of our house, Anton, his contemporary.

Anton, whom we called affectionately Antonushka, and his wife, Antonovna, were an old Russian couple who chopped wood, swept the courtyard, tended the garden, and did other chores for the family. They had helped raise my father and his older brother Samuel, and they were like grandparents to me.

My uncle, Samuel Pisar, who died before I was born, was known for his enormous strength. When the circus came to town, the strong man would clasp his hands to his head and challenge any six men in the audience to pry them away. Three men on each side of him would try and fail, and a chant would go up from the audience: "Samuel, Samuel, Samuel!" My uncle was shy, but occasionally he would oblige, and wrestle the strong man to the floor. That, at least, was the story I heard. Jews in Eastern Europe were prone to hero worship, regarding such figures among them as protectors in a perilous world.

My father was known more for his skill than for brute strength, but may have been seen as a "protector" in his own right, which made it all the more difficult for him to consider severing his ties to the Jewish community and starting a new life elsewhere. Besides, there were his properties. With his three older sisters he had inherited several houses, including a large two-story building known as Pisar Hall that served as the town's center for concerts, lectures, weddings, and other public events. He had also started the city's first taxi service, with a Renault and a Chevrolet. His own automobile, an open Ford, was one of the first cars to have been seen in Bialystok. He kept it lovingly in a wooden shed in our huge compound where my aunts and their numerous offspring also had their homes, and where my friends and I played cowboys and Indians after school.

Father was a tall, soft-spoken man, whose self-control contrasted with my mother's romantic and excitable temperament. He liked to tinker with automobile and motorcycle engines, an aptitude developed during his military service. I remember admiring him in his Polish army uniform, with his long sword, when he would go off for periods of reserve duty amid intensified preparations against the danger of a Nazi attack. I also remember his amusing me with feats on a bicycle, riding backward or on one wheel. His dexterity with playing cards, learned from a detachment of Cossack horsemen garrisoned on our property, held a special fascination for me. I watched him for hours, as he played poker with his friends, always winning staggering stacks of huge bills — totally worthless after the cataclysmic inflation — in German, Austrian, and Russian currency. I often asked him to teach me a few of his tricks. "Maybe later on," he would say. "I don't know your character yet. One day you may be tempted to use these tricks when you play for real money. I'll teach you when I know you better."

He was fairly strict with me, but used the rod sparingly. The punishment I hated most was when he would sit down to lecture me after my sister, Frieda, had complained that I had pulled her pigtails or after he had caught me smoking cigarette butts in the bathroom.

One evening he sent me on an errand to a neighbor and discovered that I was afraid of the dark. Immediately he took me to the far end of the orchard and ordered me to find my way home alone. As I walked away I kept crying out: "Papa, are you still there? Papa, are you still there?" He did not answer. When I arrived at the house he was already there. He stroked my head and said, using the Yiddish diminutive of my name: "You see, Mula, there are no wicked ghosts in the dark out there."

My parents, I realize now, personified the two conflicting traits that had tugged at the history of Bialystok ever since the Polish Count Branitzky invited Jews to come to his seventeenth-century village on the Bialy river to build a prosperous city. As the armies of the Kaiser's Germany, czarist Russia, and Napoleonic France swept back and forth across the map of Poland, the first instinct, which flared during periods of depression and pogrom, was to strike out for a freer and safer life elsewhere. Today, in New York, Paris, Melbourne, Buenos Aires, Tel Aviv, and other cities, there are substantial communities that trace their lineage to the people who emigrated from Bialystok in the late nineteenth and early twentieth centuries.

These people have made an internationally recognized contribution quite disproportionate to the city's size. It was out of Bialystok that Dr. Ludwig Zamenhoff brought his universal language, Esperanto; Maxim Litvinov, who became Soviet Foreign Minister, was born there; General Yigal Yadin, the world-famous archaeologist who rose to chief of staff of the Israeli army, and Dr. Albert Sabin, the inventor of the oral polio vaccine, also trace their origins to that prolific town. The list is long and the fraternity warm.

In the New York of today, thousands of children — blacks, Puerto Ricans, Italians, and Irish in descent — savor a delicious snack they buy from sidewalk vendors: how many of them know where the fragrant roll they call a "Bialy" originated?

Once known as the town with the golden heart, today Bialystok is little more than a cemetery without tombstones.

The other trait that characterized Bialystok — and underlay my father's reluctance to emigrate — was the will to outlast adversity until better times returned. Without that determination, Bialystok could not have survived as one of the glories of European Jewry. After 1919, when Poland won her independence from Russia, the curse of official anti-Semitism was attenuated and prospects for the new state's Jewish communities seemed improved. Was all that to be abandoned now? David Pisar was not a man to walk away from a fight when attacked; he hesitated, debating whether the Germans would dare to invade Poland at the risk of war with her powerful allies, England and France; he waited to see if the black cloud on the horizon would dissipate.

Had not Poland's commander in chief announced that the country's defenses were as impregnable as the French Maginot line? Had not Neville Chamberlain and Edouard Daladier announced to the world that a generation of peace was at hand after their Munich agreement with Hitler? Could he, a simple citizen, know better than these eminent and experienced statesmen?

August 1939. Little Frieda will begin school next month. Little Mula studied hard all year. It was time for a peaceful family vacation in the country.

Those fateful deliberations in my parents' home came back to me vividly during the summer of 1978, when a wealthy and distinguished French businessman asked to see me professionally. He spoke at length about the worrisome course of events in Europe. "Our democracies are endangered from within and without," he said. "I owe it to my family to take certain precautions. You see, I have taken out extensive insurance on my life, my health, my home, my car. The only thing I cannot insure is my freedom and my peace of mind. Could you help me obtain a permanent visa so my family and I can enter the

United States at will? I would like to be sure that in the event of a war, a revolution, God knows what, we can catch the last plane or the last boat."

For some time, well-to-do Frenchmen, Germans, Italians, and other Europeans had been consulting attorneys in my New York and Paris law offices on how to organize their business affairs so they could plant one foot on each side of the Atlantic. Even the prospect of having to pay high American taxes as resident aliens did not discourage them.

In this instance I demurred vigorously. I told him that he was exaggerating the danger of a Soviet military attack or a communist takeover from within, that to abdicate all responsibility for the future of his country was to encourage the very process he feared most. History does not inevitably repeat itself, I added, and even if the dangers were there, running away from them was no solution.

"Think it over, Monsieur. America offers no more security today than any other continent. Until now she has been spared the violence of war on her soil. But even the Atlantic and Pacific oceans can no longer protect her against the technology of modern warfare. And as to economic and social upheavals, the last decade, with the erosion of the dollar and the rebellion of the young, has shown you that such things can happen in America too."

Then I stopped, dumbfounded. A man had come to ask me for advice on a means of escape and I responded with a sermon.

After that meeting I could not rid myself of a deep feeling of uneasiness. His children were now listening to the same troubled conversations that I had overheard at our dinner table forty years earlier. What right did I have, even if I found his request panicky and unrealistic, to say to him that what had happened could not somehow happen again; especially I, whose entire family had missed the last plane, the last boat?

This simple incident, which took place exactly forty years after the fraud of Munich that had promised a generation of peace, gave me more insight into the new fears that were gripping the minds of perceptive men, than did the most sophisticated political theories. It confirmed another experience I had had a few days earlier.

I had just returned from Mexico City where, at a gathering of several hundred heads of the largest banks in the world, I had debated with Henry Kissinger the changing international situation — a debate that, I might add, I did not take on without trepidation. The purpose of the exercise was to analyze from different standpoints — before an array of financial leaders who collectively managed over two-thirds of the world's total money deposits — the increasingly hazardous international environment in which they would now have to calculate their risks and make their decisions.

To my surprise, when David Rockefeller introduced me to the audience, he alluded not only to biographical data from my new life in the United States, but also to my Auschwitz background. Because, like Kissinger, I was an emigrant from persecution — I understood him to imply — I was an American in the most traditional sense.

Kissinger and I certainly knew something about persecution and the tragic side of history that the average native-born American did not. Our views of the future were indeed colored by something more than what we both had learned from our studies and research at Harvard, or from our experiences in Washington — mine, of course, at a level not comparable to his. But, in Mexico, I was startled at how my global outlook differed from that of the former Secretary of State.

While he saw the world in classic geopolitical and balance-of-power terms, I stressed the economic, social, and human problems that were eating away at the West from the inside: energy shortages, inflation, unemployment, declining productivity, the weakness of the dollar. He emphasized Russia's growing military might but I felt he did not sufficiently appreciate Russia's abysmal weaknesses: the inability to feed its people, the backwardness of its civilian industry and technology, the size of its own and its satellites' hard currency debt, the discontent of its consumers, intellectuals, and ethnic groups.

He placed an overriding priority on America's and NATO's defense budgets. I shared his concerns, but considered that our freedom and safety were threatened as much by internal weakness and by the dislocation of our alliances as by the growth of the Red Army. No nation, not even the United States or the Soviet Union, has the means to fight endlessly on two fronts without bleeding itself white: to keep on building ever-more-costly military arsenals and also to direct essential resources to the festering problems at home and to the misery and anger that are boiling in the Third World. And even if one side were to succeed in obtaining total superiority in the arms race, or in the generation of international upheavals intolerable to the other side — the other front might still collapse and move us all toward a universe of camps and gulags.

Before the Holocaust, Henry Kissinger had been lucky. He and his family were able to take the last boat before the night closed in on my family and me. His father had guessed right; mine had guessed wrong. But today there are no havens to escape to: survival must begin at home.

On the eve of the German attack, gas masks were issued to all the children in my neighborhood and we were drilled daily for air raids. But when the first bombs destroyed the Bialystok railway station, the sirens that had wailed so often during our drills were not even heard and we never made it to the shelters.

Father was among the first to be mobilized, and, because of his skill with cars, was attached to the army general staff. In the debacle that saw elegant Polish cavalry thrown against German panzer divisions, and the Nazis roll over the country in a matter of days, he managed to spirit several generals across the border to Lithuania — a feat for which he was decorated with a medal of military valor.

Then he was back. And so were the Russians. In the secret partitioning of Poland prearranged by the pact between Hitler and Stalin, the Bialystok region was consigned to the Soviet zone and the Red Army marched in from the east to take its share of the spoils. What I saw then the world has since seen reenacted at Budapest, at Prague, at Kabul. Even so, the Pisars were lucky, and I did not mind giving up my bedroom to a family of Jewish refugees from Warsaw who had fled east before the Nazi bestiality.

For almost two years we lived under the Soviet occupation. Then, on June 22, 1941, the bad was succeeded by the worst. Out of nowhere came the thunderclap of Germany's assault against Russia. The supposedly invincible Red Army crumbled under the onslaught of the Third Reich, and the treason, incompetence, and indifference to the communist ideology from the inside. I observed the sordid spectacle as a youngster and it is an experience to which I shall return.

The Nazis shock troops that entered Bialystok wasted no time in implementing the Führer's racial plans. On the first Friday of the occupation, over a thousand Jews were herded into the Great Synagogue, which was then set aflame. The following Sabbath, after a house-to-house search, hundreds of able-bodied men, among them my cousins Isaac, Grisha, and Frol, were rounded up, lined up in a field, and cut down by machine-gun fire. That was the beginning.

Having established its reign of terror, the Nazi command issued an order: all Jews were to move to a designated slum section of the city, whose non-Jewish inhabitants would be resettled in the abandoned Jewish homes. The order was to be carried out within twenty-four hours.

With our bags packed we gathered in our living room — my father; my mother; my sister, who was then eight; my mother's youngest brother, Memel; my grandmother, who had hoped to join her two other sons in Australia and whose travel documents were ready, alas too late; and myself, then twelve. This was now the immediate family. My other grandparents had died from natural causes.

It was a hot summer day, but father had built a roaring fire in the fireplace, and into this he proceeded to throw our most cherished possessions — mementos, photographs, letters, family heirlooms, things we could not take with us and did not want to fall into strange hands. We stood in a semicircle around the fireplace, father dressed in a khaki winter suit, with a thick leather belt and high riding boots. His resemblance to Gary Cooper, about which mother used to tease him constantly, was more striking than ever. The yellow Star of David we were required to wear on our chests made him look even more like a sheriff of the American Far West.

"We are living," he said, "our last moments in our home. We don't know when we will return. We don't know who will move in here after we are gone. Each of us is allowed to carry one bag. That means we can take only the barest essentials, only what will help keep us alive. Everything else must be left behind."

"But father," I protested, "what about my bicycle? And my ice skates? And my stamp collection? And my —"

"Bicycles are not allowed. Your ice skates will be useless. As for your stamp collection, take it along. We may be able to trade it for food. But that's all."

Mechanically, with no sign of emotion, he kept tossing item after item into the fire. When he came to a small bouquet of white artificial flowers that my mother had held in her hand on their wedding day, standing next to him under the marriage canopy, he hesitated.

"This bouquet . . . ," he began, and his voice faltered. "Anyway, by throwing it into the flames, here, as we all stand together, we make it eternal. When Frieda gets married" — he stroked my sister's hair — "we will get her a bouquet of her own."

The nosegay disappeared in a spurt of flame. Mother was still and expressionless. Only grandmother, I remember, gave a tiny sob.

My father put his arm around my mother's shoulders. "Helaina," he said (I remember being frightened by the solemnity of his use of her full name; I had always heard him call her Hela), "it is time to go."

We picked up our bags and walked out of our house — across the great courtyard, with its old well where peasants bringing produce from the country watered their horses; out past the orchard where raspberries and cherries and apples grew in sweet profusion in the flowing seasons of the year; out into Botanical Street, where my father's other houses were. Antonushka and Antonovna stood at the gate, crying and crossing themselves. As we moved on, huddled together, we saw groups of other dispossessed men, women, and children with suitcases, bags, or satchels, trickling into a widening stream toward the wall, topped by barbed wire, that had been erected at Germen behest to mark off the ghetto. Trying not to look at the machine-gun posts, we walked through the ghetto gates.

At the outset, life in the ghetto did not seem all that unbearable. We were assigned a small room and kitchen in a wooden frame house. I slept with my parents, Frieda with my grandmother, and Uncle Memel on a door that he would take off its hinges at night and put back in the morning.

One of the two windows overlooked a tiny plot where we were able to plant a few vegetables. I remember the thrill of watching the seeds sprout; the little tendrils pushing out of the mud, were, to me, an affirmation of life. I could still read books, visit my former classmates, kick a football, solve chess problems. And there was Ben.

Ben was a boy from a poorer background who had gone to a less prestigious school; we had met about a year earlier playing soccer, as members of our respective school teams. In those days sports were my passion and soccer became a bond between me and this rather reserved boy with blue eyes and blond hair, whose father had died when he was an infant and who felt an affection for me that I reciprocated. Ben was somewhat shorter than I, though a year older, but he was tough and quick-tempered and would pounce on any kid who made anti-Semitic remarks.

My parents made every effort to preserve a semblance of normal life. Since there was no school in the ghetto, an emaciated young man studying for the rabbinate agreed, for a bowl of soup a day, to prepare me for my bar mitzvah and to teach me the rudiments of Hebrew. He also taught me French. My mother's parents had sent their son Lazar and their daughter Barbara to study in Paris at the Sorbonne, and I suppose that even as our world sank before our eyes, similar dreams were being dreamed for me.

Ben, who lived with his mother and four sisters, would join me in these lessons now and then. We were reluctant pupils, and the poor rabbi was hard put to adduce convincing evidence that the world still turned under the watchful gaze of a just God.

Amid the violence and hardship, a moral rot set in everywhere. Among the first signs: our vegetables were stolen during the night just as they were ready to be picked. The winter of 1941 was marked by famine and a total lack of fuel, electric power, transportation facilities, and even regular supplies of drinking water. Hunger and cold completed the destruction of community spirit. One morning we woke to find our fence gone — stripped for firewood.

The more life deteriorated, the more people tended to say that things could not get much worse. If only they knew. But how could they? What lay ahead had never been done to human beings before.

⁂

Every Sunday morning we received a strange visit. An old man and an old woman, kept at a distance by the barbed wire and the guards, would stand silently on the other side, looking at us, and we would go out of our house to look silently at them. It was Antonushka and Antonovna. With our departure into the ghetto, their world had collapsed too. And there they would stand after Sunday-morning mass, immobile, too far to say a word or to throw over a loaf of bread, making the sign of the cross on their chests and tilting their heads toward heaven.

On my thirteenth birthday I was bar mitzvahed in a shabby little synagogue, just inside the barbed wire, in full sight of the Nazi sentries who were marching back and forth with their fingers on the triggers of submachine guns. I was not animated by any great religious fervor, and at home my parents observed High Holidays more out of respect to their parents than out of deep faith. But reading the Bible in my captivity brought home to me truths that seemed timeless. The aescetic-looking rabbi talked to me about the eternal persecution of Jews by the pharaohs, the Babylonians, the Persians, the Romans, the Spanish Inquisition, the Russian czars, and now Hitler's Reich. I felt close to those families which through the ages had to celebrate the bar mitzvahs of their sons clandestinely, not knowing what the future might bring. I understood their eternal quest for freedom and knowledge, and how the timeless bonds of suffering that tied them together had forged the identity of a people. I felt privileged, perhaps because the persecution was now at its highest point, to belong to that people for better or for worse.

When I stepped away from the scrolls of the Torah to make my ritual speech the words came naturally: pointing through the window of the synagogue at the tall fence outside, I said: "As always let us turn to pray toward Jerusalem, but today our Wailing Wall is right here."

Ben was first to congratulate me on becoming a man in the eyes of God. My former school friends came over to embrace me and to offer me gifts ingeniously improvised from the poor belongings their families had managed to retain. I did not know that I was seeing them for the last time.

❖❖❖

My father, who spoke fluent German, worked on the other side of the barbed wire, maintaining automobiles for the Nazi governor of the town. It was to him that he traded, after a long conversation in which I gave my solemn consent, the stamp album I had assembled — stamps on letters from Uncle Nachman and Uncle Lazar in Melbourne, featuring long-tailed Australian lyre birds and kangaroos; from Aunt Barbara in Paris, depicting the Bastille and the Eiffel Tower; from relatives in Boston, New York, and Cleveland, showing a bewigged George Washington and a bearded Abraham Lincoln. Every evening father would return home with scraps of food and give me exaggerated credit for having supplied the means.

While road-testing the cars in his charge, he would occasionally spirit from the ghetto children whose parents wanted to give them to non-Jewish peasant families in the hope that this would offer them a better chance to survive. One day my mother told me they had thought of giving my sister away.

"I hope," I said, "you weren't thinking of giving me away, too?"

"No," she said, but her look was strained.

I recalled that conversation only recently, after I had begun writing this book. I woke up in the night with a start.

My God, my parents were willing to give me away! But only, I argued with myself, to save me. Yes, but . . .

The realization stunned me. Such memories have an unimaginable power to hurt.

One morning my father kissed us goodbye, and we never saw him again. What happened I have put together from bits of evidence that drifted back to us in the succeeding weeks. He was caught in his clandestine activities, tortured by the Gestapo, and executed with a group of other prisoners in a forest several miles from town.

My mother clung to hope that he was still alive. Once before, after the Polish collapse, she had waited for weeks without news of him, yet he finally had returned. I had played a role in his homecoming on that earlier occasion. Antonushka had got me out of the house after dark, saying that my father had sent for me and that I was to speak to no one. I found him in a little park across the street, thin, exhausted, unshaven, his uniform grimy and torn.

"Go," he said, "tell your mother there is someone who wants to see her. Someone from the same army unit as Papa." He explained he wanted to prepare her gradually. I did as he said. She followed me anxiously to the park gate. A tall shape stepped out of the gloom.

She rushed forward. "My God, David, you're alive!"

And now, in the ghetto, I tried to buoy her up with lies — that I had spoken to someone who had been inside the Gestapo compound and had heard of Papa, that someone who took food into the prison reported seeing him there . . . Ben joined me in these inventions, but she must have seen through our childish imaginations even though she pretended to believe us, for very quickly her hopes sickened and the very wish to live, without this man whom she had loved more than anything in the world, seemed to go out of her. She still sang occasionally while preparing our meals, but only the mournful refrains composed under the occupation, about those who had been executed on Thursday and on Friday and on Saturday, and so on.

The ghetto was thinning out bit by bit. Every morning stacks of emaciated corpses were taken to a new cemetery not far from our house. The living also were being herded out in families and groups. Everyone lived in fear of the next SS evacuation patrol. The end was drawing closer.

Sometimes the Nazis would take hostages and offer to free them for ransom. Destitute relatives would then plead from door to door for jewelry or gold in hope of obtaining the release of a husband, a brother, a son. I saw my mother drop her earrings into a hat.

One day the SS took my grandmother and her son, Uncle Memel. He, a fine athlete, could have escaped if anyone could. I guess he did not want to see his elderly mother sent to her ordeal alone. Soon afterward Ben also disappeared.

In our little room we were now three — my mother, my sister, and I. Our meager supply of flour and potatoes was dwindling. Through a friend of the family I landed a job at a locksmith's. He put me to making keys. When I handed mother my first pay envelope, containing food-rationing coupons, she kissed my grimy face and said, "You are now our breadwinner."

Finally, the ghetto was razed. Incredibly, many young Jews, both men and women, tried to resist the military assault, killing a handful of Nazis. Unarmed, their resistance was as heroic as it was futile. All were mowed down. One, Malmed, threw a bottle of sulfuric acid into the face of an SS officer, blinding him forever. I saw Malmed's hanged body that night in the middle of Commerce Street, the main ghetto artery.

For the rest, all I remember is flames in the night — the three of us scurrying past burning houses, over dead bodies littering the streets —

and hiding by day. Somehow we found ourselves in an underground bunker where some thirty people had been holed up for days. By the glow of a candle I made out the features of my teacher of Latin and history. Professor Bergman, a fragile and kindly man, was rocking his infant son, trying to stop his coughing. On the other side of the trapdoor above us came the shouts of German search parties and the barking of their dogs. We all fell silent; only the baby's coughing continued. "Shhh," hissed a burly man near the door. The coughing did not stop. The man crawled over and placed a hand over the baby's mouth. The coughing ceased. Minutes passed. The child sank limply to the ground. All the while, Professor Bergman sat petrified. I knew he was not a coward. Even then, I understood that if he could think or feel anything at all, he was weighing one life against thirty, even if that life was his own son's.

The next day we found refuge in a private hospital. Its director, Mr. Kniazeff, had been Uncle Nachman's best friend. Other fugitives also clamored for shelter. He let us in when he saw Mother at the gate. Another night passed. At dawn, an announcement was made that the SS would evacuate the hospital compound. We were to be taken elsewhere. The men, we were told, would go separately from the women, the children, and the sick.

We had fled our room with our last few belongings. Now my mother folded my clothes for me as calmly and methodically as though she were sending me off to summer camp.

"Do you think you ought to wear your short pants or your long pants?" She was thinking out loud.

She hesitated for a moment, looked at my sister then again at me, and said, "If you're dressed in short pants, they'll let you go with Frieda and me. If you wear your long pants, we'll probably be separated. You will go with the men. You're a big boy now, maybe it would be better if —"

"And you?" I asked. "And Frieda?"

She did not answer.

Only one thought was in my mind: "What will become of them, and what will become of me, without them?" In my despair, I could not even begin to find an answer. I feared the worst.

We had been living for months in an atmosphere of absolute terror. All around me people had talked about death and I knew perfectly what it meant. But for my mother, still so young, for my little sister, and for me to have to die without having really lived seemed inconceivable.

Oblivious to the bursts of machine-gun fire outside, we savored our last moments together, precious, fragile moments, full of tenderness and even an occasional smile.

Mother was thin and drawn, but with her pale skin and long black hair she seemed more beautiful than I had ever seen her before.

My sister cuddled up against her and fell peacefully asleep.

In the morning the storm troopers broke in. With the butts of their rifles they drove everyone, wounded or not, out into the street. A grim figure with the emblem of the skull and crossbones on his helmet walked up.

"I want that."

"What, sir?" my mother said.

"That ring on your finger."

It was her engagement ring, a gold band with a small diamond in a cluster of tiny rubies, shaped like a heart. She tried to get it off, but her fingers were puffed from stress and fatigue.

The SS man pulled out his bayonet. "Quick, or the finger comes off with it."

In my terror I remembered a cake of soap she had packed in my suitcase. I got it out, spat on her finger, and rubbed the soap fiercely into the flesh. The ring slipped off. I handed it to the Nazi.

"Here, *mein Herr*."

At that moment I felt something snap inside me. I think I became someone else . . .

More orders, and we were separated into two groups — women and children in one, men in the other. Thanks to the long pants I was wearing, I passed for a man.

We were marched off. Helplessly I looked back. Mother and Frieda were being marched the other way. My eyes were glued to the two frail shapes as they moved off in the distance. With one hand my sister held on to my mother; with the other she clutched her favorite doll. They too looked over their shoulders. Then they disappeared from sight.

Could my mother have sensed — she could not have known; none of us knew anything — that a young man able to perform physical labor for the Nazis had a better chance of surviving than a child classed as useless, unneeded, an extra mouth to feed? Did she, in pushing me away from her into the cruel adult world, hope to give me a chance at life, if only one chance in a million? That moment when I saw her for the last time pursues me to this day with its load of agony and guilt and unquenchable anger.

When the two lines of prisoners separated and I could see them no longer, a rage against man and God tore through my breast. Choking with tears, I raised my fist to heaven in a blasphemous cry against the Almighty: "*Gazlen! — Monster!* How dare you!"

Two decades later, I returned to Bialystok. In 1961, after serving on one of President Kennedy's electoral task forces, I became an adviser to the Joint Economic Committee of the United States Congress. With a group of legislators led by Senator Jacob Javits of New York, I visited NATO headquarters in Paris to discuss with members of the German and French parliaments new ways of coordinating Western aid to the developing countries. We also traveled to Warsaw, Prague, and Moscow to explore the prospects of East-West trade. In Warsaw, on an impulse, I decided to make a side trip alone. Without going into explanations, I told the American ambassador, Jacob Beam, where I wanted to go and he kindly offered me the use of a chauffeur-driven limousine. I arrived, on a gray day, in the city that was only a ghost of its past.

My purpose was not to search for roots; there were none left where I was going. My roots, my branches, my blossoms were now, and forever, on the other side of the Atlantic.

I wanted most of all to find my father's grave. But whom to ask? Out of Bialystok's sixty thousand Jews, only a handful remained, nine to be precise, and as for the rest of the population, they had no reason to remember. When I reached, at night, the outskirts of town, near which I knew the executions had taken place, I stopped to ask directions. In an eerie encounter, a couple of deaf-mutes, who seemed to know what I was after, gave me directions in sign language. In a snowfield lit up by the headlights of my Cadillac, I found a monument, a stone cross with an inscription that said that hundreds of men — Jews as well as non-Jews, I assume — taken from Bialystok's Gestapo prison had been executed there. That cross, near the village where our family used to spend its summer vacations, marks, I believe, my father's last resting place.

In the city, a few landmarks remained. The Catholic church spire that soared so high in my childhood memory was modest in height to me now. I directed the driver to our house. Children who were playing in the courtyard stopped their game and ran behind the limousine as we drove in. The courtyard was still large, even to my adult eyes. The orchard where my father taught me not to be afraid of the dark was gone. But there was the shed where he kept his old Ford, the alley where he taught me to ride a bicycle, and the pond where Frieda used to feed the ducks. The house still looked solid and inhabited. A wisp of smoke floated from the old chimney.

''How long have you lived here?'' I inquired of the small crowd that had collected around me.

''Since the war.''

''What happened to the former occupants?'' I asked.

An old man volunteered: ''All killed by the Nazis.''

''All?''

''All but one,'' he said. ''A little boy seems to have survived. There was something about it in the papers. He works in Washington, they said.''

I turned away, trying to hide my emotion. To cross the threshold of that home, to give in, even for a moment, to the pain that I had so carefully kept under control year after year, was more than I could face.

Instinctively, I felt for the U.S. diplomatic passport in my breast-pocket. Without another word I got back into the car and asked the chauffeur to drive quickly to Warsaw, turning around only once to take a last look at the place where all my beloved had departed from this earth.

My mother, Helaina

My father, David, and
my sister, Frieda

My mother's parents

Uncle Memel in his Polish army uniform

Frieda feeding the ducks

The cross marking the mass grave where I believe my father is buried

My mother and father on their wedding day

My sister and me, shortly before the beginning of the war

2

IT was almost night when the heavily guarded column of men — I, with my long pants, one of them — arrived at the immense field where we were to spend the night. Alone among thousands of strangers, I stumbled around looking for a familiar face. Then, seeing a distinguished-looking gentleman stretched out on the ground, I walked up to him and asked, "Excuse me for disturbing you, sir, but would you mind if I lay down next to you?" Immediately I had an awkward sensation that my polite manners were out of place in my new surroundings, for the man did not answer. His eyes glazed over, he just kept staring into space. I put down my suitcase for a headrest, covered myself with the heavy winter coat my mother had insisted I take so I could be warm when winter came, and closed my eyes in a desperate effort to summon her face.

It was still dark when I awoke from what I thought, for a happy second, had been a nightmare: "Papa, are you still there? Mama, are you still there . . . ?" But then I realized that what had roused me had been the shouts of our guards and the barking of their dogs, and it hit me for the first time that I was totally and irrevocably alone, that I had no one to count on but myself.

By hundreds, we were lined up in groups, facing the long train of cattle cars, their doors open to receive us. Women and children were facing the train farther to the rear.

After a long wait, one group after another, we were ordered to run on the double across the field in a single line toward a designated car. As we ran, a gauntlet of SS men, in their black uniforms, struck at us with canes. Ahead of me I saw some of the prisoners fall, try to rise, and then collapse, done in. Suddenly, it was my turn. I ran, hunched over, holding on to my small suitcase with one hand, shielding my head with the other. I felt the blows on my head and my hands and smelled the blood on my face. I could not see but I knew that I had to keep running, I had to, at any price, for if I fell it would be forever. When I finally made it to the railroad ramp and the interior of the car, it was like a haven.

The car filled up quickly and the heavy door slid shut, casting us into total darkness. Outside we heard screams and more doors sliding shut. Then there was silence. Quickly, the stench and closeness inside became suffocating and it was only by finding a crack between the floor planks and pressing my nostrils against it, that I was able to breathe freely.

Where in the world were they taking us? I remember thinking how scared I used to be at the thought of ever having to move to another neighborhood, to another town, to another school. Now I felt so strangely unafraid, so strangely calm, while all these men around me were becoming more and more agitated, groaning, pushing, shoving, yelling at each other. No point in that, I kept repeating to myself; better save energy.

After seemingly endless hours we heard whistles and more shouting outside, and the train began to jolt into motion. Gradually I made out a flicker of light at the far end of the car and I squirmed toward it through the densely packed bodies. Someone had pried open the cover of the small skylight. Seeing me, a boy, smaller and lighter than anyone around, two of the men lifted me onto their shoulders so I could poke my head through the skylight and report what I saw.

Thank God, fresh air! I filled my lungs.

I was told to signal when we were passing through wooded country, and at each of my signals I was lowered and one of the men climbed up, crawled through the skylight, and jumped off. From what I could tell, several of them jumped unnoticed, rolling on the ground toward the trees. The third or fourth time this happened, as I was lowered, I saw that the man being boosted through the skylight was a teenager — maybe five years older than myself — wearing the jacket of his school uniform. His hands clutched the rim of the skylight and he hung suspended for a moment, as if hesitating. Then he gave a heave of his body and pulled himself up and out. Bursts of machine-gun fire from the sentries posted on the roofs of the cars broke the rhythmic metallic thuds of the wheels against the rail joints. When I stuck my head out again I saw that many of the escapees from other cars had been mowed down.

Then the train stopped. I was again raised to the skylight and saw that we were at a huge crossing with multiple railway lines going off in different directions. I looked for the station, as we were obviously near a large city, but could see nothing, only a field and a thick forest in the distance. Several wooden signs marked the place. Painted on them was the word "Treblinka." After a few hours, the train jolted back and forth a few times. I stuck out my head and realized that the rear cars had been uncoupled; they remained motionless in the green peaceful landscape as the rest of the train, transporting us men, moved off.

All those slow, winding trains, which converged from all parts of Europe toward the death camps — how many who saw them pass by could have guessed what was inside? Without schedule, shunted aside any time a civilian Pullman or military convoy claimed priority, standing immobile on side tracks in the blistering sun or the freezing cold — who could have guessed that they were transporting perishable cargoes?

Who could have imagined that the parched, anguished, extinguished human beings, who spent the last hours of their agony behind the sliding steel doors of these rolling coffins, were preparing the most radiant of posthumous victories? These shadows without graves, martyrs of the greatest holocaust of history cry out even today to those who continue to betray the calling of man — tyrants, through madness; democrats, through blindness.

The State of Israel was created by them. They have populated it, they have armed it, they have defended it.

One evening in June 1967 when I returned home from the office, I saw an unbelievable, an unimaginable, sight on my television screen: Israeli soldiers, white prayer shawls covering the machine guns on their backs, steel helmets serving them as yarmulkes, praying at the foot of the Wailing Wall. Suddenly, I burst into uncontrollable sobs, sobs of which my children never thought their father was capable, sobs from the depth of my being and from the wells of time.

My mind, my training, my experience told me that the sight I saw was pregnant with unfathomable complications. I was aware that to follow to the comma the strictures of an ancient book about the sacredness of this or that speck of soil was an oversimplification that bordered on the fanatical. I knew that the legitimate rights and ageless passions of others were also involved. But the memory of what I had lived through, of what an entire nation had lived through for millennia, had broken the emotional dam in front of this eternal symbol of sorrow and of hope.

Yes, on that day, the trains headed for Treblinka, Maidanek, and Auschwitz had finally reached their destination.

❖❖❖

Those trains! Those cargoes! Those destinations!

Prime Minister Golda Meir, the eyes in her tired, wrinkled face fixing me with all of their tenacious, penetrating force, took another deep draw of her ever-present cigarette. As I listened to her in her small unpretentious frame house near Tel Aviv, she seemed to carry the entire tragedy of the Jewish people on her frail, hunched shoulders.

For our first meeting, in the autumn of 1972, her assistant, Ambassador Symcha Dinitz, drove me to her door, which she opened herself.

"What? No coat? You will catch a death of cold."

My God, I thought, just like my grandmother. The reincarnation of the grandmothers without number that I saw deposited by those trains at the doors of the gas chambers.

"What is this poor State of Israel all about? What is the meaning of our work? What is the point of our sacrifices, if the Russian Jews cannot come here to live in freedom and dignity?" she began, her voice transmitting frank emotion. "Your ideas on peace, on coexistence, on trade between East and West, have found a worldwide audience. You should think a little more about how all this can help our people."

Her hands were now together, in a prayerlike attitude, as if I, too, needed convincing that what she was saying was important. Then she cut herself short. "Forgive me, Samuel. For a moment I forgot who you were. I confused you with the other foreign dignitaries who come to discuss with me their abstract theories — who want me to look at things diplomatically, but who refuse to remember the bloody tragedies that have darkened our history so recently and so often in the past.'' For her, anything that touched on the survival of the Jewish people was beyond politics, beyond statecraft, beyond rationale almost. It was tied to the very purpose of her life.

''Come, Shmuel,'' she said in Hebrew, using the Hebrew name of the prophet now, ''I'll make you a cup of tea.''

Looking at her, talking with her for hours, listening to her humorous stories, stories that only those who have read Isaac Bashevis Singer and Sholem Aleichem in the Yiddish vernacular can appreciate, I understood how she managed to have such a hold on her sons and daughters all over the world. I understood how she managed, when she went to Yom Kippur services at the Moscow Synagogue after becoming Israel's first ambassador to the U.S.S.R., to bring out of hiding thousands of Russian Jews who had been deemed lost to another culture and another faith.

This mixture of tenderness and authority, this rock of courage, was no blind, religious fanatic. She was simply determined to struggle on until her last breath in order to make sure that those trains would never roll again.

No air, no water, no food. How long we were inside these cattle cars I don't really know. I remember someone saying seventy-two hours. We were horribly dehydrated. I saw people with faces that were literally blue, licking their own sweat; there was urine and excrement all over the floor. It was like a sewer.

When we stopped and the doors were opened, blinding floodlights lit up the night. A long line of SS men, each holding a restive police dog on a short leash, stood along the ramp. A short order — EVERYTHING OUT — and several of the great beasts leaped into our car. In the space of seconds, two or three of the half-conscious prisoners were torn to pieces. Horrified, the prostrate men dragged themselves up with their last ounce of strength and staggered out. Other bodies lying on the floor the dogs did not touch; they were dead. Of the hundred or so men in the car, more than a score had succumbed along the way.

On the railroad platform there was panic — blows, screams, and the gruff barking of the dogs. I held my suitcase up against my chest for protection as I stumbled over corpses. But I don't remember being particularly terrified. Despite all that had happened in the space of a very few days, I felt more sure of myself, more controlled, as if I had suddenly aged several years. What I remember clearly is being numb and yet so thirsty that I thought I would die if I did not have some water.

In the chaos, I walked up to a guard who stood on the other side of a line of barbed wire encircling the station. He pointed his submachine gun at me. I unlocked my suitcase and pulled out a package my mother had placed in it — my father's pocket watch, with its long gold chain. I opened the package and offered it to the German. What gave me the idea, I think, was the trade my father had made with the Nazi in Bialystok: my stamp collection for food.

The guard studied the package as if he could not believe his eyes.

"Tie it up, throw it to me."

"*Wasser,*" I said. I had to have water.

"Throw it to me!"

"*Wasser,*" I repeated.

I knew, of course, that he could shoot me. But then he would not have his booty, because he was on the other side of the wire.

He left. After a few minutes he was back with a bottle. He pushed it through the wire and I threw my package over. I think now of that trade as the most fruitful I have ever engaged in. It probably saved my life.

I brought the bottle to my lips, took a long gulp, then another. Before my thirst could be slaked there was a clamor, and a dozen of the deportees descended on me from all sides. Judging by their wild cries and faces I thought they were going to kill me; I surrendered the bottle and jumped aside. As outstretched hands grasped at it, the bottle dropped and broke. The men fell to their knees to lick up the moisture with their parched tongues as it slowly seeped into the ground.

As I observe the world scramble, on its knees, one might say, for the last barrel of oil, I cannot help recalling a proposal put forward by two Americans, experts on the problem of overpopulation, William and Paul Paddock. Their idea was that in dealing with underdeveloped countries in dire need of Western aid, we proceed on the principle of "triage" — although a plainer word, such as selection, would mean the same thing. In brief, the industrialized nations would decide which of the needy countries were to be helped along the road of development and which were to be left to their own devices. We would identify, on strictly utilitarian grounds, the countries that were better able to contribute to our own economic and strategic objectives.

I think I can say that I have a certain feeling for a desperately impoverished people asked to line up for this sort of triage. Will they be found too feeble or otherwise unsuited to do the donor much good, and be told to step aside and accept their unenviable fate, or will they be found sturdy and worthy enough to be helped to work and survive? Because, more than once, I faced the anguish of being "triaged" myself.

The first time was when I got off that train. I didn't know where we were. No one knew. We were marched to some place with a wall, which I couldn't distinguish very well in the darkness, and ordered to undress for a shower. There I recognized Dr. Kaplan, our family doctor who had brought me into the world. Before I even had a chance to speak to him, we were lined up, naked. We filed past an SS officer sitting at a desk, who cast a quick eye over each man before him and gave one of two orders — "Left," or "Right." I reached the point where the line divided; I was just behind the doctor. A bent and frail man of about sixty, he held a long, broad elastic bandage in his hand.

"What is that?"

"For my hernia, sir."

The officer said tonelessly, "Leave it here and go left. You will get it back when you come out."

Then he looked at me with surprise.

"How old are you?"

"Eighteen. I'm small for my age, but I'm strong."

"Go right."

"Can't I go with Dr. Kaplan?"

"Right!" he repeated.

And that, I realized later, was the end of Dr. Kaplan, and a further lease on life granted me.

Later, at Auschwitz, I was "triaged" by Dr. Josef Mengele himself.

Will it be to the right or to the left? You watch your judge's eyes, his gestures, anything that might give you a clue to whether you are about to die. A random puff on his cigarette might break the rhythm and send you one way instead of the other. Those who passed such tests, which took only a few seconds, joined the company of the elite among slaves. There were no old or weak or sickly among them, and certainly no women and children, and they enjoyed their furlough on life for a few days or a few weeks or a few months; but not many lasted much longer than that in what was, for most of them, an antechamber of death.

⁂

Like the others who had been told to go to the right for a shower, I was allotted a pair of wooden clogs, a jacket and trousers of striped cloth, a round cap, and a metal bowl I was always to wear at my belt. Our own clothes and our last possessions — anything that could remind us of our former life — which we had been told would be returned to us after the shower, we never saw again. My head was shaved clean, a pungent white disinfectant was smeared between my legs, and I was assigned to a barrack. Two boards, one above the other, ran down each side of the barrack, like shelves, with a space in between. A line of tiny openings near the roof filtered in some light and air. The dozens of other barracks were all the same. We learned that we were in a concentration camp called Maidanek.

At the first whistle we lined up for chow. I looked down distastefully at what was being poured into my bowl, thinking that tomorrow would be time enough to get used to my new diet. An older man sitting opposite me on the floor tapped my clog with his:

"Son, you listen. Do you want to eat that soup or do you want to croak? . . . Then don't give yourself any airs. Your mother isn't here to make you potato pancakes — eat. Or else give it to me."

I forced the stuff down my throat. I didn't know yet how right he was, how missing one meal in my weakened condition could make the difference between life and death. I didn't even begin to realize what his words would mean to me later, what it is like to be crazed by hunger, when a helping of lukewarm liquid in a rusty container makes the emaciated body tremble in anticipation.

You cradle your bowl lovingly, looking for a quiet place where you can eat undisturbed. With closed eyes you sip mouthful by mouthful the ambrosia inside, dragging out those precious moments during which you know you are working at your survival. You lick the bowl clean, then your lips and your teeth, and like a Pavlovian dog you begin thinking of that distant hour when the whistle will sound again.

The hunger becomes psychological, hallucinating, obsessive, the first sensation on waking in the morning, the last before falling asleep at night. All other sensations, even the feeling of pain or the fear of death, become secondary, precluding any concentrated effort of thought. The animal instinct to eat, no matter what, no matter where, no matter when, remains the only predominant reality.

How to explain the daily quest for nourishment among those who suffer from permanent starvation all over the world, to our leaders, our policymakers, for whom often the greatest dilemna over food is posed by a solicitious waiter: "Would you like your steak rare, sir, or well done?"

Standing at attention at roll call, we could see a complex of structures with brick chimneys, which occasionally gave off smoke. But we did not yet connect the smoke with our own fate. We had seen enough people killed by gunfire and succumbing to extreme physical hardship, to know we were in mortal danger, but the knowledge of the crematoria and the gas chambers had not yet gotten around. Even when their purpose became unmistakably clear, many among us refused to believe that anyone, even the Nazis, could sentence a whole people to extermination. Some time would pass before I learned, without much chance of error, that the women and children whose cars had been unhooked from our train at Treblinka were taken straight into the ovens.

As we made contact with prisoners in other barracks who had been in the camp for some time, as we saw groups of our comrades suddenly disappear and new groups arrive, we realized that we were in a place organized solely for our physical annihilation. Vaguely, I began to understand that whatever strength I had left and whatever cunning I possessed had to be devoted to the postponement of that event.

One evening, after an endless roll call, an order was issued: All who are tailors by trade remain standing at attention; the others fall out.

If they needed tailors, I reasoned, they would keep them alive. My instinct told me to stand still.

The SS officer who went down the line inspected me with mild amusement and disdain.

"So you think you're a tailor."

"No, sir, I am not."

"Was your father a tailor, then?"

"Yes, sir, and my grandfather, too. I was the *Knopflochmachinist.*"

"*Knopflochmachinist,* eh? What's that?"

"The buttonhole maker, sir, on a very big and complicated machine. You try to sew buttonholes by hand, it takes forever. On the *Knopflochmachine* it takes only a few seconds."

On the street where we lived there had been a tailor's shop, and in the shop there was a huge buttonhole machine that fascinated me. I would sometimes hang around there after school, and since I was the landlord's son the operator would let me push the pedal to punch out a few holes.

The irresistible logic of my explanation — that wherever tailors are needed, buttonhole makers are needed too — must have impressed the SS officer, because he waved me to one side, the side of life. For the second time in a matter of weeks, I had saved my skin.

There was something in this, I feel now, of the ancient instinct for survival that runs through the history of the Jews, an instinct that has been honed by repeated national tragedies and traumas.

That evening, in my bunk, I fancied myself a young Daniel who read the writing on the wall at King Belshazzar's feast and escaped alive from the lion's pit in Babylon. I fancied myself a young Joseph carried off to Egypt by the Ishmaelites, alone in a dungeon, improvising the means of his salvation. The pharaoh has dreams about seven lean and seven fat cows. Is there anyone in the kingdom who can read dreams? Joseph becomes an interpreter of dreams and wins his life. He has invented his buttonhole machine.

The next day our entire contingent — the others all bona fide tailors — was piled into trucks, and after two days of intermittent driving and stopping, was unloaded in a place called Blizin.

My joints were stiff and I could hardly move when the order was given to undress and wash in a freezing swamp. We realized with some relief that there was no gas chamber in the guise of shower installations.

Blizin was a labor camp situated in the bleakest countryside I had ever seen. Like most camps, it was surrounded by a thick forest. But inside the barbed-wire fence, dominated by machine-gun towers every few hundred feet, there was no sign of nature: not a single blade of grass, not a single weed; only black crows occasionally circled overhead, never deigning to alight. The entire compound was covered by gravel and rock, constantly swept and replenished by teams of skeletal prisoners.

After the usual processing as new arrivals, and assignment to barracks, we were taken to a huge hangarlike brick building that housed a factory for the manufacture of German army uniforms. In the warehouse section of the factory where I was put to work, I saw a familiar shape, his prison garb striped like mine, his head shaved like mine. He was standing with his back to me, but there was no mistaking him.

"Benek!"

He whirled around. "Mula!"

His eyes were larger than I had remembered them. He had aged several years in the space of a few months. Like myself he must have lived things in minutes that usually take years. It seemed to me that he talked now like an older boy, and he must have felt the same way about me. We embraced, slapping each other mightily on the back. Then we both started at the same time, "How did you—?" and stopped, laughing.

Ben had been taken to Blizin directly from Bialystok. Like me, he had been separated from his family at the train station.

He couldn't tell me much more; a foreman, with a long whip, ordered us back to work. Along with the new arrivals, I was to sort out old uniforms, which were to be turned and restitched.

Ben knew his way around the camp and that evening he managed to get me into his barracks. In the darkness, after roll call, we talked in whispers for hours, reminiscing about our schools, our classmates, and about all that had happened since his disappearance from the ghetto.

The High Holidays arrived after we had been in camp several months. Our barracks became an eerie synagogue. In the darkness, after work, without a Torah, without prayerbooks, without candles, with prison caps for yarmulkes, every man stood in front of his bunk, facing Jerusalem. Without the chants of a cantor to guide him, every man mumbled softly, lest we be heard by the roaming guards and their vicious dogs outside, whatever prayers he could remember. On this Yom Kippur the fasting came easier than the atonement.

The conviction that my mother and sister were gone forever had settled on me again when I looked at the desolate expanse of Blizin, and now, at the age of fourteen, I wanted to join them, I wanted to die. Death seemed such a relief. What right, I asked Ben, did I have to live if my father, my mother, and my sister were all dead?

"But supposing," he snapped in anger, "your mother and sister are still alive? You really don't have the slightest proof they are dead!"

He confessed that he, too, had thought of giving up. But now, he said, he and I had to reject all such thoughts. If our mothers and sisters were still alive, it was our duty to stay alive also, to survive until the day we could be reunited. There was always a chance. "In a soccer game," he said, "you don't stop trying even if you are three goals behind. You never know what the next ten minutes can bring."

I agreed. No more talk of suicide, of passive acceptance of the worst. My mother had given me life a second time on the night we were parted. This second birth had been much more painful for her than the first. My life, I felt, was no longer entirely my own. That part of her, of all the others, that was within me would have to live on too. Maybe one day, if I was spared, I would be able to wreak revenge, to bear witness in America, in Australia, in France, wherever members of our family might survive, to the unspeakable depth to which a perverted world had sunk. It was my duty to struggle on.

Ben and I knew that we had to keep our heads, to stay cool. We had to act like grown-up men. There were tricks to be learned. The trusties and foremen were a dangerous lot, but we could get around some of them and get extra scraps that could keep us going. Ben had found an old pair of canvas shoes; maybe we could filch another pair, so both of us would have something better than wooden clogs. Also, with the onset of winter, we would need bits of cloth to piece together so we could have something more than straw to warm us at night.

The German that we had learned as a second language in school was now a godsend, for it helped us catch on faster than the others to what was really happening. We soon discovered ways to swap our clothes when we alternated between day shift and night shift, so that the one who was out in the cold would not freeze. We realized that at the very beginning or at the very end of the servings, the gruel was often thicker, and depending how deeply the trusty manipulated the ladle, we would be either first or last in line. We knew that we had to keep clean, even if that meant washing with rainwater from potholes or with snow from the ground.

We knew that we could not afford to make any mistakes, that we could not, as we used to do at school, first make a draft of our homework and then rewrite it clearly before handing it in to the teacher. In every situation, we only had one opportunity, at the most, and our decision had to be fast and correct, or else.

Together, we would be more than just two boys, more — in terms of ability to survive — than a grown man. We swore a pledge to share everything, to stay close, to hang on.

We had sealed the Benek-Mula pact: the will to live!

3

ALEXANDER SOLZHENITSYN's chronicle of life in Stalin's labor camps has stirred the conscience of men everywhere. The daily quest for survival against all odds, against all logic, the feeling of total abandonment by the international community — I have lived it all, and on reading his books, I relive it again.

We have been at the bottom of the human rubble heap, he at the age of thirty and I at half that age. Our innermost thoughts and feelings are, therefore, also essentially alike.

When a *Pravda* editorial suggested that my views on coexistence between free-enterprise and state-enterprise societies contributed to international détente, I was not too astonished. But when Solzhenitsyn, the Kremlin's most severe critic, discussing the link between East-West trade and human freedom, also wrote, in *The Oak and the Calf,* that "Pisar is one of the few to see clearly," I was as pleased as I was surprised.

The paradox is not difficult to understand. Although all totalitarian systems are basically the same ugly beast, I have come to feel, perhaps more strongly than he, that a decisive new dimension has entered into our relations with major powers whose political systems we may despise. Our planet now lives under the threat of an atomic holocaust. Men and women can no longer thrill as once they did to Patrick Henry's fiery eighteenth-century slogan: "Give me liberty or give me death." Liberty today can no more be won by poetic fervor than it can be conquered by force of arms. New means have to be brought into play, means which in another book I have called "weapons of peace."

Solzhenitsyn, on the other hand, seems to favor a return to the policy of confrontation with Russia and to feel that this, rather than negotiated, broader contacts, could force its system to change. For my part, I continue to believe that in the Western world's historic contest with communism, our most effective weapon is not our costly and far-flung military establishment but our superior capacity for economic progress, and the human rights that must go with it.

Our resistance cannot be limited to the tyrannies inherited from the past. New dictatorships are on the rise and the slide toward totalitarianism may become widespread as country after country braces itself against the onslaught of economic and social chaos. We must combat Hitler's and Stalin's heritage not only because they left disciples, but because the conditions — unemployment, inflation, disorder — that brought fascism and communism to power on the crest of an authentically popular wave are threatening us again.

What I have in common with the great Russian dissident is, however, infinitely stronger than our differences in approach to the issue of coexistence with the U.S.S.R. We share a sacred bond of brotherhood and honor, common to all survivors of the camps and the gulags — to resist torturers and executioners wherever they may be.

I read with fascination Solzhenitsyn's first book, *One Day in the Life of Ivan Denisovich,* and almost regretted not having shared his lot. The narrative of his day-to-day existence in the archipelago of Stalin's gulags is, to a point, virtually a page-for-page description of my own existence in Hitler's camps. It is so accurate and precise that for me to describe in the same detail a day in my own captivity would be repetitious. Certain differences did, nonetheless, strike me as fundamental. His gulag, horrible as it was, was not, like my camp, a place of extermination. Nothing can equal life in the shadow of a continuously active gas chamber.

That prisoners could wear felt boots, socks, and underwear was unimaginable for us. But more important, the gulag inmates could look forward to receiving letters, parcels, even visits from family or friends who were still alive. What respite, what consolation, what life-energy those links, no matter how tenuous, with the world outside must have provided.

I know how grotesque it must seem to make comparisons between these two ultimate forms of barbarism. And neither of us will ever be able fully to convey to others the total horror of the thoughts and memories that haunt us, the premonition that our experience was a precursor of events to come. For we are among the very special few who know from life in its rawest state that man's capacity for evil, like his genius, has no limits.

If I draw a distinction between Solzhenitsyn's inferno and mine, it is because I feel an obligation, to the memory of those who agonized and perished in the Nazi death factories, to make sure that the historical record is not blurred, that the vocabulary of the Holocaust is not deprived of its unique value as a warning for the future.

For sheer demented horror, Treblinka, Maidanek, and Auschwitz were in a class of their own: the end of the world, the end of creation. They were no more in a category with the gulags than the ghettos of Bialystok or Warsaw can be compared to the ghettos of Harlem and Watts or the favellas of Brazil. Nor can the massacre at My-Lai — or even Hiroshima or Nagasaki — approach the delirium of death that swirled through the Nazi extermination camps. The Jews had attacked no one. Acquiescence, surrender, conversion — nothing would satisfy or appease our executioners. Simply and indiscriminately, we had to be expunged — our blood was tainted.

From Blizin, Ben and I, along with several hundred others who had stubbornly refused to die, were transported to Auschwitz — the crown jewel of the star-studded Nazi archipelago of concentration camps. And Birkenau, Camp D, where I was immediately consigned, was like the center court at Wimbledon — the ultimate.

Upon arrival, the vast dimensions of the camp stupefied me. The gigantic masterpiece was lined with barracks laid out as straight as a ruler. Only the odor marred the sense of propriety that must have inspired its German builders. The tall brick chimneys that poured smoke and shot flames at the camp's far end suffused everything with the repulsive smell of burning flesh.

A 2500-calorie intake is needed to keep a person productive. At Blizin, we were worked to death on food rations of 600 calories a day. But we were in a labor camp, and we knew that if we died it would be from hunger, dysentery, or typhus, or as a penalty for some conscious or unintentional infraction of the rules. They wanted to get some work out of us before we gave up the ghost and made room for another shipment of deportees. There were no gas chambers or crematoria —no technologically organized death.

Auschwitz, the end of the line for the long cattle trains creeping day and night from all corners of occupied Europe, was a place where the scientific method of extermination was elevated to a supreme art, dominating the ephemeral existence of its transient guests. Having surmounted the first obstacles in the race with death at other, less scientific, camps, its shifting population of 200,000 to 300,000 persons was the remnant of an already stringent elimination process. The dread of selections was constantly present. A lineup, a chance look from an SS officer or guard, a word, a nod, a shrug of condemnation could cut a person down like a scythe. A life expectancy of a few days or a few weeks was all one could hope for. A few months would be a miracle.

Utterly lost, Ben and I wandered among the prisoners — all anonymous numbers like ourselves — till one day I saw a familiar face. I stared at the man in silence. There was no doubt. I now recognized him clearly. He was a good friend of my parents, who used to visit us often in Bialystok. He never failed to bring Frieda and me little presents: candy and toys that I still remembered. And he is here, in the camp, I thought; Ben and I won't be so alone anymore. I ran up to him, elated.

"Heniek!"

He pinned me with a cold stare. I could see he recognized me too. "Get away from me," he snapped.

Sheepishly, almost ashamed, I held out my hand. "I'm not asking for anything, Heniek. I just want to talk to you."

He looked around worriedly. "Get lost."

I retreated, stunned, almost in tears. I could not understand why this kindly man who used to spend hours chatting with me, as a grown-up will with a boy full of questions, should have rebuffed me so unfeelingly.

Later, I understood. In the conditions that prevailed at Auschwitz, it would take a rare person to befriend a youngster. Every human tie implying dependency or sentiment threatened to bring on complications that, at any moment, could mean the difference between life and death. It was a hard lesson, but it was to stand me in good stead. Years later I would rediscover it, from another perspective, in an old Chinese proverb. I was so bewildered, I had to read the words many times over, realizing how precisely they reflected my experience of life and death: "If you give a man a fish, he eats once. If you teach him how to fish, he will eat all his life."

With his rebuff, Heniek taught me that I must fish for myself and probably took his place among those who saved my life. I learned from his example and others to be hard and to keep myself rigorously apart. At the right moment, no one and nothing could impede me from doing what had to be done to retain a chance of survival.

Within myself, I put aside all sensitivity, all modesty. I became cautious and resourceful. I forced myself, although only a child, to be "tough" in order to get by in the merciless grown-up world around me — a world whose reality one cannot grasp if one depends on such abstract concepts as honor, dignity, or human rights. At Auschwitz, these luxuries were useless and even detrimental. What counted was the basic animal instinct to endure.

Of course, the lesson did not apply to Ben. He and I were more than ever committed to "total partnership." In Auschwitz, we grew ever closer. Like me, he had no grown-up to talk to. We could talk — really talk — only to each other.

Then, after three or four months, I made another exception to my rule of self-reliance, as did Ben. We made friends with Niko.

In a chow line, a German convict who had been in the camp from the time when it was still mostly populated by hardened criminals, sexual deviants, and Soviet prisoners of war had pushed in ahead of Ben. My partner had a notoriously short temper and what ensued was an unequal brawl between two boys and a burly street fighter. Almost immediately, a command in a strangely throaty accent came from the back of the line. "Cut it out!" Before I could grasp what was happening, our aggressor lay writhing on the ground. The inmate with the throaty accent had struck a blow that could only have come from a karate expert.

Niko, whom the other prisoners called "the wild Dutchman" and whose cattle car had come in from Rotterdam, was around thirty. His parents had been gassed on arrival. Tall and slim, he stood out from among the other prisoners because of a swaying elegance in his stride and a sardonic wit. His sharp, ironic eyes could size up a situation at a glance.

From that moment on, Niko was the third member of our triumvirate and a resourceful older ally in the daily struggle against death. With Ben, he became my constant companion in the concentration camps. With Ben, Niko became my brother.

No bed, no sheets, no blanket, only a plain wooden plank shared with other prisoners who are inevitably encumbering. I lie freezing, my teeth chattering, in my wet rags. The day has been full of beatings, hard labor, and tension. I try to sleep, thinking of life outside, but with little hope that I will ever taste it again.

I cannot share my anguish with any of my fellow sufferers. And yet their anguish is the same as mine.

Illness drains me and wears down my resistance. Every morning I scrutinize the faces around me and try to compare their state of decay with my own, wondering which of us will survive the next "selection."

In the center of the barrack, a large pan serving as a urinal overflows, its contents sploshed across the floor. I am awakened long before dawn by guards who unbolt the door, yelling and striking out indiscriminately with whips and sticks. I scramble up. On the way out I shake someone who is still asleep on a lower bunk. I shake him again, since the slightest delay for the lineup can mean punishment.

Roll call! I turn one last time toward the motionless comrade, to wake him, to warn him, to help him. I grab him by the shoulders and turn him over — he is cold, stiff. No time to think. If I linger on with the dead, I will join them. The roll call takes priority over all else.

Under the goad of whistles and shouts I hurry out of the barracks to my place in line, while others clear out the "refuse" — the corpses and the urine from the night. For in this world of "law and order" the rules are followed meticulously: the dead are laid out on the ground in neat rows, next to the living, for the final count.

Across the length of the death camp, thousands of gaunt and cringing shapes, grotesque enough to outdo the weirdest imaginations of a Hieronymus Bosch, waver in ranks like the dried-up sweepings of subhumanity. The roll call is an elaborate ritual, a macabre mass.

The smallest mistake in the checkoff and the count starts anew. Twice a day, I stand immobile, sometimes for hours, in icy winds and freezing cold that can drop to 15 degrees below zero, numbing my limbs and my senses. What day is it, what month, what year? Nothing that happens is happening to me. Only the number tattooed on my left arm reminds me that I still exist.

How to make the most of my chances of putting off being sucked into the deadly funnel? The first rule is absolute submission. I found it hard at first, humiliating; anger mounted inside me. But after a while it became second nature, for the slightest murmur or pause, look, or gesture that could be interpreted as lack of humility was seized on by the SS as sufficient reason for condemning a person on the spot. The same was true of the kapos, the trusties chosen from the ranks of the inmates, mostly for their brutal and sadistic qualities — which, needless to say, were developed to the full in the inhuman conditions in which we foundered. We pressed ourselves against the wall when an SS or a kapo walked into our barrack; we froze and snatched off our caps when we met a German crossing the yard; we tried to be behind the guard or kapo when he turned this way or that, to avoid his glance if it wandered in our direction. We did everything possible, in short, to make ourselves invisible.

One day I passed an SS officer without pulling off my cap. It was no gesture of defiance: my head was simply down and I didn't notice him. At lineup that evening, my sentence was announced. It could have been death. Why it wasn't, I don't know. Perhaps he was a shade more merciful than his men.

"Number B-1713, for lack of respect, twenty-five lashes."

Stripped half-naked, I was tied to a post in front of the others. The leather thong tipped with lead tore across my back and buttocks.

"One . . . two . . . three . . . four . . . five . . . six . . . seven . . ."

Each stroke of the whip seared into my groin. Yet, out of some childish pride or some thought that it would count in my favor, I didn't let out a sound.

The SS man put his whip down. "Well! what have we here? A prisoner who is immune to pain? Very well, let us try it another way."

He resumed the strokes: "Seven . . . six . . . five . . . four . . . three . . . two . . . one . . ."

Then he started again: "One . . . two . . . three . . ."

The whip cut my flesh like a knife. My sight dimmed. Silence. I heard a shout — some prisoner betrayed by my punishment into the audacity of raising his voice. It was Niko's voice: "Howl, you fool, or you'll croak!"

Ben told me later I had received more than thirty lashes, still mute, finally unconscious, before the punishment was done.

I came to in the barrack, my back a bloody pulp, in the arms of Niko and Ben. Slowly they helped me out of my blood-soaked rags. I felt the acid fire of the rough cloth as it slid over my wounds. At just that moment, there was a whistle and everyone had to pile out for another lineup.

They stood me up and helped me dress. The cloth soaked up the blood. I leaned against a post. I tried to walk, but fell. They stood me up again. I was going to faint. No, I had to make it, at all cost: I had to take my place in line!

Somehow I did, and that pertains to the second rule of survival burned into my mind: never admit the least sign of infirmity. A sore throat or a cough threatening to develop into something worse? A cut or wound or sore that might be protected against a fatal infection if you can scrounge up a piece of cloth? A back or leg injury that makes you stoop or limp? Don't improvise anything that the guards can spot as a makeshift bandage. Hide any mark of illness, no matter how serious or how slight. Remember that you live under the precept — however lunatic it may sound in a pit where all are condemned to destruction — that the weakest, and often the bravest and the best, go first.

Granted there are no medicines in the barracks, no doctors or nurses to be called to your side — there is, for all that, an infirmary in the center of the camp; and, if you ask, you may be taken there. They will receive you and will sit you down. And then, when you are warmed and feel better, they will use you as a guinea pig for pseudomedical experiments — a brutal castration, perhaps — and in the end they will lead you off and cast you into the rooms with the hissing gas.

What we were primarily up against, Ben, Niko, and I, and all the others, was the constant pressure on Auschwitz to fill the extermination quotas handed down from Berlin as the trains with their loads of *Untermenschen* — Jews mostly, but also Gypsies, Poles, Russians, Frenchmen, Greeks, and other undesirable subhumans — converged from the four corners of Hitler's empire.

In our motley international microcosm — the perfectly planned and integrated society — all racial, ideological, and religious differences quickly disappear before a common fate. We were all in a utopia where equality reigned supreme: we all had an equal right to hunger, to torture, and most of all to death.

The new arrivals, particularly the close to half-million Hungarian Jews who were shipped into Auschwitz in the summer of 1944, kept straining the gas chambers and crematoria beyond their capacities.

Make room, make room for new arrivals! Six thousand, seven thousand, eight thousand persons disposed of in one day. Still not enough. Yet another higher quota is set! Ten thousand a day! The death factory works around the clock, trying to break its own previous records, and the trains keep arriving, day after day after day.

Constantly, the deliveries at the doors of the gas chambers keep on increasing. I watch them: men, women, and children massed up against the portals, the SS becoming more and more brutal, as though themselves touched by some form of death fever. The heavy metal doors close on the victims. A few small cries and the sound of prayers rapidly intoned, then silence as the cyanide does its work.

In three minutes it is all over. The gas chamber is just as efficiently aired out, the doors open and the corpses tumble out like a pile of dirty laundry. Now it is the turn of the *Sonderkommando,* a particularly hardened class of inmates, themselves slated for gassing, who pick over the bodies for gold fillings, hair, and anything else that can be sent to Germany for industrial processing.

Even if you kept out of sight, hid your physical impairments, and remained deaf to offers of kindness, the odds of the infernal lottery were overwhelmingly against you. At any moment, for no reason other than that the quota that day was still underfilled, you could be designated at a lineup or anywhere else, and that was the end of you.

One day I found myself among the condemned. We stood in a group in front of the camp gate. We stood for hours. Except for a slight sensation of nausea in the pit of my stomach, I remember feeling almost reconciled with my fate.

And then, for some reason, other groups were placed ahead of us. They had priority, we were told. Whether we had been rounded up ahead of plan or the authorities had slowed down the day's production schedule, German efficiency remained paramount and after a while we were taken back to our barracks. The next day was a new lottery, a new turn of the wheel.

A few months later and I am selected again. This time our group is placed in a halfway barrack to have our numbers checked off and to wait our turn. I manage to wave goodbye to Ben. It is harder the second time, somehow.

We stand closely packed in a dread silence, the faces around me flushed with the rage of helplessness, or some crazed hope of last-minute deliverance, or the hallucinatory peace of the imminence of death. At the back of the room, in a space clear of prisoners, I see a barrel of water, and alongside it a pail, brush, and rag.

Slowly, I creep forward on the floor. The people whose legs I touch are too benumbed to notice. Reaching the pail, I wet the brush in the water and begin scrubbing the floor.

I go over one section, then another, scrubbing and drying vigorously as hard as I can, like a good worker performing an assigned task. Slowly, I inch my way toward the exit. Now, one of the guards who had brought us in catches sight of me through the open door and looks indifferently the other way, supposing I am carrying out orders. Another calls out to me:

"Hey, asshole, over there, that part's still dirty."

My heart thumps as, gradually, I cover the cleared area and work my way ever closer to the door, past the legs of the other condemned prisoners too terrified to notice that I am one of them. I am close to the threshold when the same guard calls out:

"Hey, you, get back here. Clean that corner, you lazy slob."

I lift my pail and slouch back to where he stands. "Yes, sir."

The corner cleaned a second time, I resume my slow progress toward the door. It seems forever before I reach it, and when I do, I begin scrubbing the floor in front of it with a conscientiousness calculated to earn a pleased nod from the most demanding kapo. I dry the floor as though I want it to glow. Then, and only then, do I allow myself to stand up. Carrying the pail, with the brush and rag inside, I walk slowly to the door, then out into the open. I expect to be stopped — a cry, an order, a blow on the head. Nothing. With slow, measured steps I walk toward the other barracks and lose myself in the anonymity of the camp.

Ben, lying on our bunk, jumps up when I come in. He is wild-eyed, as though I have returned from the dead. Our pact, too, is resurrected.

Before sinking into sleep that night I see my mother's face. Could she have imagined how resourceful her little boy would become by himself in this unspeakable world; the little boy who, she was always afraid, might have an accident crossing the street, who would go out into the cold without his scarf, who did not like the taste of vitamin drops in his milk?

Sometimes you did not think you could make it one step farther. You heard the whistles that meant it was reveille and you thought: To hell with them, I'm not getting up; let them do what they will. Partly it was exhaustion, but partly it was despair: what was the use? Why pour all this energy and willpower into the struggle to get through yet another day when your days were numbered and the most you could gain for yourself was a brief additional span of hardship? It was so easy to put your hand on the electrified barbed wire.

But you overcame the despair because you had vowed not to give in to the bastards — or to yourself. You did not go through so much for so long to give up now. So you forced yourself up and stuck out your chin, and got into line and grabbed at the piece of gray bread, which, along with the gruel, whose stench you no longer noticed, lay between you and a lethargic death from starvation. And you felt that there was no limit to what you could endure.

Ah, that bread! What rituals were not performed in the slicing of the loaf that was rationed out for a certain number — the man entrusted to slice it measuring it out adoringly by millimeters, another turning his back so he could not see the pieces while calling out the names of those to whom they were to be apportioned. They snatched their slices with exclamations of joy or anguish, depending on whether a man thought his portion slightly larger or slightly smaller than it should be, the tiniest differences elevated to impassioned quarrels, envenomed hatreds, sleepless nights. And, eternally, that hard choice: Should I eat my slice now or should I store it up for the next day, when the rations may be reduced still further or there may be no bread at all? And if I keep it overnight, where shall I hide it? Where can I put it so it won't be stolen?

I remember a man of about forty-five, a dignified man in spite of his emaciated state, who was in my barracks. He had a son of about twenty. One evening the son ate his own piece of bread, while the father placed his under a crumpled piece of cloth that served for a pillow. The next morning the father let out a stricken cry: his bread was gone. It was easy to see what had happened. The son, lying next to him, had eaten it during the night.

The father was plunged into an inconsolable depression. That his own son could do such a thing to him — the knowledge shattered him. The next day he was dead.

Strange, how an organism that can go beyond the limits of physical endurance will often give up under a blow against the mind.

In this world without mirrors, with nothing that could give us even a faint reflection of ourselves, we were psychologically vulnerable to others' estimation of our physical state, and in our camp there was a terrible sentence that one inmate could pronounce on another: "You are a Musulman."

Where the expression came from I don't know, but it meant that, with the practiced eye of an observer of death from privation and despair, the man who rendered the judgment had recognized in the other the unmistakable signs of imminent collapse. I saw it work, time and again, with the potency ascribed at other times and in other places to the power of the Evil Eye. "You're a Musulman!" — and the person thus condemned was left feeling he had exhausted his last reserves of strength and hope. Men who had contrived to cheat the exterminators for weeks or months on end could be so struck by the verdict that in a day or two, not much longer, all the fight went out of them and they died with one conviction: nothing could be done and, anyway, no one cared. They expired on their bunks or dropped lifeless during the head count in the yard or at their place of work.

And what "work!" The motto over the main gate, "Work Brings Freedom," mocked us as we marched in step out of the camp like some lower-race variant of the joyous labor battalions of Adolf Hitler, with — the final indignity — our music-loving kapo ordering us to lift our voices in a song of praise for the Führer and the Reich. I recall even now, word for word, some of the lyrics: "March on, march on, with a quiet, sturdy stride . . ."; "Today Europe is ours, tomorrow the entire world."

The work of the unit I was placed in was to collect garbage inside the camp and take it to a huge pile some distance away, and then to turn this refuse into compost heaps to be mixed with human ashes and used for fertilizer. This malodorous heap was the rendezvous place for the most unbelievable of amorous adventures.

Contact with the opposite sex was unimaginable at Auschwitz. Every day separate columns of marching men and women would cross each other. In the circumstances, only one thought prevailed: "For us it's horrendous, but what must it be like for them?" That was how men and women "met" at Auschwitz.

The men who pushed the garbage carts were for the most part privileged kapos — big, sadistic brutes who enjoyed a certain freedom to satisfy their whims. The women selected to push the carts from their camp were the youngest and prettiest girls. They had no notion at first of the fate that awaited them. Close by our compost heap stood a small dilapidated house, its attic filled with straw — Auschwitz's improvised brothel for the prisoner elite.

I witnessed some of the orgies, being charged with keeping the participants supplied with water. After the first moment of panic, the instinct for survival made the young women overcome their revulsion and even pretend to enjoy the privilege of submission to our obsessed little gods: because if not pleased, gods can punish. A girl whose embrace proved unsatisfactory would have a black mark against her, the kapos warned, and would be beaten or executed on her return to camp.

It was an indelible experience for a fifteen-year-old, a shocking vision that was sometimes, against all expectation, touched by a hint of tenderness and beauty. Truly, humanity, even at its cruelest and most depraved, can be softened during the intimate surrender of the sexual act. A kapo who has been violent and cruel suddenly plants a tender kiss on a girl's lips and sinks helplessly and quietly away from her arms. Such sights contributed, perhaps, to my emotional development, leaving me with a sense that nothing that lives is quite beyond the reach of Eros, and that even among the most wicked or the most damaged, some wisp of human feeling can be found.

⁂

Not all kapos were totally sadistic tools of the Nazis. Otto, my kapo at the garbage heap, a small, almost dwarflike man with a long criminal record for armed robbery and an insatiable appetite for the youngest girls, was more interested in his diet and appearance than in beating up prisoners all day long. He made me his valet and gave me the immense privilege of shining his shoes, keeping his clothes in order, and preparing his meals. Otto knew that I was helping myself liberally to the leftovers.

One day, when Otto came back from the garbage heap with a bag of potatoes, I got the wild idea of making potato pancakes, the way my grandmother used to make them; I crushed the potatoes in a piece of cloth by pounding them against a stone wall and fried them in Otto's special ration of pork fat. My kapo hated the delicacy I served up before him and it almost cost me my job, but that evening Ben, Niko, and I had an incredible feast on our bunk. It brought us a vague taste of home.

Otto was very particular about his clothes: he had his uniform recut by one of the prisoners who had been a master tailor at home and the made-to-fit ensemble elevated him in sartorial elegance way above the other prisoners. I asked the same tailor-prisoner to refashion my cap so the vertical stripes on the sides would coincide perpendicularly with the stripes on top. After that, every prisoner who saw the astounding symmetry of my cap assumed instantly that I had some kind of special nitch in the camp hierarchy. It was a protective "hands-off" signal to anyone who wanted to take advantage of my age.

The work at the garbage dump had one major advantage: almost every day we uncovered edible scraps. Only the exquisite work contingent known as "Canada," which cleaned the cattle cars of the incoming trains, could rival ours in terms of the food that could be found in the garbage. We called it "Canada" because in our minds that word signified a land of great abundance. With pieces of bread, sausage, and other valuables I found in the garbage, and with kapo Otto's approval, I was able to arrange for Ben to be transferred to my group. Alas, this "nutritious" period of our captivity was very short-lived.

The oncoming winter was particularly hard. The cold was intense and the rations were reduced to a point where the inmates were falling like flies. One evening an announcement came over the loudspeakers in my part of the camp. Children and adolescents were to assemble after the first roll call for a supplementary ration of white bread and milk.

White bread and milk? We had forgotten what they looked like. That evening, troubled discussions took place in the barracks. Could the Germans be believed? Was it a ruse? For the cunning of the guards was another constant source of danger.

There were some other teenagers at Auschwitz, mostly Gypsies and a few Jews who, like me, had survived the first selections. For some of them the temptation was too great, and the next day, hesitant and full of fear, a group assembled at the appointed hour; they were given the promised food.

That evening, the offer was repeated. The following day, a few more children turned up. Again, all were given the precious white liquid and the unbelievable white bread.

For several days the miracle continued. The guards who distributed the rations were kindly for the most part. A sort of muzzy sentimentality descended on the camp. Against our common sense and everything we had learned, there spread the notion that someone in authority had been revolted by what was going on and that somewhere, at some command level, perhaps in Berlin, perhaps even at the level of the Führer himself, it had been decided to sustain the youngest victims — a simple humanitarian act.

I could have joined those getting the bread and milk, for I was still only fifteen, but something kept me back when the others would troop off for the distributions. The fifth or sixth day was the last. The children lined up with their bowls for the milk. But the rations did not arrive. Instead, there was a blast of whistles the length and breadth of the camp and a platoon of SS men burst into the compound. In a few minutes, the children were thrown into trucks. Some were taken to the "clinic" for medical experiments; the others went directly to the gas chambers.

Why? The most obvious answer is that the number of young people who had made it into the camp had become a problem: useless mouths to feed. They also seemed more resistant to the effects of extreme privation than the older folk and were not dying off fast enough — a fact of scientific interest to the Nazi doctors.

The simplest solution was to persuade the victims to cooperate in their own execution, just as it had been easier at earlier stages to lure the grown-ups into the gas chambers by telling them they would have to take a shower for sanitary reasons while their clothes were being decontaminated.

✣✣✣

In the winter cold at Auschwitz, typhus was a powerful instrument that helped to keep the death quotas filled. Anyone who caught it was usually dead within a few days. Covered with lice, wallowing in mud when it rained, living in the stink of human excrement — the inmates were allowed to go to the latrine, without paper and for ten seconds each, only once a day, and some went the rest of the time wherever the need overtook them. We tried to observe certain primitive sanitary precautions, knowing it was hopeless if an epidemic struck. But the hopelessness that outweighed all else was the prison of the mind. More than the barbed-wire fence with the searchlights and the machine-gun towers around us, the impossibility to glimpse some ray of salvation was the ultimate source of despair. The only way out of this place was through the chimney.

What was happening in the outside world? Did anyone out there know what was happening here to us? Did they care? Where was God? Where was the Pope? Did anyone anywhere still think that we had the right to live? Was there still an outside world? If Ben and I did not despair quite as much as the rest, maybe it was because we were too young to know the indifference that can inhabit the hearts of men.

Was the war still on? Were there no Allied aircraft to bomb the busy railway and crematoria installations of our camps? From the boasting of our guards, we had every reason to believe that all of Europe was under German occupation, even the Soviet Union beaten, the Red Army smashed. What chance had England not to fall to the seemingly invincible forces of darkness?

And America, America, are you still there? The United States was unprepared and far away. How could she be expected to reverse the remaking of the world at this penultimate juncture? Auschwitz was perhaps the entire universe. What miracle could prevent the millennium of the Third Reich?

And so time went by, and we lost count of the months; only the cold of winter and the heat of summer marked the passage of the seasons. One day was like the other, and we hid our injuries and puffed out our rib cages to show our sturdy health and forced our swollen legs to carry us on. We cringed before our guards and began to accept the cuffs and punishments as normal, arriving finally at an acceptance of ourselves as indeed subhuman and inherently inferior to the lords of creation who asserted their right to dispense life and death in the only world left under heaven.

Every other Sunday we were excused from work and could stay inside the camp and enjoy our free time. Groups of inmates lay about like refuse, or weaved their way along the barbed wire like the restless spirits of the damned, or jostled feebly around a faucet for a splash of water on the face or hands.

In the summer, during these hours of surcease, we sat in the open, warming our wounds in the sun when no guard or kapo was about, grateful to our masters for this enormous luxury — grateful that the trains with their limitless human cargo would cease roaring up to the gas chambers for this one day.

4

JUNE 6, 1944, when the Allied troops landed on the beaches of Normandy against Nazi cannon and machine-gun fire, was for us in Auschwitz a day like any other. The day's toll in the gas chambers was greater than the invaders' casualties on this, their longest day.

It took weeks for the news of the heroic invasion to slip into the camp with the Polish day workers who made deliveries to the Germans. Among the inmates it was whispered that the Russians had also mounted a powerful drive on the Eastern Front.

Incredible! God had not turned his face from the world after all. The impossible was perhaps no longer unthinkable. Oh, to hang on! To hang on a while longer, until liberation reached us from the west or the east. We could see from the Germans' increasing nervousness that, with the English still fighting and the Red Army on the offensive and America's full might mobilized and thrown on the scales, the weight of battle was changing decisively. It was now the Third Reich's turn to fight for its life.

Although the unexpected glimmer of hope boosted our morale and strengthened our determination to go on, for Ben, Niko, and me things were not easier. As still fairly able-bodied males at a time when the Nazis were becoming desperately short of industrial manpower, we were among a group of prisoners placed aboard a train and taken deep inside Germany. We did not know where we were being taken, but we were aware that to leave Auschwitz by the same gate through which we had entered was little short of miraculous.

After brief stopovers at a huge regrouping center near Berlin, and a stretch of several weeks at Sachsenhausen, a major concentration camp reserved largely for German dissidents, we were dumped on a snow-covered moor in the heart of Bavaria. Our new camp, Kaufering, had to be built from the ground up. This we did in the raw cold of early winter. Many men died from exposure, hunger, and punishment while putting up the barracks and workshops, but at least the blueprints did not call for the construction of a furnace.

Once the rudiments of the camp had been erected, we wondered about the productive labor purposes for which we had been dragged such a distance. It turned out that we were in for a period of respite during which no work of any kind was required of the bulk of the prisoners. Most of the days were occupied by long roll calls. The prisoners had to march in step or to run on the double around an alley, along the barbed-wire fence.

In the camps, the main problem was the German shepherds that the guards used to terrorize the prisoners. The dogs were trained to rip, on their masters' orders, at the buttocks of anyone wearing a striped uniform. Some of the dogs were specially trained: on the first signal, they grabbed the victim by the collar and pulled him to the ground; on the second signal, they put their muzzle on the victim's throat; on the third signal, they bit. The guards would regularly engage in this sport, occasionally going as far as the third signal. Remembering the tenderness and affection I saw the guards lavish on their beasts, I decided that a person who loves animals does not necessarily love people.

My first job reminded me of the house by the garbage dump at Auschwitz. A transport from Budapest brought several hundred young women, originally intended for the Wehrmacht on the Eastern Front, now rerouted into Germany for other purposes — birth-control experiments, someone said, to ensure the Master Race's future fertility and the future sterility of other races. I was ordered to search the girls as they were shaved, disinfected, and processed into the camp. This meant inspecting their most intimate parts for items they might have hidden on their bodies. Although my searches were cursory, the valuables I found even so were enough to open a small jewelry store. The instinct of all deportees was to take along their most precious possessions, especially those that could be easily hidden. The SS in fact encouraged them to do so, as it made the confiscation process easier.

Following the integration of the women into a specially zoned-off section of the camp, I became the only male regularly allowed to pass the barbed-wire separation. I functioned as liaison between the two barrack compounds, reporting to the main workshop what essential repairs were required in the girl's compound or alerting one kitchen of the camp that there was a shortfall or surplus of rations in the other. My fellow prisoners envied me my soft indoor job and my unheard-of proximity to female company. Niko and Ben ribbed me about what they called my eunuch life in the harem.

I enjoyed hanging around the women's compound and I became particularly fond of one of the girls, Bela, who was eighteen. When it was her turn for inspection on the day the transport arrived she looked so beautiful to me — even with her shaved head — and so shy that I did not have the courage to search her. We expressed ourselves mostly in sign language, as the only Hungarian I had picked up at Auschwitz was a vile lexicon of swear words. But even though we could not communicate well, feelings stirred in me that I had not experienced before — sparks that flared each time I saw her. As a seasoned prisoner I took it upon myself to teach her how to survive.

Although considerably older that I, Bela was like a child. She could not stop crying over her separation from her parents, who had been taken early in the summer of 1944, when she was away from home. I did not have the heart to tell her that I was certain they had gone straight into the ovens of Auschwitz with all the other transports that came in from Budapest at that time. Later, I realized it would have been better to force her to cut her umbilical cord and make her understand that she was alone and had to fend for herself.

Bela could not make the adjustment to camp life, even though she experienced no real violence or hunger. Ben was more than a little angry; he felt I violated our partnership when I gave her whatever extra food I could promote. She refused to eat it, even after I had repeated with her the scene at Maidanek when I had been ordered by a more experienced prisoner to gulp down that first bowl of disgusting gruel. Bela was becoming a Musulman before my eyes and I felt guilty that, by trying to help her, I was instead preventing her from standing on her own two feet. In the low-pressure conditions at Kaufering I became momentarily sentimental and unable to transmit to her the lesson I had learned so quickly from Heniek. By making her lot a little easier, I deprived her of a chance to fend for herself.

Ben's assignment — felling trees in the icy forest — was less delicate than mine. Niko was given an important supervisory function. Kaufering, a brand-new camp without any established prisoner hierarchy, allowed him to rise to a position of responsibility among the prisoners. The camp administration noticed his qualities of leadership and a situation that developed naturally was soon ratified. Niko became the *Oberkapo* of the camp, with authority over several thousand prisoners.

The kapos in general were a gruesome bunch and after liberation the first impulse of many survivors was to hunt down and lynch those responsible for the death or torture of their fellow prisoners. Once, later, I was beaten up by some former inmates when, yielding to the pleas of his girl friend, I testified on behalf of one particular kapo before an Allied investigative body, (untruthfully) saying he hadn't been as bad as some of the others. No one, however, had any complaints against Niko, despite his high rank in our camp.

Niko's main interest at Kaufering was less in asserting his authority than in getting admitted every night after roll call into the barracks holding the Hungarian ladies. The diets of a number of them improved extravagantly after Niko resolved the problem of admission, with the help of his friendly eunuch. Otherwise, Niko's standard stratagem, as *Oberkapo,* was to be tough in words when the SS were close by, and mild in deed when they were out of sight.

One day, Niko was ordered by the SS to hang three men for stealing cigarettes from the guardhouse. They fell on their knees before him, crying and begging to be saved. More than one kapo had been executed for not carrying out orders to the letter. But, instead of hanging the men by the neck, Niko strung them up on a makeshift gallows by their feet and told them to howl at the top of their lungs. Then, at inspection time, he ordered a whipping. The SS found the spectacle so amusing that they contented themselves with an additional twenty-five lashes and let them go.

Niko seldom spoke about his past. He had been a seaman and had worked for the Holland-America line, crossing the Atlantic many times. He had learned fluent English and German from the passengers. In brawls he exhibited the skills of a master. No one who picked a fight with him ever remained standing for long. There was talk among the prisoners that Niko had been a gangster or a gigolo on the Rotterdam waterfront. I did not believe it. In any event, I did not care. With Ben, he was my best friend, and I would not trade him for a dozen of my acquaintances who today pass through my life as upright and distinguished citizens. Who among them, I wonder, would have in similar circumstances shown the daring, the energy, and the generosity that Niko gave proof of day after day?

Under Niko's protection, no other kapo dared to mistreat me or Ben; in many respects, we had never had it so good. But this situation did not last long. Unexpectedly, I was tapped for transfer to another camp and not even my *Oberkapo* could change the verdict. Ben was working in the woods when my group was marched out, and there was no way even to say goodbye to Bela. Once again, I was on my own.

My new destination was Dachau, near the city of Munich — an immense installation filled for the most part with German common criminals, political prisoners, religious dissidents, and homosexuals, as well as some foreign nationals. I wasn't there long enough to remember much more than the physical symmetry and perfect organization of the camp. Everything ran with the efficiency of clockwork, possibly because there were so many Germans on both sides of the wall.

My most vivid memory of Dachau is the drill my camp group underwent. For several hours a day, we practiced the exercises I had acquired great expertise in during my days at Maidanek. The exercises consisted of a series of orders that the prisoners had to execute simultaneously, within a fraction of a second. Those unable to keep up were punished on the spot:

"*Attention!*" A thousand heels clicked together, yielding a single, solid sound.

"*Caaaps off!*" The thumb and index finger of the right hand had to snatch the cap off and bring it down in one continuous motion with a thud to the right hip, again in perfect unison with all the others.

"*Caaaps on!*" The cap had to be thrown quickly and as best one could, on the head, and the hand brought back to hip.

"*Rectify!*" The thumb and the index finger had to grab the cap, center it on the crown and bring back hand to hip in one single, solid motion.

"*At ease!*" The prisoners resumed dancing in place their weird little jigs and blowing on their cupped hands, in a futile effort to keep warm.

Between commands, the SS officer noted all prisoners from whose direction the click of the heels, or the slap of the hips, had not been perfectly synchronized, or those whose caps had fallen to the ground. These were marked for special drill, all day long, after the rest of the camp had been permitted to disperse. Prisoners incapable of coordinating this succession of movements often ended up with their skulls cracked open.

Soon I was moved to yet another camp. I began to hope that all these frequent and incoherent transfers were due to the chaos now gripping our German masters as their armies retreated on all fronts.

Leonberg, near Stuttgart, is a German town with clean streets, prosperous shops and *gemütlich* beer halls — in short, typical. On its outskirts there is a mountain called Engelberg — the "Mountain of Angels" — beneath which today a two-way tunnel serves the busy traffic of the Autobahn. This was not always the tunnel's function. In my days, the Mountain of Angels housed a major underground aircraft plant invulnerable to aerial attack. In that cavernous installation I worked for months riveting the fuselages of fighter bombers, put in hectic production against the Allied onslaught.

We lived in a camp which was close enough to Leonberg so that we occasionally saw the local citizenry standing with their children, on an elevation near the camp, and observing the spectacles inside: a shooting, a hanging, a whipping, or perhaps a routine evening roll call with its rhythmic "caps off — caps on" that made any military parade, even a German one, seem loose and uncoordinated by comparison.

Conditions at Leonberg were considerably better than at Auschwitz, with respect to both food and lodgings, for my comrades and I had been promoted to the status of slave laborers, at the heart of the Nazi's military-industrial complex. Our work was important to the war effort.

In our Vulcan's forge, we worked twelve-hour shifts and almost never saw the light of day. When we were inside the Engelberg in daytime, we would be marched to camp for the night, and when we were inside it at night, we would be marched back to sleep during the day.

The attitude of the German engineers who supervised us at work was by and large more humane than anything we had experienced until then. One of them, an elderly man, asked me how old I was and told me he had a grandson my age. He occasionally slipped me a piece of bread or sausage out of his lunchbox. Paradoxically, it was the Nazis' sudden concern with our physical safety that almost did me in.

The Reichminister for Armaments, Albert Speer, had decreed that aircraft workers were vital to defense and were to be carefully protected against loss of life or limb. Whenever a bombing alert occurred while we were in camp, we were rushed to the mountain, and to safety underground. As air raids became more frequent, we were shunted back and forth. We would complete the night shift and go to our barracks to sleep when the sirens would sound and — *"Achtung!"* — back into the mountain until the all clear. Or we would work the day shift and collapse for the night back at the camp when — *"Achtung!"* another air raid — and back underground. Sometimes we'd be shunted back and forth between mountain and barracks several times a day or night.

More effectively than hunger, more than illness or mistreatment, the systematic denial of sleep over a protracted period of time drained us of our last reserves. We would have given anything, even have risked death by Allied bombardment, for a few hours of uninterrupted sleep. The constant state of exhaustion decimated the population of the camp. Men, eyes glazed, would for no apparent reason suddenly go raving mad. They would be taken outside and shot.

A human being faced with the harshness of nature will somehow manage to survive even against seemingly impossible odds. But when hardship is placed in his way by the deliberate act of his fellows, the solution to the problem often is beyond human reach. Even at its cruelest, nature is kinder than man touched by evil.

✣ ✣ ✣

In early 1945, wave after wave of RAF bombers and American Flying Fortresses pounded our area, often catching us in the open. A night bombardment, with the spluttering lights of the attackers' flares, was a festive fireworks for us prisoners. It put us on a level with our Aryan masters, as they hit the dirt in fear and consternation. It even made us feel a bit superior as we listened to the flying shrapnel with the mystic confidence that a man who had survived under the scourge of Nazi brutality could not be earmarked for death at the hands of friends. These raids, more than anything else, gave us hope that deliverance might not be too far off.

The raids interrupted our work schedule in other ways. Sometimes we were marched into Stuttgart to dig out the wounded and the dead. As we rummaged about in the apocalyptic landscape, our interest focused more on warm underwear than on cold bodies, and what I cannot imagine myself doing today I did as a boy of fifteen, without the least compunction. Stripping a corpse? What did it matter next to the mountains of corpses I had seen?

I remember the mangled body of one old woman — she looked no less mortal than our dead in the camp. Crushed pieces of plaster stuck to her blood-caked face. She must have been in her kitchen during the raid, for there was a frying pan resting on her shoulder and a jar of marmalade nearby. I helped myself on the spot.

The guards under whom we worked grew tense as never before. They feared that it was the beginning of the end and lost no opportunity of impressing upon us that our turn would come before theirs. We took them at their word, but also sensed that they were becoming panicky. A few actually became downright considerate, hoping, I suppose, that we might put a good word in for them when the Allies arrived.

One night the silence of the camp was torn by a barrage of explosions of a different kind, far away in the unbroken darkness. Inmates with military experience thought it sounded like artillery. A few nights later we were awakened by a deafening blast, a rolling explosion that shook the whole camp. At dawn, part of the mountain was missing. The entire installation had been sealed off by the Nazis and blown up, together with the machinery. Many of the prisoners working the night shift were buried under the wreckage.

The next morning, the rest of us were marched to the railroad station to be evacuated ahead of the "enemy advance." These forbidden words, never before heard, were now murmured. We were beside ourselves with excitement. What "advance"? British? American? Soviet? At the railroad station, pandemonium reigned. Our group became mixed up with groups from other camps and with civilian labor teams from various parts of Europe. I had an inspiration. I would pass for an Aryan. My German was now fluent enough for me to pretend to be a convict born abroad of part-German extraction. An Italian laborer gave me civilian pants and a jacket.

I shed the biblical name my parents had given me, which until then had been a passport to the crematorium, and baptized myself "Gerhardt." I felt no less iota Jewish than before, but I was sure that as a non-Jew my chances to survive Germany's collapse would be greatly improved. As it turned out, I was wrong.

We were packed into a train and sent off on another endless journey, stopping and starting, going this way and that, to keep out of the way of army transport. Suddenly, the landscape became familiar, and a few hours later we were marched back into Kaufering. Ben and Niko were still there! Bela, as I had feared, had died.

Our reunion was wild. We laughed as if it were funny. My physical condition, however, had deteriorated badly due to the prolonged lack of sleep. I was wracked with spasms of coughing and spit blood. I had almost become a Musulman. Gradually, Ben and Niko managed to build me up with special food rations from the kitchen, which *Oberkapo* Niko procured without too much difficulty. They also got — I don't know how — dressing for my sores. When my strength returned, Niko teased me: "Off he went, this young jerk, thinking he could do better on his own, and what do you know? Now he comes running back, all skin and bones, begging to be forgiven."

It seemed that no one, nothing, could keep us separated for long! Ben and I almost came to believe in some form of divine intervention, although Niko, with his skeptical outlook, said it was just fool's luck.

✣ ✣ ✣

The war was coming to an end — that was clear. But as the end approached and the hope of pulling through became more real, the danger increased as well. With the advance of the Allied armies, the ground shrank under the Nazis' feet and, when they found themselves without room to retreat, doubtless they would destroy us, as I had seen them destroy my comrades at Leonberg. The final solution must be completed, and the witnesses and evidence of the crime wiped out.

What should we do — lie low, waiting for liberation, in the hope that in the ultimate confusion the Nazis would forget us? Or take things into our own hands and try to escape? We weren't the types to bank on a miracle.

We formed a plan: Ben, Niko, I, and about ten others. We would create a diversionary incident in the camp, a big, noisy brawl just before curfew, cut the barbed wire while the roving searchlights pointed the other way, and crawl through. It was a terrible risk — we would be executed if caught — but it was worth taking, given the fate that awaited us.

Niko's role was essential. As *Oberkapo,* he would be able to get the wire-cutters that we needed from a workshop outside the camp. Of the others, nothing was required except secrecy and presence of mind.

I still remember the looks the others shot at me and Ben: why did they need the burden of a couple of kids? But they knew that if they wanted Niko, they had to accept us.

As we waited for a dark moonless night to make our break, events beyond our control overtook us. Without warning, one day we were ordered to form two columns, Jews in one, non-Jews in the other. The women were to line up at the tail end of the Jewish column. Niko and Ben decided that my hanging on to my new identity of Gerhardt made sense, considering my serviceable German and my long absence from Kaufering; the kapos seemed not to remember me from before. So now, as they entered the Jewish line, I joined the other. And, as I had hoped, in the confusion, there was no identity check.

We started through the main gate, my column first, when an irresistible impulse seized me. I stepped out of line and darted back into the other column — the column of Jews. When I came up to Niko and Ben, I was knocked to the ground by a blow in the face. Niko had hit me, and now Niko, glaring with anger, pulled me to my feet. "Idiot," he railed at me as I fell into step, "now you are going to be roasted with the rest of us."

Perhaps I was an idiot, but we were together still. I had almost, by being too clever, sundered our mystical union. I could see that Ben was half sorry and half glad, as was Niko, behind the show of anger that often was the only way he knew to express his love.

In fact, had I followed through with my Gerhardt ploy, it would have been my end. Before long, the German front line buckled; the non-Jewish column had come too close to the war zone to suit the Wehrmacht commanders and the whole group of several hundred, along with some Soviet prisoners of war, was mowed down by the SS guards.

Our Jewish column of several thousand was marched along back roads. Down the line word spread that we were being taken to Dachau. Dachau, that huge and elaborate installation which I had seen with my own eyes, could mean only one thing at this eleventh hour: certain death.

The men who had accepted Niko's leadership in the original escape plan were still marching along directly behind him. Now came the whispers of a new plan: when the opportunity presented itself, we would make a break for the woods. Our success hinged on the likelihood that the guards would be unwilling to risk losing a whole column by going after a dozen escapees. Niko was grim. All he would say to Ben and me was: "Just stay close to me."

We were on the road without incident for two days and two nights, stopping only rarely for meager rations of bread and water. In the late afternoon of the third day, several Allied fighter planes — someone said they had American markings — mistaking us for German troops, swooped down low, strafing us. Our SS guards flung themselves to the ground, their machine guns blazing wildly in all directions. We stared at the planes, transfixed by the thought that our liberators were only a few feet above our heads.

Then Niko shouted: "Come on!"

I kicked off my clogs and bolted after him; Ben too. Our whole conspiratorial group made a clumsy, uncoordinated run for the trees. Then others broke away from the column. German fire caught most of them. The only ones who made it to the woods were Niko, Ben, and I, and three others.

We ran and ran and ran, gasping for breath, finding strength we did not know we possessed, until we could not run any longer. There was no sound of pursuit, only the thunder of our beating hearts. From the direction of the road came an occasional stutter of machine guns. We stumbled on, I don't remember how long, our feet sore and bleeding, trying always to work our way deeper into the forest. Then it was night, and Niko decided that we could rest. I plunged into sleep and woke up with the young spring sun in my eyes and the long-forgotten sound of birds chirping in the ears. I looked around and, for the first time in four years, I saw no barbed wire and no guards; there would be no head count to line up for. Yet it was not freedom either.

Because I looked least suspicious, least like an escaped prisoner or convict, it was up to me to find food and water. I also was charged with getting some civilian clothes. I broke into a nearby farmhouse, in broad daylight, under the nose of an old woman who was there milking cows. I thought her husband must be out in the fields. I thanked God that she had not noticed me, because, under the circumstances, I would have had to do her harm.

For myself, I appropriated a peasant outfit, including a pair of short Bavarian leather pants. Mother's idea served me well this time too, for now, almost sixteen, to be safe I needed to look younger.

We thought it would be better to move toward the Western Front than to stay put, and Niko figured out the direction by the North Star. We moved by night and hid during the day. But I had difficulty keeping up with the others. Of course, when I had opened the pantry of the farmhouse kitchen, I'd been mesmerized by what I saw, and so my first order of business had been to eat on the spot about a pound of raw bacon, washed down by a bottle of sour cream. Not enough. Walking back to the forest where my comrades awaited me, I had two baskets full of food in each hand, as if I were a peasant boy taking produce to the market, and had stopped here and there to drink a few raw eggs. Now, as we moved through the night, I was caught in the grip of uncontrollable nausea and diarrhea. I wanted never to look at food again as long as I lived.

My friends said that I should be happy if I survived my little feast, seeing that my body had been practically without fats or proteins for years. Niko, of course, was furious and said that I should have been left behind with the column; but I knew he didn't mean it.

We entered a densely populated area where it became more and more difficult to keep out of sight of police and army personnel. Anytime we passed a German in uniform it was difficult to restrain the compulsion to snap to attention and reach for the imagined cap. The habit inculcated over years had created a conditioned reflex.

When, one night, a week or two after our escape, we almost blundered onto an airstrip swarming with troops, we decided we had better find a hiding place in which to wait until the German retreat had passed us by. On the outskirts of a village called Penzing, we found what we were looking for . . . an abandoned barn.

We were holed up for several days and nights. Then, in the stillness of one bucolic afternoon, lying in the hayloft, I suddenly became aware of a hum, like a swarm of bees, growing in volume. A machine gun opened fire alongside our barn and, when it stopped, there was that hum again, only louder, unearthly, metallic.

I peeped through a crack in the wooden slats. Straight ahead, on the other side of the field, a huge tank was coming toward the barn. It stopped, and the humming ceased. From somewhere to one side, machine guns crackled and the sounds of mortar explosions carried across the field. The tank's long cannon lifted its round head, as though peering at me, then turned slowly aside and let loose a tremendous belch. The firing stopped. The tank resumed its advance, lumbering cautiously toward me. I looked for the hateful swastika, but there wasn't one. On the tank's sides, instead, I made out an unfamiliar emblem. It was a five-pointed white star. In an instant, the realization flooded me: I was looking at the insignia of the United States Army.

My skull seemed to burst. With a wild roar, I broke through the thatched roof, leaped to the ground, and ran toward the tank. The German machine guns opened up again. The tank fired twice. Then all was quiet. I was still running. I was in front of the tank, waving my arms. The hatch opened. A big black man climbed out, swearing unintelligibly at me. Recalling the only English I knew, those words my mother had sighed while dreaming of our deliverance, I fell at the black man's feet, threw my arms around his legs and yelled at the top of my lungs: "God Bless America!"

With an unmistakable gesture, the American motioned me to get up and lifted me in through the hatch. In a few minutes, all of us were free.

II
Redemption

Unearned suffering is redemption.
— Martin Luther King, Jr.

5

THE GIs say, "Hi, kid." I reply, "Heil Roosevelt." I have been adopted as an army waif. I am fed with American government rations. I am dressed in American government issue. I am safe. I am alive. But I am not content.

I have developed the heart of a warrior, become a sort of mini-Patton. I want those tanks with their white stars to roll on at once into Berlin, Treblinka, Bialystok. Who knows, maybe someone — I dared not think who — might be found alive. Why don't these tanks keep on rolling?

My new American friends understood my impatience. A few of them spoke halting Yiddish, learned from their immigrant forebears. A Jewish major from Chicago traced his family back to a village near Bialystok. He had taken part in the liberation of a death camp, farther west, and speaking about it still went white. Others in the regiment questioned me for hours on end. They sat silently, listening, their faces dark with outrage. The major warned those who went out to comb the woods for enemies that all German prisoners, even the SS, must be treated in accordance with the Geneva Conventions, on pain of court-martial.

One day a jubilant announcement comes over the regimental loudspeakers. Hitler has committed suicide! Germany has surrendered! The Third Reich is no more . . .

The army camp explodes with joy. Liquor flows. Officers and enlisted men hug each other. Ben, Niko, and I go off by ourselves. We should be ecstatic, but we feel strangely empty. Is anyone celebrating in Rotterdam? Is anybody celebrating in Bialystok?

No, for us this was not the happy ending. It was the beginning of something unknown, disturbing.

My mind flinched at the thought of a journey back to Bialystok. For what — to search in the bloodstained sand for the blown-away traces of the dead — those nightmarish visions which repeatedly invaded my sleep? I knew, once the war was over and once the reasons that Ben and I had given ourselves for staying alive had served their purpose — to lend us the will to stay alive — that the hope against hope to which we had clung was only an illusion, a hypnotic refusal to believe. There were too many eyewitnesses with too much evidence, informing me that my father and mother and sister had died, for me to undertake any insensate pilgrimage into the burned-out cauldron of my private hell. Had I been older, perhaps I would have done it anyway. At sixteen, I could not bear the thought.

Then what? What should I do? Who was I? I felt lost. Peace had come to Europe; I could go where I pleased. But where could I find a place called home? Where?

Of the three of us, only Ben still refused to accept that his family was dead. He wanted to go back to Bialystok to look for his mother and sisters. Vaguely haunting both of us was a strange, half-submerged sense of guilt at having survived. By what right were we alive when so many others — the best — were broken and killed?

I made an effort to dissuade Ben from returning. Bialystok was now occupied by the Russians. In Soviet eyes, he and I were undoubtedly still Soviet citizens — a status foisted on us when Stalin and Hitler divided Poland between them in 1939. We might even be drafted into the Red Army, or be refused exit visas to leave the Soviet zone. And having sampled Soviet occupation, neither of us had much taste for the communist paradise. We wanted freedom; we wanted to live.

Ben left, nonetheless, hitching rides in army trucks. On roads choked with hordes of displaced persons and a flood of refugees from the east, he eventually came across people from the Bialystok region. They gave him a firsthand account of what had become of the town — the entire Jewish population massacred, the Soviet Army in tight, iron-handed control — and had persuaded him not to go farther. Within a week he was back in our village — Penzing.

With defeated Germany in an anarchic state, long-harbored dreams of revenge were discharged by masses of foreign nationals awaiting repatriation and by others who, like us, were displaced persons with no papers and nowhere to go. A climate of abuse and violence developed. The Germans, for the most part, were cowed and submissive.

Some camp survivors banded together to track down former SS who had served as concentration camp guards. We could usually spot the type among the throngs of haggard soldiers in their dirty uniforms, and even when they wore civilian clothes; the proof was the blood-group designation tattooed under their armpits. The temptation was strong, but I could not become a killer, not the son of David and Helaina Pisar. I never even enjoyed beating up those despicable creatures; nor did Ben. About Niko I can't be sure.

One of the more determined Nazi hunters among us was "Warsaw Moshe." Moshe, who had taken part in the Warsaw ghetto revolt, had been with us at Auschwitz and had seen his wife and five children exterminated there. Mad with grief, he would set out each morning to track and kill an SS, or a kapo, or any former prisoner who had been an informer or collaborator of the Nazis.

We three could not help but breathe the atmosphere around us. Not that we went about with vengeance in our hearts — we were, rather, three lost souls groping along, unsure of our footing — but stirred and stimulated by the heady air of a brand-new world in which everything was possible and everything was permitted. We thrived in the middle of chaos and destruction.

One of the first acts we undertook as free men was to "requisition" three huge German army motorcycles from a demobilization depot. Mine had a beautiful chromium-plated sidecar.

On those powerful machines, we spent days hurtling through the outskirts of Penzing, the village where V-E Day had found us, enjoying the wide-open spaces around us. The nights we passed with an assortment of German women. This was now Niko's chief occupation and Ben and I modeled ourselves after him as best we could.

One day we drove our motorcycles into a farm and asked the farmer politely for milk, butter, cheese, and eggs. I fondled a stolen Mauser that I always carried with me. The German obliged without a murmur.

After we loaded up, and before speeding off, I put a much-folded piece of paper in his hands. When he unfolded it, he would read: "Merciful God will pay you. Samuel Pisar."

One act of lawlessness makes the next one easier, and where we had come from, the ethic was that to follow the law meant certain death. Pretty soon we were foraging everywhere and provisioning ourselves regularly and royally off the countryside.

Nor were we beyond looting. Joining a group of liberated Russian prisoners who ransacked the area, we broke into a large mansion on the outskirts of the village and helped ourselves to its contents — shoes, shirts, pants, whatever we could find. I spotted a beautiful Leica camera, which I grabbed and slung over my shoulder. Our scavenging was interrupted by a frightened but extraordinarily beautiful young woman, who came down the staircase. Addressing herself to Niko, she pleaded for some items that were of sentimental value to her family. He looked at her appreciatively and told us to stop and to get out. Ben and I were not surprised, but the others left only grudgingly and one, as he went out the door with an armful of loot, shouted over his shoulder: "What's the matter, Niko? You want to keep all the Fräuleins for yourself?"

On another occasion, one of the local farmers had the nerve to say we were behaving like bandits. We broke all the windows in his house and called him a Nazi, even though he obviously was too old to be one.

After a while, we lost our enthusiasm for these raids. Yes, we were on the winning side for a change. But along with the initial exuberance it brought, we began to get an inkling of the emptiness of victory.

Yet we were intoxicated with freedom. Ben and I, who spent two years under Soviet occupation and four years in captivity, and Niko, who was confined even longer, began to find Penzing too small for us.

We moved our activities to a bigger town, Landsberg, where, by greasing the palm of an old German housekeeper, we got ourselves a three-room flat, on the main square, that had belonged to a family killed in the war. It took us a while to get accustomed to sleeping between white sheets that were changed every week, to use the bathroom at will, to have running water. Niko even started perfuming himself with after-shave and putting oil on his newly grown hair. "How many times have I told you two punks," he would yell, "to use your own fucking toothbrushes?"

✣✣✣

The whole Allied occupation zone of Germany was open to us for exploration. The Americans were easygoing. Our camp-learned guile, placed at the service of our unbounded energies, needed a broader outlet. We thought we saw one.

The Germans lived mostly in abject poverty, the Americans in isolated abundance, accompanied by unbelievable waste. I can still remember my stunned amazement the first time I ate breakfast in the army mess hall. Rows of stainless-steel containers, two feet by three, heaped full with scrambled eggs, half of which would be thrown out, together with whole loaves of day-old bread. I couldn't believe my eyes. We could act as middlemen between these two contrasting worlds.

For a carton of Lucky Strikes, or a pair of nylons, we would put a black GI in touch with a willing German Fräulein. But our principal medium of exchange was coffee — practically unobtainable then in Germany. Ben found a job as assistant cook in an all-black American regiment. He had a thing about getting close to where the food was.

Every morning, when preparing breakfast, he would pour a few extra sacks of the aromatic beans into the urns, so there would be plenty of grounds left over after each meal. I would drive up on my motorcycle, pile sacks of wet grounds into my silver sidecar, and take them home. There I would toast them in the oven of the old brick kitchen stove and pack the recycled coffee in small brown paper bags. We would then market our product as "real Brazilian coffee," exchanging it for valuables of any sort. There was almost nothing the Germans would not part with for a taste of real coffee, and the long years of drinking ersatz had made even our grounds seem like the real stuff.

We diversified. A certain Herr Pflantz had despaired of his shoemaking business on account of the worthlessness of the German mark; we bought up his stock at two pounds of coffee for a pair of shoes and bartered our new line off for a healthy profit. As the months went by, we acquired a certain notoriety.

Niko blossomed into a man-about-town. With a white silk scarf thrown casually over a dark blue overcoat, he cut a figure with the ladies, of whom he never could have enough. He knew how to play the harmonica and had a beautiful voice. Before long, Niko was singing all the GI songs and, although I did not understand the words, I hummed the melodies of "Sentimental Journey" and many others.

Niko became friendly with a young upper-class married German woman named Mimi. She was ready to abandon everything for him but he shied away from the responsibility and lived with her only intermittently; she bore him a son whom she named after Niko's father. When her husband returned from the war, Mimi went back to him and they both moved to another town where she later died.

Mimi's mother treated Ben and me like members of the family and I learned again about human warmth. I liked to threaten her, only half in jest, that if her son, who had been a member of the Hitler Youth, ever came home, he would be ripped apart. He never did. I would not discuss with her, or any German, my own family.

But she once showed me a photograph of him in uniform, saying: "He was only a boy. I wanted to keep him out of the Wehrmacht."

I looked at the picture. He was a good-looking boy about my age. He was wearing short pants.

In Landsberg, I discovered that Germans could be human beings like any others, a realization that shocked and upset me then. Since the age of twelve, I had considered all of them, without exception, to be monsters, and believed that the only good German was a dead German.

The first time I held a German girl tenderly in my arms, I'm not sure I knew what my emotions really were: genuine feelings for her, a tinge of racial revenge, or simply the first stirrings of manhood. I still don't know. All I am sure of is that I was grateful that she was so alive.

Although I followed Niko's example in most areas, my true love was my motorcycle. I tried cars too, however, and on my first attempt to drive I completely demolished a cream-colored Mercedes that Niko had quite simply taken from some former Nazi's garage. Dressed in a Gestapo-like leather coat and high leather boots — oblivious of the irony — I could not be parted from my 500cc BMW bike, morning or night. I would show off on a bet, with acrobatics, risking my neck in ways that today give me shivers just to think about. We were all ready to try anything and everything, so long as it was new, amusing, daring, dazzling.

One hot summer day we drove out to Lake Ammersee, near Munich. Niko undressed and jumped in. Seeing him execute a spectacular dive, sailor that he was, I jumped in after him, not stopping to think even for a second that I had never learned to swim. Swallowing water and unable to scream, I was sure my hour had struck this time. My thrashing around looked like clowning to the onlookers, until Niko realized that I was desperate, and pulled me out.

Years in the death camps had convinced me that I was now immortal; flirting with death — an intimate companion — had become a habit. We might easily have been killed a dozen times in our folly, our frenzy, to live every day, every hour, every second, to the hilt.

Our fall, when it came, was abrupt. We expanded our commerce when we found a German with a well-stocked liquor cellar. (Fortunately, there were no drugs then.)

A pound of coffee returned us a bottle of first-class schnapps. A GI who drove a gasoline truck would siphon off part of his load regularly for five bottles and a docile blonde. Gas at that time was severely rationed and our new business prospered so spectacularly that, as new cellars brought us a widening clientele, on the one side for the whiskey and on the other for the gas, we were bidding to render the United States Army nonoperational in the state of Bavaria. The army did not fail to react.

One fine morning Niko set out on his rounds and landed in prison. He was picked up in the home of the daughter of a former Wehrmacht general by two white-helmeted American constabulary who transported him to jail in a jeep marked MILITARY POLICE.

I was outraged: that Niko, ex-prisoner of the Nazis, should be imprisoned again by our liberators — by the same people who had defeated his former jailers — that dear, brave Niko should be thrown into a German prison, and, ugly irony, the very same prison where, twenty years earlier, in the aftermath of the Munich putsch, an arrested agitator named Adolf Hitler had sat and written *Mein Kampf*. It struck me as monstrous. What had Niko — what had Ben and I — done? Facilitated with skill and success the workings of the laws of supply and demand, nothing more. Couldn't a man be free anywhere in this world?

In truth, the viciousness of camp life and the amoral jumble of the postwar scene had badly impaired my sense of right and wrong. It could hardly have been otherwise. Today, when I marvel at my escape from the Holocaust, I thank providence not only for sparing my life but for saving me from the spiritual debasement toward which I was heading, a kind of postwar juvenile delinquency, in the rubble of Germany. I bribed a German warden at the prison fortress (which, at that time, held very few prisoners) and was led down a long echoing corridor to Niko's cell.

After a quick look through the spyhole, the warden sifted through his enormous key ring, finally coming up with the right one. "Visitors time!" he squawked. The lock creaked and the door sprang half open. There was Niko, sitting on a wooden plank, half-naked, beard stubby, almost like in camp. He stared at me dumbfounded.

"It can't be true! What are you doing here?" he asked. "Are you nuts?"

"I've come to rescue you."

"What?" He sounded displeased.

"No, I've thought it all out. I've got one of the prison guards in my pocket. We'll plan an escape."

"Look," Niko said, disgusted. "We're not in camp. These Americans aren't Nazis. Besides, they've got nothing on me. I'll be out of here in a couple of days."

He wasn't. Instead, Ben and I were picked up at our apartment. The charge sheet was as long as your arm: black-marketeering, theft, assault . . . whatever they could think of. They had had it, and wanted to be rid of us. Ben went into the cell with Niko. I, being a year younger than Ben, was put in a juvenile detention home. I was furious. To be separated from my two companions, to be in prison without them! I made such a racket that I was thrown into solitary confinement. From that cell, I continued hollering, demanding to be transferred to the main prison and urging the older youngsters to rebel. Notified by the guards, the prison director, in person, paid me a visit.

"Quiet down, young man. I warn you. Otherwise . . ."

"What do you mean? — *otherwise!* You lousy SS! They should put you away for good in one of your own concentration camps! Instead of letting you go on with your dirty work here!"

The director was just a petty bureaucrat in the German penitentiary system, doing his job. He probably figured it would be dangerous to punish a victim of racial persecution, so he just threw up his hands. He got hold of the American military authorities and asked permission to transfer me to Landsberg fortress.

Once there, I insisted on being put in with Niko and Ben, and found them sharing a large cell with a half-dozen hardened criminals.

"Hello, you guys!"

"How the hell —? Impossible! How did you manage this??"

"I told them that — "

Suddenly, I smelled something burning. The back of my jacket was aflame — some kind of initiation rite for new prisoners. I rolled on the ground to smother the fire, amid unfamiliar peals of laughter. Then Niko, Ben, and I exchanged looks and threw ourselves at them.

It was rough in that cell. Like being in the middle of a perpetual gang war. After several days of brawling we convinced them to leave us alone. Luckily, Niko was still the old pro, despite the new perfume and brilliantine. His punch was dynamite, and it worked with marvelous precision. It was my forte to go for the legs, while Ben specialized in the half nelson. We had gotten through much worse in the camps.

A week went by without any indication that our case would come up. I persuaded a guard to let me use a phone in one of the administrative offices. I had make it past the prison check-in with a few gold coins in my shoes, and a couple of diamond rings acquired in the course of my recent "business" activities. The search had been even less thorough than the ones I had made of the Hungarian girls imprisoned at Kaufering. One of my coins did the trick.

I told the guard, who held on a short leash a huge, implacable German shepherd, to get me UNRRA headquarters in Munich. Since our liberation, we had seen representatives of the United Nations Relief and Rehabilitation Agency everywhere in Germany — helping DPs get food and shelter and arranging their repatriation to the homeland. From the very beginning, we gave them a wide berth, for we had no desire to be put into a refugee camp, or live on public welfare. Now, however, the time had come to avail ourselves of their services and our rights.

When I finally got through to UNRRA, the voice on the other end was speaking German with an American accent.

"Goldberg here."

A Jew! I let out a yip of relief.

"*Shalom!* — Listen here," I said, "I am sixteen years old. I spent four years in the extermination camps. Auschwitz — ever hear of it? Then no sooner am I liberated than they throw me in prison. You know *which* prison?'' I paused. ''The very same one where Hitler was once held, and where he wrote *Mein Kampf* — Landsberg. Nice, eh? And do you know who's one of my fellow inmates now? Krupp, that war criminal who used us as slave labor to build arms for the Nazis. This is a disgrace. You've got to get me out of here. With my friends.''

''What's your name?'' he asked, in a voice that shook.

''Samuel — Shmuel, like the prophet,'' I corrected myself, ''Shmuel Pisar.''

I gave him some facts about myself, Ben, and Niko, and about Bialystok and Rotterdam. I laid it on. I had no compunction about exploiting the past. And I glossed over our black-market exploits as innocent pranks.

Goldberg, whom I later met, was a sensitive young man who had only recently arrived in Germany. Like so many other American Jews he was guilt-ridden in the face of a European Jew who'd survived the Holocaust — because he had not suffered.

It worked. Two days later, we were out of prison and in the custody of a UNRRA official who came for us in a jeep with documents issued by the American occupation authorities — all the doings of the admirable Goldberg. But our freewheeling days were over.

We were driven to Munich and put in a refugee center on the city's outskirts. The officials at the center, though at a loss about our future, were solicitous of our requests. They tried to persuade us to go to Palestine. We had heard about a man called David Ben-Gurion who came from Tel Aviv to speak to Jewish survivors about Zionism and the homecoming awaiting us in the land called Israel. But Niko felt that living in collective settlements wouldn't really appeal to us. Besides, we'd heard stories about boats full of Jewish survivors, bound for Haifa, getting stranded on the high seas when the British administration under the Palestine Mandate refused to let them disembark.

An extremely wealthy Jewish couple from South Africa visited the DP camp. They desperately wanted to adopt a child. They promised me everything: they said I would have anything I wanted in their Johannesburg home. I turned them down flat. I needed no one but Niko and Ben. They were my only family.

We spent most of our time outside the camp, at the movies or in beer halls. The UNRRA officials let us go into town whenever we wished, but to preserve appearances, someone in authority was supposed to accompany us. Although we found it a soft life, we missed the action left behind. We'd become hooked on that.

So one day we just walked out of the refugee center, took the train to Landsberg, and picked up where we'd left off.

Yet it wasn't the same. Goldberg's Boy Scout eyes, the earnestness of the UNRRA officials worrying about what would become of us had had their effect. A bad conscience can take many forms. For us, it led to a kind of impatience with each other.

"Look," Niko said, "you two little bastards can't go on pissing your lives away. You've got to do something sensible."

Ben said, "I want to — well, I'd like to *learn* something."

As soon as he said it, I knew that's what I wanted, too. Niko nodded. "Sure. What you two need is some education. You don't know beans. You know how to survive, but you haven't learned how to live."

We asked around for a teacher and found a German professor, a war veteran.

"What would you like to learn?" he asked us.

Ben shot me an embarrassed glance.

"As much as possible. What can you teach us? A little Latin, a little arithmetic, and geography. A bit of everything."

Our thirst for an education was matched by the professor's longing for coffee. We made a deal. In exchange for some of the brown bags of which we still had large reserves, we'd receive daily lessons.

Our good intentions didn't last more than a couple of weeks. For boys whose only schooling, for five years now, had been in physical survival and semilegal barter, the intellectual effort which even the most rudimentary of educations demanded proved too much. Poker was more in our line. We dropped our professor and began spending our nights at the card table, with hard-boiled gamblers from the local underworld.

One night I hit a losing streak playing with a bunch of real pros. I lost all my money, then my hoard of rings and bracelets; I had nothing left.

"You've still got your motorcycle," said one of the gamblers. I fingered the ignition key in my pocket and the pistol next to it.

"No," I said, "I guess not."

I rose from the table, flushed and angry . . . at my father. Why had he refused to teach me those sleight-of-hand tricks and his magic way of handling cards? Much later I decided that, had my father given in to my pleadings, I would certainly have ended my days in some smoky card room — with a knife in my guts. I never played cards for money again.

We prospered. We hired a cook and thought of opening a store, When I walked down the street, the Germans, out of servility, treated me like a big shot.

"Good morning, Herr Pisar."

When the three of us walked into a restaurant, or a movie theater, with a waiting line of Germans, Ben or I would yell out: *"Achtung!* The Herr Director is here!" The line would move over, and Niko would walk in with the two of us in his wake.

Could this be us, the nameless numbers, the village rakes, now big-town worthies, prospective tradesmen? *Was it progress?* In my heart, I wasn't sure. Landsberg was a decompression chamber for us, an extraordinary no-man's-land between the dark depths of the past and the gradual surfacing to new life. If we wanted to remain in Landsberg, we had to be prepared to adapt, to realize that freedom had to have some limits. It wasn't a very tempting prospect.

❖❖❖

One day, as we were having lunch, Regina, the cook, came up from the first floor. She looked at me, "There's someone in uniform to see you."

Our eating stopped. No one operating just this side of the law is happy about an unannounced visit from somebody in uniform.

"Say I'm not in."

And the three of us climbed out the kitchen window and dropped into the backyard.

A few hours later, we thought it safe to return. But then Regina came in again. "The man in uniform is back. He says he's got to see you. He says he's a relative."

I was at a loss; the idea that I could have any family left had been far from my mind.

"What's he like?"

"He speaks German with a French accent. I almost forgot — he says he's married to your aunt."

Memories floated vaguely in my head. The fireplace in Bialystok. My mind tumbled through the photos my father had tossed, one by one, into the flames before we were hounded to the ghetto.

My mother had a sister who was a student in France. That which minutes before seemed impossible suddenly was plausible.

His name was Leo Sauvage. He was a slight, finely boned man in French uniform, who introduced himself as a journalist, married to my French aunt, Barbara. We stood facing each other, uncertain of how to proceed. He looked at me through thick glasses. I judged him to be thirty, but his hesitant tone and awkward gestures made him seem my junior. I could also see that he was taken aback. It was not hard to understand why. He had come prepared to find a pathetic starveling, sifted out of the ashes. Instead he saw before him a well-built, healthy-looking gallant of independent mien, evidently rather satisfied with himself and the world around him.

"My God!" said my French uncle, "how you resemble your aunt." After I introduced Niko and Ben to him we took a stroll.

We spoke in German. His was cramped. Slowly but precisely, as we walked up and down the street, he told me what I wanted to know.

My aunt Barbara had corresponded with my Australian uncles, Nachman and Lazar, and with our relatives in the United States. Their letters were weighed down by the horror of what became known of the fate of Europe's Jews. My relatives sought to discover if any of the family remained alive, but their queries all drew a blank. Then, on a list of people liberated from the concentration camps, compiled by the U.S. Army in Munich and circulated around the world, they saw the name Samuel Pisar. Could it be little "Mula"?

Samuel had been the son of David; he could have been only ten at most when Poland was divided between the Soviet Union and the Third Reich; it seemed impossible that one so young had survived, when millions of adults perished.

"So your aunt sent a telegram to Brussels, to the address on the army list. And she got a reply: 'Dear aunt, I am sick, I need you, please come.' It was signed with your name."

I laughed. "That's not exactly my style."

"Just wait. Your aunt went to Brussels, found the street, the house, and walked up to the eighth floor and knocked on the door. An old man opened up. He was bald and, clearly, he was very sick.

"She asked, 'Are you Samuel Pisar?'

" 'No,' the old man said, 'my name is Stachelberg.'

" 'I received a telegram from . . .'

"The old man sat down on his mattress. Silence. Then he said, 'I am all alone, and sick. I was in a concentration camp. When I got your telegram, I thought I could borrow this name, Pisar, so you'd help me a little.'

"Your aunt was speechless.

" 'And you don't know where this Samuel Pisar lives?'

" 'I never heard of him.' "

It was a terrible disappointment to my aunt, and to my other relatives. They did not know what else to do.

As a war correspondent, Leo Sauvage had freedom of movement in the Allied occupation zone of Germany, and wherever he went he asked to see the DP records. In Munich he saw, again, the name Samuel Pisar. The person has been placed in a local refugee center but had disappeared. The only address that existed was Landsberg, where he had spent time in the prison fortress.

Leo Sauvage had hurried to Landsberg. He checked the town hall registers, the jail. Nothing. He went to a café. "Have you heard of anyone named Samuel Pisar?" he asked the waiter.

"Herr Pisar? Of course! We buy coffee from him." And the waiter directed Leo to our apartment.

We stopped in front of our house and he studied me intently. Delighted as he was to find me, I sensed there was something about me he found disquieting.

"Your aunt entrusted me with the mission of bringing you home with me if I found you."

"But I'm fine where I am. I have my friends, I have my — uh — occupation . . . my work."

He didn't object. I knew what he was thinking: first win the boy's confidence, then we'll see.

"Here's a little present from your aunt. She put it in my pocket just in case."

It was a wristwatch, plain metal. Yet given the wartime shortages, it must have represented a tidy sum in France.

"Ah," I said, "it's nice," accepting it indifferently.

He saw my massive gold watch and gold chain and hid his thoughts behind the acrid smoke of one of those dark French cigarettes he was constantly lighting. It was his last one and he crumpled the package.

"Here — uh — Uncle. Come with me."

He followed me inside. In a room full of whiskey bottles, coffee sacks, and powdered-milk cans, I pried open a big wooden crate where we had stored a hundred or more cartons of Lucky Strikes.

I offered him a carton. "I only smoke American. You don't mind?"

He accepted it without a word, biting his lip.

❖ ❖ ❖

Aunt Barbara arrived within a week after Uncle Leo had left. With uncommon determination she beat down the bureaucracy, which did not want French civilians roaming around occupied Germany. Her husband's report had thrown her into a panic. Twenty-nine, pretty, high-spirited, and refined, she came prepared for a long siege. She announced that she would camp in our apartment. Niko graciously gave her the bedroom he used for his conquests and moved in with Ben and me.

I warned Niko, "Listen, one false move with my aunt and I smash in your face."

She did not start her appeals at once; these, she knew from Leo, would have to be carefully timed. I was charmed by her French humor, her French lightness, and she in turn was amused and a tiny bit enticed by our raffish existence. But even though she did not know about the secondhand coffee and the schnapps and the gasoline, she was well aware of the deadly dangers around us; and after a while she brought the conversation around to how much she and Leo would like it if I came to Paris to live with them.

I rebuffed her, even when her entreaties became tearful, all the while wondering how long I'd be able to resist. Finally, she played a trump card, the one argument that carried everything before it:

"For your mother's sake, you must come!"

Pictures from the past conjured up in my mind, faces as they looked at me for the last time . . . I was trapped. "All right! I'll go to Paris if Ben and Niko go with me. Otherwise, I stay."

After long negotiations we reached a compromise. I would leave as soon as my papers had been arranged, on condition that once we got to Paris, she and Leo would do the same for Ben. It appeared that Niko would have to join us later. There were problems in his past, so it would take a while to get him approved for residence in France.

It was hard to break the news to Ben and Niko that once again we would be parted, though with a far better chance, this time, that it would be only for a while. They, it turned out, had never expected me to hold out for long against my determined aunt. But neither did they expect me to stay away for long. They remembered what had happened with the German professor.

The American colonel who reviewed my record received Barbara and me in his Landsberg office without much warmth.

"I'll be glad to give you the authorization you want," he told her in fluent German, "but are you sure you know what you're doing?"

In the light of my black-marketeering wheeler-dealings, arrest, and imprisonment, my conning of UNRRA, and my flight from the DP camp, he put little stock in Barbara's hope for my moral regeneration. He heard her out and, before signing the paper, said, "Madame, your nephew is a hardened case. If you ask me, he belongs behind bars." But then he added, as an afterthought, "Look, you couldn't take all three of them, could you?"

Barbara and I drove to Munich together on my motorcycle, she in the sidecar. The French consul there was a functionary of a zealous stripe.

"What's your nationality?" he asked me in German.

"I guess I don't know."

"What do you mean, you don't know?"

"Well, I was born in Poland, so I was Polish, then the Russians came, so I was Russian, then the Germans came and took me to Germany but they sure as hell didn't make me into a German. . . ."

After we left, Barbara translated for me the conversation that had followed in French between her and the consul.

"He told me it was required to have your identity card, Mula, and a certificate from the civil authorities at your place of birth. Then he went on: 'We must also have a medical certificate and three references attesting to his moral character.' "

Barbara had stared at him in disbelief, and then had exploded: "Monsieur, don't you realize what sort of person you are talking about? The city where my nephew was born has been razed to the ground. The records are all destroyed. His whole family was exterminated. The only identity card he has is the number on his arm."

The consul had shrugged, looking ill at ease. "I understand the situation, Madame, but there's nothing I can do."

Barbara had risen out of her chair and flung at him: "You're worse than the Nazis!" The man had paled.

"Look at him!" She had flung her arm toward me dramatically, and I had watched, tickled by her dramatic vehemence, though already I could see this interview would have an unfavorable outcome. "He is condemned if he does not quit this horrible life; this horrible country. And you, Monsieur, are delivering the coup de grace!"

We had stamped out of the consulate, Barbara completely undone and I rather annoyed for her sake.

I was already fond of this young aunt who was showing such concern for her fragile, helpless little nephew, who constantly begged him to mind his table manners and watch his language. "Where on earth were you brought up?" she would exclaim absentmindedly and then catch herself and turn away her face to hide her tears.

The idea of going to Paris, the city of lights about which I had heard so much, in Bialystok, began to intrigue me. "Look, Barbara," I said, "don't worry! Go back to Paris! I'll join you there, and *soon,* I promise."

She looked at me. "You? What can you do against these clerks?"

I smiled as one smiles upon a fretful child. "I'll think of something, you'll see."

Barbara did go back, because there was no point to her staying on. "I'll resume my campaign with the French authorities, Mula, when I get home," she told me. "I'll speak with my husband's connections.

If that doesn't work, we'll spread it across the front page of every newspaper in Europe. It's a disgrace.''

A week later, Ben and I rang the doorbell of her Left Bank apartment on the Boulevard Saint Michel.

How did we do it? This is one incident I prefer not to expose. Let me just say that, at about this time, a Polish military mission crossed the German border into France. When it proceeded on its journey, after a stopover at the city of Strasbourg, it was lighter by two Poles.

Barbara and Leo were stunned, overjoyed but also worried. It would take all of Leo's high-level contacts to regularize my situation with French officialdom. The need to intercede on Ben's behalf as well would make it doubly difficult. I didn't see the point of all of the formalities.

''We're here, aren't we?'' I argued.

But they were adamant that we should have regular papers and somehow they prevailed. Our identity cards were stamped ''Stateless.''

Once that happened, I reminded them of their promise about Niko. ''We left everything behind to join you: our flat, our comforts, our bikes. We've got to have Niko!'' But that was more than they could manage.

❖❖❖

Paris was more sumptuous, more inspiring, more colossal than anything I had imagined. Its gardens, palaces, and cathedrals were of storybook grandeur. The encounter between Europe's greatest historic capital and the stateless, anonymous adolescent who had known the normal world only at the level of Bialystok and Landsberg, and long rows of wooden barracks otherwise, would develop into a lifetime affair. But in that winter of 1946, Paris was cold and gray and poverty-stricken; the rationing that was still in effect was hard to take after the luxury to which, lately, I'd grown accustomed. Since my aunt and uncle, with their two-year-old son, Pierre, lived in a small apartment, there was no room to spare: Ben and I were domiciled separately with friends, he on Boulevard Raspail, I with a professor of the Sorbonne opposite the Luxembourg Gardens. Gradually, I awakened to a new and delectable world.

Until now, the lessons learned in camp had governed all my actions.

I'd had to keep myself hard, invulnerable, suspicious of sentiment. For the first time — through Barbara and Leo and their friends — I learned to surrender to the normal. I didn't give in easily. They wanted the oddest things from me — that I eat at regular hours three times a day, that I sleep in my own bed every night, that we visit their relatives on Sunday, that we hand over good money to a bus or metro conductor.

The ravishing young women who were a part of this way of life made the routine more acceptable. Soon I began an affair with one of them. She was quite a bit older than I, and called me her wild fawn who needed domestication. I thought I'd surprise her with what I knew, but I learned from her much more than I taught. I moved in with her and for the first time, I think, my behavior was not conditioned by external pressures but internal feelings.

In Australia, my uncles Nachman and Lazar rejoiced over my springing to life out of nowhere, and importuned me to join them. I was not averse to the idea of emigrating to that new continent, whose advantages they described so energetically. They understood that Ben had no one left in the world and agreed to bring him over, too. And they promised to do everything they could regarding Niko.

It was pleasant to bask in Barbara's and Leo's affection, and the joys of first love were a novel experience, but I had sold all my ill-gotten valuables and was growing tired of being without money. The best job my aunt had been able to find for me was developing films in a darkroom at a photographer's studio that specialized in French movie starlets; and, for Ben, an apprenticeship in an electrical supply shop, learning to repair radios. I gathered Barbara and Leo were praying that we two young monsters would learn some kind of trade and hold down steady jobs. But that was not our idea of life. We needed a couple of motorcycles. We needed elbow room. And, most of all, we needed Niko. I wrote to my uncles, restating my conditions and giving my consent.

The papers did not take long to arrange. The ticket arrived, with money for the trip; I would proceed to Southampton and board a seaplane, which would fly me in stages to Melbourne. We said our goodbyes, Barbara and Leo and Ben and I. My other parting was more difficult but she had wisely known our liaison could not last, and her tears were quickly dried.

As in a movie reel, the French farmland flitted past my train window, the English Channel foamed underneath, a train very different from all the trains that had carried me before slid into a railroad station, and a taxi driver — responding to the only English I could summon: "Hotel, please" — bounced me across war-scarred London, to a mansion whose luxury far exceeded anything I had ever seen: It was the Mayfair Hotel in Berkeley Square. I realized, a few days later, after being presented with a bill on a silver tray, that the cabbie had taken my measure by the cut of my Landsberg clothes and the heavy gold watch and chain. I promptly corrected that mistake by pawning most of my possessions and moving to a dilapidated hotel on Russell Square that charged five shillings and sixpence a day, breakfast included.

The dark green of the English countryside opened out before me during the bus ride to Southampton, where a great water bird waited to swoop me up. I buckled my safety belt, ready for a flight to another planet. Without regret, I was abandoning the psychotic and suicidal continent of Europe, forever. An essential gulf was being created between me and my past.

In my coat pocket I had a letter from Niko. I reread it on the plane. In his ironic manner, he wrote about the latest in Landsberg. Feeling guilty, I had to admit that the details of what until recently had been my whole life now seemed remote, colorless, part of something I was pleased to be leaving behind.

Me, several months after liberation by the U.S. Army

ABOVE: *Niko on his machine*

OPPOSITE ABOVE: *Ben on his machine*

OPPOSITE BELOW: *Me on my machine*

Ben and me after our release from the Allied prison at Landsberg

Niko posing for me at the desk of the U.S. military governor of Landsberg

Barbara and me on the way to Munich to see the French consul

Aunt Barbara and Uncle Leo in Paris

6

BENEATH me: Naples, Athens, Cairo, Tehran, Delhi, Bangkok. One after the other, sweltering cities and harbors teeming with the strangeness of Asia appeared before my bewildered eyes. I gaped, every stop making me more and more conscious that I was being severed from Europe, the only ground I ever knew, by a voyage of no return. Still, my mother's dearest wish was coming to fruition. In two days I would reach Australia. The sun was melting over the horizon when we set down in the bay of Singapore and I looked out the window at the tropical landscape.

I was carrying my suitcase to the bus that was to take us to an overnight hotel, before going on to Melbourne, when I spotted an imposing stocky figure planted twenty feet away, across my path. He was staring at me intently.

I stopped. Yes, there was no mistaking it. Those pictures of him. That memory of him, though I was only eight when he left Bialystok.

The man who now took a few hesitant steps toward me, his blondish hair disheveled by the wind, his green-blue eyes fixed on me, his face tense with emotion, was Uncle Nachman, my mother's brother.

"It is you," he said.

He stood before me, this rock, this family legend who had foreseen our gruesome fate, whose entreaties that we leave Poland as he had done had not been heeded in time. He shook his head, as if trying to dislodge the disbelief from his eyes. He trembled as he hugged me. He was crying. I was embarrassed.

We stood there for a long moment. He kept shaking his head: "It's really you." Then he dried his eyes with a handkerchief and gave me a timid smile. He put his arm around my shoulders and picked up my suitcase.

"Come on," he said in Yiddish with a firm voice. "I flew to Singapore from Melbourne to have a talk with you."

"Plenty cheap, My Lord! Take you anywhere! Plenty cheap!" A skeletal rickshaw puller tugged at my uncle's sleeve. A slave, a horse? I thought that men like this lived only in my past.

Uncle Nachman hailed a taxi. "Raffles Hotel," he said. "Raffles," he added, conversing as though to fill in time, "is a landmark of the British Empire in this part of the world."

"We will have this talk" — he paused for a moment — "just once, only once. After that, we will forget everything, absolutely everything, that has been said. I want you to arrive in Australia with only your new life ahead."

Uncle Nachman and I had separate rooms. He sat in mine after dinner, questioning me.

I saw that he blamed himself for not doing enough to save our family, the only survivor of which was now sitting in front of him, and for being far away and secure and not having suffered himself. I became aware that, for him, I was a symbol, a precious remnant of what once had been. His precise, pressing questions, his tragic gaze, made me ill at ease. I thought that he was punishing himself in vain, that it was useless to add further suffering to all the suffering that had come before. Besides, I didn't want to talk about those things. I had talked about them already with Barbara and Leo. I didn't want to talk about them with Uncle Nachman too.

The night was hot and humid. My answers grew terser as my depression increased. I was young, I wanted to live, to forget. I didn't fancy myself as a cult object. The past was past.

Uncle Nachman sensed something was wrong. We sat for a long time in awkward silence. Outside, night had fallen and the harbor lights twinkled over the water.

"You remember your friend Kniazeff?" I asked. I wanted to show him that not everything about him had been ineffective, that he had been useful, even from afar.

"Kniazeff? Of course — my best friend! When was it that I saw him last? Ah, yes — at the Sporting Club in Bialystok in 1937, just before I left."

"He saved our lives."

I told him how the SS had assaulted the Bialystok ghetto and how my mother and sister and I had fled through the carnage and massacre to the gates of the old hospital.

"There was Kniazeff, trying to reason with the crowd clamoring for admission. Mother called out to him: 'I am the sister of Nachman Suchowolski!' Kniazeff heard her and instantly made a path, for the three of us, through the crowd and into the hospital."

Uncle Nachman listened, petrified.

"That was our last night together. In the morning, the Nazis separated us and I didn't — I never —"

Something at the pit of my stomach rebelled. I felt a little nauseated and went to the open window. The night held a tropical fragrance. I felt better, breathing it in. No, damn it, I hadn't taken on this Australian journey to relive all that! I looked at Uncle Nachman, bowed in his armchair, his eyes caught in an empty stare, and walked out of the room.

In the corridor I heard music and, following the sound, I strolled downstairs into the hotel nightclub. It was almost empty. On a small stage by the dance band an Asian girl was singing. She was pretty and wore a brightly colored sarong wrapped gracefully and intricately about her waist. I took a nearby table, admiring her openly, and she smiled at me when our eyes met. After the music ended, I asked the Malayan waiter to see if she would join me for a drink. The waiter said she did not drink with the customers at the nightclub, but afterward, if I wished . . . ?

At breakfast the next morning, Uncle Nachman was withdrawn — tense. I, on the other hand, was feeling better — more communicative — enjoying a hearty feast of papaya, mango, passion fruit, and other things I hadn't even known existed.

My little adventure of the night before, with an all-too-palpable present, had pushed the depressing past back where it belonged, and made me more appreciative of this strong-featured relative of mine who had come all the way to Singapore from Melbourne so he could draw the whole story out of me, never to oppress me with the subject again. My grandmother was his mother, my mother was his sister, and he had a right to his full hour of the kind of grieving that, with me, had been parceled out in spasms. I decided to let him have it, once and for all.

By word and gesture I conveyed to him my change of heart, and he, I believe, understood and regretted the stress to which he had subjected me the night before. From that morning on, there was a change in his attitude toward me. I think he realized that he had been treating me as a symbol, and that I was not to be typed; I was an individual with my own inner reality and more than my share of quirks. From then on Uncle Nachman and I talked unconstrainedly, and by the time we arrived in Australia, three days later, I had poured out to him a great deal of what he wanted to know.

In Melbourne, Uncle Lazar welcomed me; he was my mother's other brother, who had left Bialystok to study in Paris when I was an infant. Uncle Lazar had the keenest and kindliest eyes of any man I had ever known. Since he was a bachelor, it was thought better for me to stay with Uncle Nachman and Aunt Rachel, who had two children; they would give me a sense of family.

Australia's beauty was striking — its marvelously fragrant eucalyptus trees, its extraordinary wildlife, its naïve and gentle aborigines, its endless deserted beaches washed by a gentle surf. But after several weeks, my irritation returned. It was only natural that the two brothers should invite relations and friends to meet the nephew they had plucked from the embers of Europe, yet I couldn't help feeling at those interminable parties that I was on show, like some freak, some kind of memorial for public wonderment. Besides, life with Uncle Nachman and Aunt Rachel was even more family-centered than with Barbara and Leo, and much too tranquil for my taste.

Nachman wanted me to become a child again. When I reached for his razor one morning, thinking it was time to begin to shave, he looked at me sadly and said: "I know you have lived more than many grown-up men, but what's the rush? You have time." He wanted me to recover all those years that had been stolen from me — but I was now seventeen.

"Where's Ben?" I demanded of my uncles. "You promised you'd get him over."

"We're doing it," said Uncle Lazar. "We got Stachelberg over —

that old man in Brussels who pretended he was you. Why wouldn't we do the same for your Ben?"

"He'll be here soon enough," said Uncle Nachman. "Meanwhile, it's high time we thought about getting you back to school."

"I'd rather have a motorcycle."

"You can drive the Buick as soon as you get a driver's license."

"I don't need a driver's license. I've driven cars before."

They ignored my brashness. I appreciate now the tact and determination they used in a mission they considered sacred — to rescue the son of David and Hela from the dehumanized heritage that otherwise would strangle his life.

"We've arranged for an interview tomorrow morning," Uncle Nachman said. "You haven't opened a book in six years. We must see what we can do about that."

Professor George Taylor headed a special school for dropouts. Seated in his office between my two uncles who were briefing him on the tortured itinerary of my life, I chaffed under his penetrating stare. Uncle Lazar said something to him, and then Uncle Nachman, and then the professor spoke, looking grave and drumming his fingers on the tabletop. I guessed he wasn't quite sure he could handle me, and I wondered whether, perhaps, my case was more desperate than I had imagined.

Uncle Lazar spoke again with great intensity, and Uncle Nachman interjected his views in a similar tone. They were trying to impress upon the professor that even if full rehabilitation was impossible, whatever still lived within me must not be allowed to die. He, George Taylor, an expert in such things, must provide me with a modicum of education.

I remember the Australian pedagogue gazing thoughtfully out of the window, pondering, I now suppose, whether this youngster was to be considered no longer recoverable — whether he was to be given up on, as the U.S. Army colonel in Landsberg had recommended that Aunt Barbara do — or if some chance remained to bring him back. He must have been wondering whether what had happened to me at so early an age, and for so long, had pushed me beyond the point of no return; whether his science was up to the challenge of this extreme case.

Then he spoke again, and my uncles smiled and nodded emphatically. I had never really considered my lot as desperate, but now, suddenly, I felt as though, once again, I had passed "selection."

"Truly he is an exceptional case," said George Taylor. He got up to shake hands. "His fate moves me deeply. We'll see, perhaps we can come up with a special program."

I would start next morning, but he did not think he could put me in a class. Instead, I would get private tutoring. First, I would have to learn some English.

Miss Lockwood, my tutor, was a sour-looking old maid, but I was determined to show her — and that professor, and my uncles — that I wasn't as retarded as they supposed. I applied myself to these lessons as I had applied myself to outwitting my camp guards and to selling our "real Brazilian coffee." After a few weeks, Miss Lockwood asked Professor Taylor to free her from her other duties so she could devote all her time to me.

I suppose the chagrin that led Ben and me to search out the Wehrmacht officer in Landsberg as a tutor was now rekindled in circumstances that threw my past deficiencies in even bolder relief. Or, perhaps, certain hereditary qualities that had been pinched off like flowers in winter were reasserting themselves. At any rate, this time the impulse to learn was sustained. A few weeks short of my eighteenth birthday, I entered what would become a regenerative phase in my life.

After six years living as an animal, aware only of the physical and the immediate, cut off from nourishment for the mind, I soared in dizzy excitement at Miss Lockwood's expressions of delight with my progress, and my uncles' satisfied looks.

I threw myself into the study of English, possessed by a rage to learn. I knew that Professor Taylor had expected to do no more with me than inculcate a working vocabulary stamped with an immigrant's accent — enough to be able to find and hold down a job. Within several months, however, I could understand everything he said.

Within a year I was exploring corners of the language he had never imagined I would discover. The English language quickly became my very own. It also became for me a marvelously unencumbered vehicle to the world of knowledge, a vehicle that did not carry with it, as did all the other languages I already knew, the emotional baggage, the fears and terrors I carried from my violent past.

Soon I was going to classes in history, geography, math, and other subjects, along with the Australian boys at the school. My mind soaked up knowledge like a dehydrated sponge. I set myself the task of learning in the shortest possible time everything I should have acquired by degrees since the age of twelve. There was something fanatical about me, and even my uncles began to inquire with concern if I wouldn't like a break from time to time, to go to a movie or a concert or a dance. No! I dug myself into an armchair — to discover Dickens or cudgel my brain over Shakespeare, or memorize Milton's "Paradise Lost," or the Gettysburg Address, as if my life depended on it. I commandeered Uncle Nachman's nine-year-old son, Sym, and read passages out loud.

"I want you to listen. Correct me when I mispronounce anything."

Abashed at the ferocity of this strange kin, the poor lad would lift a timid hand from time to time.

"Yes?"

"Just a little mistake. In pronunciation."

"Good. Which word?"

I kept him prisoner for hours. One day he lifted his hand, again.

"Yes?"

"I want to go out and play!"

I could see he was near tears. "All right. But remember, tomorrow, at the same time."

I now enlisted Uncle Lazar. Having studied mathematics and science in Paris, he was well versed in arithmetic, algebra, geometry, chemistry, and physics and he coached me so well that, before long, I was outstripping the other boys in those subjects.

My life, I now understood, had been at a dead end. Physically I had escaped, I was breathing, but Hitler had programmed my mental and moral destruction from his grave. The struggle for survival was going on once more, survival through study. It had to be waged with the same determination, the same fury.

One evening, Uncle Lazar looked up from the algebra book. He paused.

"When you sit flushed like that," he said, "your eyes shining, you make me feel my sister has been resurrected. She had the same love of learning, at your age."

That was the only time he allowed himself in my presence to go back to the past.

Some months later, Ben arrived by boat. He was welcomed like a member of the family, put up in the bachelor home of Uncle Lazar, and taken to Professor Taylor in his turn. Half-scornful but half-awed at my transformation into a bookworm, he showed a different bent and soon was studying electrical and mechanical engineering in a vocational school. I was delighted to have him with me again, but now something began to worry both of us.

Niko had stopped writing. In fact, my uncles' efforts on his behalf had proved unavailing — something in his background had prevented the issuance of an Australian immigration visa — but that would not have caused him to ignore our letters. We sent telegrams: no reply. Ben and I feared Niko had been arrested, or worse. One thing we felt sure of: he would never willingly break his ties with us.

I discovered that my uncles were intercepting our correspondence. They had accidentally come across one of his old letters and were disturbed by its content and its cynical tone. They had also noticed a return to some of my old wildness, a relapse that I too was aware of; it was mainly a reaction to becoming what Ben called "a learning machine." But my uncles attributed it to the letters from Landsberg, with their whiff of the old life; and they were doubly afraid of Niko's appearing in person, were he able to make it to Australia on his own. They decided that my contact with Niko should be cut, lest he undermine all their efforts to have me return to a normal life.

Who knows — given my restless mood, Niko in Melbourne might indeed have had just the seductive and disorienting effect my uncles were afraid of. But at that time, the mystifying silence from Landsberg only added to my unsettled state.

I still was given to flashes of violence. One day, in chemistry class, when I dug into my jacket pocket for a piece of chalk, I pulled out instead a banana peel. At the desk behind, a boy named Bill Downey grinned, chomping on a banana. With the blood rushing in my head, I swung a Landsberg jailhouse punch at him; he was knocked from his chair to the floor. The class fell silent. The teacher, who had seen the whole incident, acted as though nothing had happened. She had read my file and feared that if she made an issue of the incident, it would be the end of my scholastic career. The boy picked himself up and looked at me as if I belonged to some unfamiliar species at the zoo.

I was mortified. Fool, I said to myself, what have you done? You have reacted as if he wanted to kill you. Have those Nazis succeeded after all? It's no life to remain a savage. If you really want to make a life for yourself, you've got to become civilized. It's not enough to pass exams. You've got to learn some self-control as well. You have got to lock up the hoodlum in you and throw away the key.

I looked around the room, begging silently to be understood. The other students turned their heads. Bill Downey looked straight through me, his cheekbone splotched where I had hit him. How could I make it up to him? I had forgotten what it was to apologize. I had been in hell too deeply and too long. The next day I presented him with two pounds of bananas. He did not say a word, but he accepted them.

All in all, that wonderful continent was my teacher in the most elementary things. My first written exam, a serious challenge to be sure, did not fill me with much apprehension. But, walking into the room, I saw my classmates trembling with fear, almost sick with anxiety. I couldn't understand it. If they failed, what could anybody do to them? Anyway, the teachers trusted them — it was child's play to cheat.

Australia taught me initially unfathomable lessons: about the senselessness of cheating, about fair play, a sense of sportsmanship, about "what's done" and "what isn't done" — those things that make a gentleman and were not part of the education of Auschwitz and Landsberg. "Down Under," these attitudes were preserved to an even greater degree than in England, which bequeathed them. Australia was a temple to the virtues of the pioneer, to open and unlimited spaces, the principles of individual responsibility and playing the game. Its banner flew high on the fields of amateur sport throughout the world. In swimming and tennis, in running and cricket, the Australians dominated. I threw myself into long hours at the pool and the track. I even tried to play cricket, hoping naïvely to make up for the lost adolescent years, to show my new classmates that I was to be regarded as one of them.

They, for their part, were more than ready to accept me. Several future Olympic champions and world-ranking tennis players became my friends. The great runner John Landy, who broke the world record by running the mile in well under four minutes; the swimming champion Junior Foster; the Davis Cup star Neal Frazer were all in my class. Their exhausting hours of training every day, for no evident purpose, seemed like some form of idiocy to me at first, and although I realized that I would never be a star athlete myself, the physical, mental, and moral disciplines of the world of sport gradually became my new creed. I suppose even there I overdid it — it's the curse of people who surmount impossible odds that they must focus too singlemindedly, forever after, on whatever they undertake, even when the obstacles are long gone. For me — who had known contest almost exclusively in the conditions of the death camps — to see men battle without quarter and then go off as friends was a revelation.

It was close to two years since I'd arrived in Australia — and already the country had taught me more than all the subject matter of my school curriculum.

I graduated from high school, the proud possessor of a diploma, like all the others. I was just nineteen, a little old for that stage, but determined to catch up along the way.

The code of honor at college bowled me over. For instance, if a student didn't know the answer to a question posed in class, the others would pretend they didn't know either, so as not to show him up. What nobility, I thought, what a fine grace! I copied these niceties like a monkey, for the first time in my life eager to take a back seat, to defer for the sake of politeness. It took Harvard and Washington and all that followed to knock some of this new stuffing out of me. The wider world, I was soon to learn, was not organized around the rules of the University of Melbourne. But I am glad to have profited from the fin de siècle manners of that sheltered grove, and I count myself lucky that the acquisition of a proper sense of modesty and proportion in dealing with others was part of my passage from barbarity to civilization.

In the spring of 1948, Ben and I went through an emotional crisis. The new State of Israel, whose existence as a sovereign nation both the United States and the Soviet Union recognized and helped arm, was under assault on all sides by five Arab armies which had vowed to drown it in blood, filling our minds with visions of a second genocide in one decade. The nightmares that had intermittently been troubling our sleep since the liberation became more frequent. Although we had no animosity whatever toward the Arab people, we felt that having survived the last holocaust, it was our duty to go to Palestine to fight, and, if necessary, die in order to prevent the next. Never again!

We scouted around and made contact with a Jewish group that was looking for tough young volunteers. With some other youngsters, we were secretly trained in the use of firearms — a science not entirely alien to us — in the Dandenong Mountains near Melbourne. We suspected that the organizers were connected with the Haganah, if not the Stern Gang or the Irgun Zvai Leumi. In face of continued British refusal to admit the Palestine-bound boats of Jewish refugees, the Irgun had embarked on a wave of terrorism and blown up the King David Hotel in Jerusalem, killing British soldiers — subjects, like Ben and I now, of His Majesty King George VI.

O people of Abraham, Isaac, and Jacob, how strange is your destiny, how heavy the burden you have bestowed on your sons and your grandsons! The violence in the Middle East was, for us, yet another reminder by history that Jews, at all times and in all places, were inextricably linked by a common heritage of suffering and that they were condemned to eternal vigilance in order to survive.

Secretly, Ben and I brooded over whether moving to Israel and helping to ensure the survival of that state did not fit into the inexorable logic of our lives. Maybe we could even find Niko and talk him into joining us there. Under the law of return that granted a right of free entry to all Jews, his police record would not be a problem. But Niko was nowhere to be found. And then the war was over before we were considered ready for battle. Our training came to an end after a few weeks. And our year-end examinations were approaching.

We resolved to continue to give part of our energies to working for Israeli welfare causes. Every Sunday, with a group of other young people, we would collect, door-to-door, money and clothing to help poor emigrants from various parts of the world to resettle in Israel. As for ourselves, we decided that continuing the moral and intellectual rehabilitation we had begun, the undoing of Hitler's destructive work, even on the infinitesimal scale of two individuals, was perhaps the only meaningful form of vengeance. It seemed the best way to begin discharging our duty toward the Jewish people and toward humanity as a whole.

But it was a while before I was able to settle back into my school routine; in my discomposed state I retreated to chess. I had played the game from a very early age, as was not unusual in Bialystok, and now I spent hours over the chessboard with Uncle Lazar, who was then the chess champion of Australia. "You play a good game," he told me when he found that the pattern of my gambits occasionally needed some serious concentration on his part, "but you'll never be a champion." I think he was afraid that, given any kind of encouragement, I could become addicted to the game, become a chess bum like so many friends of his youth, and see in it an opportunity for withdrawal from the difficult choices that life was once again placing in my way.

In 1949 my university life — my thoughts of a professional career, my hopes of making the collegiate swimming and tennis teams, my plans to spend the coming vacations with my new friends — was brusquely cut off. Everything fell apart.

For some months my abdomen had ached, but I had paid little notice. One day I was seized by violent pains in my chest and stomach and was rushed to the hospital. After weeks of stomach pumping, blood tests, and chest X-rays, came the crushing verdict: tuberculosis!

In those days, before the availability of the new miracle drugs, tuberculosis was still an often fatal illness, requiring at best prolonged and uncertain treatment. There seemed little doubt that I had been carrying the germs of the disease since my camp days. Yet I was furious with myself, that I, who had coped with a host of external enemies, should have failed to notice the stealth of an internal foe against which I was now helpless.

If I were to die, could not this unsuspected enemy have struck me down earlier, before Australia had instilled in me a passion for a new life? At best, I thought, even if the spread of the disease can be arrested, I will be condemned to life as a semi-invalid. For the first time I felt that fate, by a delayed action, had sent me into the wrong column. The end of my dreams. I swayed between rebellion and despair. Had all my struggle been in vain; the *Knopflachmachinist* vanquished, helpless, ready to give up?

My uncles consulted a specialist, Sir Wilberforce Newton. He said that he would immediately reserve a place in a hospital; then, if all went well, a sanatorium. Uncle Nachman suggested I would get better care at home.

"Don't even consider it," Sir Wilberforce said. "This is a contagious disease. You have two children. Your wife will never allow it, and she would be right."

Uncle Nachman insisted. "He can be isolated in a special room. The house is big. We have the necessary means, doctor."

"Look here," said the specialist, "it's like expecting a man to do his military service by taking a correspondence course."

Uncle Lazar spoke. "Doctor, this boy was dead, and is now alive again. It's a miracle. He's a free man. Do you know what that means in his case? If you lock him up in a sanatorium, within four walls, you will take away his freedom. Don't you see, he will be interned again. His psyche will not support it and, even if he survives physically, he will never again be . . . He must remain free!"

"All right," said the specialist in exasperation, "we'll try it your way."

My year-long, interminable convalescence, interrupted by clinical treatment, calcium injections, sputum analyses, radiological tests, and drugs, was spent in a large, sunny glass room — an addition to Uncle Nachman's house, extending into the garden, built specially for me. The enforced immobility left me with only one possible occupation: reading.

By chance, I picked up a history of world literature from a shelf in my uncle's library. Although it seemed forbidding at first in its size and detail, I decided to study it from cover to cover, marking methodically the novels I intended to read. Soon I was plunged in the great masterpieces of English, American, Russian, German, and French literature.

I found myself bewitched by Anna Karenina, caught up by the sorrows of the young Werther, and I didn't know if I was provoked more by Madame Bovary or by the mores against which she strove. Until then, my view of life had been essentially physical, practical: what must I do in order to enlarge my ability to make my way in the world?

The limitless horizons opened up for me by the masters of the human psyche added a new dimension to my ken. Success did not necessarily mean happiness; failure did not necessarily mean instant disaster; everything was much more intricately and much more interestingly mixed up in the beauty and paradoxes of life. . . .

Ben, who still lived with Uncle Lazar, visited me often, but spoke only of the most mundane matters, as all visitors had been warned to avoid agitating me. One day he came into my room frowning, inarticulate. I knew something serious was up.

"Uh — I've got to talk to you. Uh — I want to get married."

"Whaaat?" I jumped out of bed from the shock. In a flash I realized that part of my life was coming to an end. From now on someone would stand between us. I was confused, hurt, angry.

"Have you gone nuts? You, marry? Tie yourself up with someone for life? Bring innocent children into this world, after all we went through?"

"I love her."

"Who is it, anyway?"

"Bebka."

Bebka Mandel was a girl from Bialystok. She was from a refined middle-class family deported to Siberia by the Soviet occupation authorities before the Nazis had arrived. After the war they had come to Australia and were frequent guests at our home.

"You want your family back. You want a sister, that's what you want. . . ." In my panic, my helplessness, I found nothing better to say. Ben left the room without a word. A few minutes later he came back.

"Uh — Mula. The wedding will be here, at Uncle Nachman and Aunt Rachel's home. I am counting on you for best man." And we fell into each others arms, sobbing like a couple of small kids, for the first time since our encounter in the Nazi uniform factory at the camp of Blizin.

❖❖❖

The world outside my window faded. I lived only with the greats: Goethe, Balzac, Conrad, Hemingway. Dostoevski shook me up as unbelievable parallels invaded my mind, in a complete fusion of life and art.

This Stavrogin, the possessed, who arrogated to himself the right to dispense death — I knew him. He was Dr. Mengele at Auschwitz. And the "Idiot" — I had encountered martyrs with something of his divine "idiocy" in the endless rows of Musulmans at roll call.

My God, despite all that I had lived I had not even begun to understand what life is all about. These authors were laying everything bare for me with nothing but a pen. Dante, how close he came to imagining my personal inferno without ever having set foot in it. The German poets — how gripping they were; their lyrical darkness I would have expected, but that such robust idealism should share the secrets of the enigmatic Teutonic soul! And what of these modern Americans? How did that comprehension of evil, of the malignancy of the universe, ever creep into Melville's tempestuous art? And then there was Faulkner, who has found such a special, vast hell inside the egalitarian American paradise.

One day I opened the covers of Thomas Mann's monumental *Magic Mountain* and was catapulted in my imagination into another world. Suddenly, I *was* in the mountaintop sanatorium in which Dr. Wilberforce Newton wanted to intern me, far away from the "healthy" flatlands of normal life. I *was* in a world where everything turned around this one disease — mine — this sickness that had been eating me from the inside and that, in Mann's symbolism, had eaten at and finally torn Europe apart.

I began to live a horrifying, fascinating spiritual adventure. An illness that until now had been nothing but a soul-wrenching riddle was beginning to yield its secrets to me: the feverish sensitivity, heightened by immobility and medication, to poetry, to love, to sex, the transmutation of anger and bitterness into new forms of mental energy. I began to measure the physical and psychological dimension of a new challenge. The poets taught me one thing more: suffering was not necessarily degrading and evil; it could purify, even ennoble — most of all, it could teach.

I would become my own physician in a combat against nature, a combat that was not all that different from the one I had waged before against man. I would scrape the floor with my nails once again to survive.

Obedient to the doctor's instructions — which at any rate were enforced by Uncle Nachman and Aunt Rachel — I switched off the light every evening promptly at nine. But my imagination raced on and on. A thought, or rather a premonition, was germinating in my mind. Thanks to tuberculosis, thanks to literature, I would be reborn once more. As on the flying boat from London, I felt myself carried along in a motion toward a larger sphere.

7

WHEN Ben saw me rigged out in tuxedo, pleated shirt, and patent-leather shoes for a dinner dance at the home of one of my new friends, he said that my exquisitely tailored Auschwitz cap would have added the perfect touch. He also suggested that I give a little less *Achtung* to my gentlemanly mien and the growing shades of Oxford in my voice. When I answered with choice bits from my vile camp vocabulary, he acknowledged that I had not lost all contact with reality.

Although the atmosphere in Melbourne was as far removed from my upbringing as could be imagined, I adapted to it easily. The marks I got in my university entrance examinations earned me a substantial scholarship. My doctors urged a life-style as free from physical exertion and mental tension as possible. In the course of my opening to literature and art, I had learned to look within myself and I was prepared to draw my principal gratifications from a deeper well than that of worldly achievement. But I was not prepared to reconcile myself to half a life — I wanted all of it. As a compromise I offered to forgo my athletic ambitions and to modulate, as far as I could, my habit of making every challenge an issue of survival.

I was torn between science and law. I had done well in physics and math, and what enthralled me about the natural sciences was their purity, certainty, and predictability. I was tempted to withdraw into the unencumbered solitude of the universe and the atom, escaping from all that was unreliable and man-made.

The study of law, on the other hand, promised to respond more fully to the emotional needs that had been generated by my checkered existence. Having lived under the most arbitrary regimes known to man, where the smallest deviation from the rules meant instant annihilation, I felt a deep reverence for human rights, the claims of the individual against the state, and the freedoms that were guaranteed by due legal process. I had gotten an inkling of the common law system with its seedbed role in Western democracy from my reading of British and United States history. But my bedrock convictions came not from John Stuart Mill's *On Liberty,* but from what I had experienced on my own skin.

Everything I had known in Nazi Germany and Soviet Russia contradicted the brand of justice that was practiced before my bewildered eyes: that a person could not be arrested or searched without a warrant; that an individual had a right of privacy; that an accused could not be detained without charge; that he could be released on bail; that rules of evidence had to be strictly observed; that everyone had a right to counsel and to appeal.

So impressed was I, in fact, by the Anglo-American commitment to the rule of law, equitably administered by trusted judges and random juries, and the infinite value attached to human life, that I decided I would be a lawyer, not a scientist after all. Who could better devote himself to the defense of the weak than someone who had seen the helpless condemned with no more judicial ceremony than the whim of a kapo or the order of an SS?

My fellow students at the university were approximately my age, but I had more in common with their parents than with them. I was twenty going on fifty. Judge Alfred Foster, a great nonconformist jurist, found it easier at times to converse with me than with his sportsmen sons. My American-born classmate, Marr, wondered aloud whether it was he or his father, Sir Roy Grounds, Australia's foremost architect, who was my closest friend. And Professor Zelman Cowen, the dean of my law school, made me burn with pride by talking with me at his level, with the irreverent airiness of adults who know too much to be earnest about it.

My walks during the last stage of my convalescence took me past the home of a neighbor, Robert Menzies, who walked regularly in the magnificent Kew Gardens. Menzies, then leader of the Opposition, who had been Prime Minister for ten years and would soon resume that office, was not averse to expounding on the international situation before an audience of one, when our paths would cross. He could not have known that his attentive listener had just left a dinner table where English was spoken with a heavy Yiddish accent, and was now concentrating as much on the great man's faultless diction as on his conservative political ideas.

Was there not something unnatural about a young man's preferring the company of people twice his age? It was as though, having once seen how quickly everything can end, I was condemned to hurry anxiously to the next phase, before the present phase was done.

In the middle of 1952, part of my new life came painfully and abruptly to an end. Uncle Nachman died in my arms. His wife, Rachel, ran into my room in the middle of the night, screaming; when I got to his bedside, he was already unconscious. He had had a mild heart attack some months previously, and this one killed him. There was a large funeral. Uncle Lazar said it was easier to accept his brother's passing because, in the five years I had lived with him, he had seen the fulfillment of his mission, the success of a personal Marshall Plan for what was left of his Europe — me.

Small consolation! Uncle Nachman was only forty-eight years old. Could not death, who had made such a feast of our family, have granted a normal span to the man who was the core of what nucleus was left? As the coffin was being lowered into the grave, it hit me with brutal sadness that we had never resumed the dialogue we had begun in Singapore. In my rush to learn, I had simply neglected to get to know him better. . . . All I knew was that he gave and gave and gave of himself; that his heart was so big. . . .

The affectionate reserve that had marked our relationship left me unprepared for my feelings of disarray, now that he was no longer there. What he had been to his wife and children, Ethel and Sym, then the same age respectively as Frieda and I when our father disappeared, is more than I can describe. I decided it was my duty to take over the role of the man of the family, to devote myself to supporting my aunt in her bereavement and helping raise her two children, even if it meant dropping out of the university.

Uncle Lazar would have none of it. "You feelings are not in question," he said. "You have them, and so do we. It is your duty to go on. You cannot let Nachman's work go for naught. You will do more for all of us by fulfilling your intellectual destiny than by getting some job. We are not destitute."

I was not blind to the quixotic element in my impulse; if it needed anyone else to point it out more bluntly, Ben filled that role.

"What's the matter?" he said ironically. "Scared to grow up? Never been away from home? The university is tougher than the camps, and you need an excuse?"

My old friend, despite our indissoluble bonds, had drifted away along the different course his life was taking. He was preparing to set himself up as a radio engineer, acclimatized completely to his adopted country. I was already hankering after something larger than a lawyer's career in Melbourne and he knew it.

To be called to the bar now seemed a limited objective. Under the special attention I was getting from a brilliant Oxford don, Peter Carter, visiting professor at Melbourne, my intellectual metamorphosis picked up speed. My thinking was becoming coldly analytical; I learned that reason must substitute for emotion. My interests broadened to the philosophical aspects of jurisprudence, as well as international and constitutional law. I became interested in the structure of federal systems, not only Australia's but also Switzerland's, Germany's, the Soviet Union's, and above all, the United States'. I also discovered that I had become something of a linguist. My English was of recent vintage, but Russian, German, French, and the other languages life had foisted upon me in the most unlikely places were tools I could now put to use in my studies.

I became an editor of the Law Review and in 1953 I graduated with one of the highest scores in my class and had an offer from an important law firm. But I was without enthusiasm for any of the alternatives before me. Then Sir Zelman Cowen (since 1977 Australia's Governor General and Head of State) intervened decisively in my life.

While in the United States as a guest lecturer, Cowen had put my case to Professors Paul Freund and Harold Berman of the Harvard Law School. On his return to Australia, he astounded me with an offer from his American friends — a scholarship and a Carnegie Grant.

Harvard! The most revered name in the world of learning, the

Athens of modern times. Should I go? Could it be that even Australia, with everything it had to offer, would not encompass the contours of my life?

Uncle Nachman would have been hesitant. He had seen me come to that beautiful land from the rubble of postwar Europe, he had seen me vanquish my illness and begin my studies. He would have said, "We must not gamble with our newly found luck. We must not tempt fate. The boy must not venture out again into the unknown." But he did not live long enough to see the serious turn my education would take, and what unlimited horizons would lie before me.

Uncle Lazar was immediately in favor, and his attitude awakened distant echos. Australia was a marvelous stop on my road to redemption, an oasis, but I must not blunt the instinct that had always commanded me to struggle on. The real world is not as calm and comfortable as it appears from here; nor does my life belong entirely to me. It remains rooted forever in the tragedies of the past and it is from these tragedies that it must draw its meaning and direction.

I left on a P & O liner, traveling by the cheapest possible class to the United States via England. At the dock, my fellow immigrant friends mingled easily with my new Australian comrades from the university. I felt light on my feet, astride both worlds. Ben and Bebka embraced me: "Don't forget to come back!" Despite the sadness I felt at leaving them, I was anxious to be off. I had understood that growth and change were salient characteristics of my odd life.

Once again, I was in motion. The four-week voyage from Melbourne to London through the Indian Ocean, the Arabian Sea, the Suez Canal, and Gibraltar re-created the headiness of my journey the other way six years before.

When I arrived, the strongest sensation I had was of being a British colonial returning to the mother country, breathing the history of his ancestors. On my previous visit, on the way to Australia, I had been an alien, stateless waif, unable to speak more than a few broken sentences of English; now I was permeated with age-old traditions and legacies that I felt were mine as much as the laws of Moses. Once, I had nearly succumbed under the laws of Nuremberg; now I knew I could not live except under the protective glow of the Magna Carta and the human rights that grew from it.

I spent some time at Oxford visiting friends and exploring with the greats of British legal scholarship what was being done in the field of comparative law. Oxford's intellectual standards were indisputable, and the discussions I had there concerning my future caused me to swing back from the practice of law to an academic career. Research and teaching seemed to be what I wanted most, after all. It was like returning, in a way, to my earlier decision to be a scientist.

I am, today, inescapably an international lawyer. But the opposing pulls of a life of action and a life of reflection still disturb my inner peace.

When I arrived at Harvard, I was totally unprepared for the siege mentality that gripped the university faculty and student body alike in the summer of 1954. I realized suddenly how apart, how isolated, Australia was, protected from the tensions that were accumulating in the world once more, so soon after the war.

McCarthyism was at its height. I remember being deeply affected by the emotion with which a professor of constitutional law, Zachariah Chafee, brought his fist down on the desk before his class, exclaiming: "This boy Alger Hiss is innocent!" I didn't then and still don't know whether Hiss was innocent. But that these Americans — the people of the white star, who in Germany had walked among us as the favorites of the gods, whose Statue of Liberty I hailed through tear-filled eyes when the *Queen Elizabeth* brought me into New York Harbor — should now visit upon themselves the same curse of anonymous denunciation that had run rampant in the charnel house of wartime Europe struck me as a tragic irony of monumental proportions.

One middle-level official, Hiss; one political drama of uncertain outcome, his trial; and a gush of paranoia and vengefulness throughout the land! Robert Oppenheimer, the great scientist who had directed the Manhattan Project that had created the atom bomb — thrown to the political dogs for having dared to question the wisdom of building worse and worse bombs, now a hydrogen bomb, and thus accelerating the arms race. Denunciations, trumped-up charges, ruined lives — the poisons of fear and mistrust of friend, family, neighbor, and government. Once again, I thought, I was witnessing human tragedy caused by ideological blindness and hysteria. In the United States, dormant subterranean springs of fear had been tapped by its "loss" of China and the incorporation of Eastern Europe into the Soviet sphere.

Coming to understand this anxiety, and its mirror image on the other side of the political divide, coming to understand the tensions which only ten years after such a cruel war were threatening the world once again, were things that would encourage me, in later years, to try to lessen these fears and show up their fundamental unreality. Spending your formative years in expectation of the very worst makes you appreciate the power of such terrors; was that why I became more preoccupied than some of my learned American and European friends with the irrational elements in the U.S.-Soviet equation?

It was a while before I understood that my early beliefs about America, acquired from afar, were simplistic. In a democracy the waters are not always calm and the sun does not always shine. Democracy can be stormy, volcanic. But with all its imperfections it seems to be the only system capable of dealing with complex human issues, in a continually decent and intelligent way.

America certainly has shown herself not to be immune from political disease, but she seems to carry within her national fiber the germs needed for self-cure. I saw that cure practiced before my own eyes by the media and political parties whose reflexes had remained basically healthy. From one day to the other, without much ado, the once all-powerful inquisitor who spread a quasi-Stalinist climate of purges and panic among so many of his countrymen was consigned to oblivion. A simple vote by his peers in the Senate was sufficient to put him in his proper place.

The longed-for America of my childhood stood up pretty well under the firsthand scrutiny of the fascinated adult.

My financial situation wasn't good. I had left Melbourne with a small sum given me by Uncle Lazar from his modest resources (I did not feel I could accept any money from Aunt Rachel). That gone, I reached Harvard knowing I would have to stretch my grant of $1,200 to cover a whole year. This money would have to take care of all my expenses, other than tuition.

With some misgiving and regret, I posted a notice on one of the student bulletin boards and sold the Leica which I had so covetously looted back in Penzing. A fellow student, now surely an important lawyer, perhaps even a judge, bought it for $95 without knowing he was receiving stolen goods — but by then the statute of limitations had run out.

Then the young *Knopflochmachinist* went busily to work. Breakfasting in the law school cafeteria, I carried my tray back for extra helpings until I thought I'd burst; for the same price, you could refill your plate as often as you wished. That meal would last me until dinner, when I was careful to keep my check no higher than ninety-nine cents; on a dollar you paid a tax and, over a year, that could make the difference between staying within and going over my budget. Would I make it to the end of the year or would I go hungry? I almost began to feel sorry for myself. How extraordinary, a man's capacity to forget. . . .

But that wasn't the real problem. The real problem was in class. Harvard was big-time; Harvard was the best. The selection process was rigorous and the breakneck competition, once you were in, was different from anything I had known.

The real world was not made of the sadism of Auschwitz or the anarchy of Landsberg; but neither, I saw now, was it the same as my ceremonious University of Melbourne. It lay somewhere in between, and I foundered in its complexities as in a tricky sea. The teaching method was unsettlingly novel. I knew there was nothing I couldn't learn, but they wanted more. You were not simply to master your material but to acquire a way of thinking, an analytical method that was meant to serve you through life. The relentless barrage of questions from the professors they called the Socratic method; a more appropriate name would have been the Spanish Inquisition.

To me, drilled to respect authority, and later trained to sit at the feet of the wise, it was astonishing to see professors interrupted, badgered, and disputed. Some of the country's leading figures in politics and the professions would come to speak, and find themselves forced to defend their views against the most intemperate criticism from the floor. And, I learned, this pitting of youthful mettle against the body of established truth was what was expected of me too if I wanted to measure up in the eyes of my teachers and fellow students.

I was ecstatic to see freedom of speech and dissent effervescing all around, for I had seen under the Nazi and Soviet regimes to what miseries blind respect for official truth could lead. But for the first time since I had found myself alone, in the line of prisoners running toward the cattle train, I doubted my ability to get through the tests ahead.

Psychologically, I had been molded to survive in the death camps, but not the Ivy League. The reflexes, the attitudes, the mental muscles, the emotional armor I had developed there were totally different from what I needed to make it here. My inventory of cunning and ruse, my capacity for physical endurance did not help one bit. Why did I take on this challenge anyway?

To move over from the jungle of animal reactions to the world of pure intellect, I had to wipe out the first seventeen years of my life. The man I used to be and the man I wanted to become could not cohabit within the same being. For this kind of combat, mind against mind, idea against idea, I would have to reinvent and reconstruct myself from the ground up. It crossed my mind that maybe I wasn't good enough or smart enough, that I should pack up and go back to Australia.

I remembered the prisoner at Maidanek who had said: "Do you want to eat that soup or do you want to croak?" My answer hadn't changed.

I plunged in, and loved it, and I would love it still. Nothing that came before or after Harvard can compare for sheer intellectual excitement. I have known other forms of intellectual gratification, such as writing a book, *Coexistence and Commerce,* which perhaps influenced some policy changes in Washington; or in publishing articles in the *New York Times, The Wall Street Journal,* and *Newsweek* and other magazines. But in these and similar efforts I had to bend to the requirements of the medium and the goal at hand. At Harvard, my mind was let loose to roam where it would. Melbourne had taught me that there was a higher level of existence I could attain. Now Harvard taught me that there is yet another level beyond the one already reached, and that trying to attain it, as long as one lives, is the process worthy of the name of life.

I spent my nights in the second basement of the law school library, breathing in the dust that Dr. Newton had ordered me to avoid. I undertook detailed and captivating research, deciphering unpublished manuscripts in several languages. As I thought back to the slogan written over the Auschwitz gate, I realized, yes, there is work that brings freedom.

New York, that inexhaustible mixture of soaring modernity and poky neighborhoods still held by the immigrant past, seemed to produce one familiar face after another, and now Barbara and Leo Sauvage were there. My uncle had been promoted to chief U.S. correspondent of *Le Figaro*. I wanted to visit them over the Christmas holidays, but the trip would be a blow to my budget, which was already shrinking faster than it should, with the first year not even half over. The campus was deserted and I was still wondering how I could do it when I got a letter from the dean of graduate studies, Professor Paul Freund.

"My dear Pisar," he wrote. "Going over my scholarship budget, I see I have a surplus of $500 I can't account for. Maybe you can use it, so here's a check. Also, two tickets for the Harvard-Yale hockey game."

My immediate problems were solved. I have known acts of kindness in other countries but somehow never as generous and unassuming as in the United States.

❖❖❖

I shared a dormitory room at Hastings Hall with a Brazilian, Sergio de Britto, and a study cubicle at Langdell Hall with an Indian, Yeshvant Chitale. On the campus one could hear the tongues of what seemed to be all the peoples of the world. There was a reason why there were so many foreign students, particularly from the underdeveloped countries. These young men were the pick of the crop, the likely future leaders of their own societies. In helping them financially, so they might pursue their advanced studies in the United States, the American government hoped to win future adherents to its global political and economic objectives.

To what extent these objectives were consonant with those countries' own best interests — and, for that matter, to what extent the returned students would be able to apply the methods and outlook of American democracy, even if convinced of their superiority — these were questions we debated. What worried the foreigners most was the inertia they would encounter on their return home.

I, having lived under Soviet Communism and German National Socialism, was innoculated against the smallpox of propaganda. Still, I had to admit that a nation that picked foreigners to indoctrinate, and placed them in its own best universities, where its program's own objectives inevitably came under merciless scrutiny, was practicing the most candid, or perhaps the subtlest and most effective, form of propaganda known to man.

In any event, it seemed to me that if there was anything the United States had to teach the world that interfered least with the tribal and peasant-based traditions of the newly emerging countries, it would be a decentralized federal system that enabled separate states to combine for economic and political advantage while guarding whatever part of their regional autonomy they wished to preserve. And this, in a more advanced form than had ever been tried, held promise for Europe as well. When my first year at Harvard was rewarded with several prizes, and I was given a $3,000 grant for my second year, I felt rich! Now I wanted to plunge deeper into the great constitutional decisions of Oliver Wendell Holmes, Benjamin Cardozo, and Felix Frankfurter. I decided to concentrate on international law, federalism and the Bill of Rights, and on how their principles could be best applied in the last half of the twentieth century.

I was twenty-five and still torn, in my plans for the future, between the attractions of a law career and those of adademe; at Harvard, I perceived the possibility of original research being carried out and applied with profound and immediate economic and political consequences. I, that nameless subhuman from Auschwitz, would help remake the world!

Will you forgive me if the ambition seems immoderately phrased? It was not specific to me; it was that kind of time and place. Beyond the Communist domain, all decision-making centered in Washington; and, at Harvard, now that the McCarthyite scourge had receded, a coterie of students shared a buoyant conviction concerning their abilities to help evolve policies superior to those that had led mankind to a series of disastrous wars.

A number were, like me, from other lands. There was young Henry Kissinger, deeply marked by his childhood brush with Nazism, developing those ideas on the paramountcy of political norms which eventually found their way into his seminal work, *A World Preserved*. There was young Zbigniew Brzezinski, whose Poland had fallen at the same time mine had, and who knew how to express himself on international affairs more eloquently than I. Professor Harold Berman, whose scholarship straddled both the law school and the Russian Research Center, called us "Poles apart" in our views of East-West relations.

There was Ralph Nader, the future consumer advocate; Joe Califano, the future Secretary of Health, Education and Welfare; Daniel Soberman, the future dean of Canada's Queen's University Law School; Antonio La Pergola, the future justice of Italy's constitutional court; and Sheikh Ahmed Zaki Yamani, the future oil minister of Saudi Arabia. There were others and, American or not, we imagined ourselves a planning elite which transcended national boundaries; I, in fact, was quietly beginning to feel American.

My wartime background was something I talked about to no one. And no one could have suspected where I had been raised. My manners and clipped speech of those days were closer to those of the British gentry than to any other ethnic group.

The reason I didn't discuss my past is one of the reasons I am writing this book. I told myself at the time that the facts were too brutal, and that I wanted people to react to me as an individual, rather than as a symbol. The shadow that had briefly fallen between me and Uncle Nachman, that had made me feel I was on show, also lay immovably between me and everyone I met.

One day, playing Ping-Pong with a West German student, I rolled up my shirt sleeves. I served; he stood stock-still, letting the ball go by. Pale and silent, he stared with horror at my bare arm.

I rolled down my sleeve, covering the tattoo. "Come on, let's play."

"*You?* I had no idea. . . ."

"It's not important. Come on. I'll serve again."

He was transfixed. "And your parents, your family?"

I said roughly, "All dead. You never read about it?"

"Of course I've read about it, but . . . how long were you in?"

"Four years."

"And you are now here, at Harvard, with all of us . . . with me . . . ?"

"Forget it! It's over."

Later, I learned that, while I was in Dachau, he was living with his family in Munich, ten miles away. Just a young boy, too.

My "case" provoked less dramatic reactions at times. For example, Clyde Kluckhohn, the well-known anthropologist, seemed fascinated by my early life, as if I were some exotic, nearly extinct animal. After several long conversations he told me with some discomfort that as a manchild I had been in the camps at precisely the right age for survival. According to him, had my calvary begun earlier, I probably would not have made it into the adult column in the first place. But had it begun later, my backbone, in a moral sense, would have been too ossified and rigid to stand up to the ordeal. I would have cracked. At the age at which I was there, I had the advantage of great pliability and adaptability. It was this that saved me from being completely broken, or warped for the rest of my life — the fate of many of my older fellow prisoners.

Our dialogue was out of a play by Ionesco!

"Professor, are you suggesting I am spineless?"

"Sam, be serious and let me ask you a few questions."

"Yes, sir."

"What do you consider your mother tongue?"

"I have none."

He looked perplexed.

"Listen, Sam, which language comes instinctively to your lips when you abandon yourself?"

"I never abandon myself."

"For example, when you dream . . . or when you make love?"

"Oh, it's a cocktail. I think in English, make love in French, laugh in Yiddish, pray in Hebrew, shout in German, sing in Russian, cry in Polish, and swear like a trooper in Hungarian."

Kluckhohn seemed a trifle exasperated.

"I guess I would have to conclude that the language of your nervous system is instinctively different from the language that could normally be considered your mother tongue."

I answered him in mock seriousness:

"Professor, I don't know if you are proposing to submit a paper on my case to the Academy of Arts and Sciences, but the conclusion you have drawn from your examination does not seem altogether false."

8

"MY little sister is coming in from L.A.," Liz said to me one day. "Come over for dinner and meet her."

"A blind date! I've never tried anything so American."

"Well, it's about time you dropped your British accent and your formal Victorian ways."

I'd been taken in tow by a visiting professor from Los Angeles, Harold Horowitz, and his good-looking and amusing wife, Liz.

Norma turned out to be a very bright and pretty girl, with dark brown hair and big black eyes. Like most nineteen-year-olds, she was delightfully open and confused. I liked her and asked her for another date. We went to hear some foreign ambassador speak at the Harvard Forum. She listened attentively and said she enjoyed it, although I think that she would rather have gone to a Saturday-night dance.

Norma lived in Beverly Hills with her father, the movie producer Lawrence Weingarten, and her mother, a medical scientist known by her professional name, Dr. Jessie Marmorston. She made these hops quite often, Norma said, through her parents feared that it was interfering with her studies at the University of Southern California.

After her departure I felt an unsettling pang of loneliness. That was a feeling I was not used to.

Some four months later I got a phone call: "I'm in New York. Why don't you meet me here?"

I looked at the Quadrangle bulletin board to see if I could get a ride by chipping in for gas.

Norma was staying in an imposing East Side brownstone. I was ushered into the living room of General David Sarnoff, no less. She came in, looking sensational, and explained that David was a friend of the family. Sheepishly, in the face of all this splendor and celebrity, I took Norma to Barbara and Leo's modest apartment on West End Avenue. They had said there'd be a party, and it was as exciting as Norma's abode was elegant; Arthur Miller was there and we had a hilarious discussion, comparing the notion of violence in the works of Dostoevski and Mickey Spillane.

I stayed in New York for several days. Norma and I took long walks in Central Park and haunted the Metropolitan Museum. She pecked me on the cheek and flew back to California.

I got a letter from her and wrote back. Our letters became more frequent and more interesting.

During the summer vacation of 1955, on the basis of an international competition, I was awarded an internship in the New York office of Dag Hammarskjöld, Secretary General of the United Nations. I had been entered on the lists as the accredited candidate of the Australian government. So it was with great glee and alacrity that I shared the news of my victory with my favorite teachers in Melbourne, Miss Lockwood and Professor Cowen, who had taken such pains to light up the road before me. Which of their other "difficult pupils" had started so handicapped and could now submit so good a report? I was proudly at work on the thirty-eighth floor of the U.N. building, overlooking the East River, when I got a phone call. Everything seemed to happen by phone in the United States.

"This is Dr. Jessie Marmorston."

"Oh, you're Norma's mother!"

"Mula," she said — Norma was by now one of the few people I knew who called me by that name — "I'm in New York for a few days. I've heard so much about you. Won't you have dinner with me?"

I found myself in General Sarnoff's study this time. Dr. Marmorston was a brilliant and beautiful woman with an alabaster complexion and reddish hair. We hit it off at once. On this occasion, I even met Sarnoff, who was still the active head of that gigantic empire which included Radio Corporation of America and NBC. Sarnoff was delighted to be able to exchange some humorous stories with me in Yiddish, remembered from the days when he arrived in New York from his native Ukraine as a little immigrant boy. Norma's mother knew I had grown up in Poland, but she knew nothing of my years in the death camps, and neither did Norma. I still obsessively kept that part of my past dark.

In the fall, back at Harvard and studying for my doctorate of juridicial science, I got a call from Los Angeles, this time from Liz. "Won't you come here for Thanksgiving? You could stay with us."

"It's sweet of you," I said, "but I can't."

I couldn't afford the trip, but the real reason went deeper. I was afraid. Things were getting serious. I was prepared to change the world but I wasn't prepared to become involved in it personally — not to the extent of getting married and having children.

I had told myself I would not be responsible for bringing children into a world where they could suffer as I had. I had told myself I would never get married. I told myself I would not go to California for Thanksgiving. And, of course, I went. And, of course, things got blurred, and Norma and I fell in love. And I went again for the year-end holidays.

Just before Christmas Jessie fell suddenly ill. She called me into her room.

"Sam, I love you like a son. If anything should happen to me," she said in deathbed tones, "I want to know that you will always remain close to our family, that Norma . . . that you . . ."

Her eyes were filled with tears.

Norma and I had talked about marriage, but she saw no reason to rush things and neither did I. I liked the warm, harmonious, and cultivated atmosphere that prevailed within that family in which not only uncles, aunts, cousins, and nephews participated, but also Nobel Prize–winners, artists, and film stars. But how could I explain to them my fears, my doubts as to whether I was really born for happiness?

And what would my mother have said? In my thoughts, I had once consulted her during a moment of weakness and despair over a beautiful Australian girl who had helped me through my convalescence. Had my mother been alive, I would have probably told her — as many a Jewish mother is told today — that my marriage was *my* business. But because she wasn't there to be argued with, and for the reasons why she wasn't there, it was *her* business. Now, I had to think of such things as the more than five-thousand-year chain of history. When you are the only link left in that chain, you're not free to break it.

But how to interpret the silence this time. At twenty-six I stood before a decision that for me came close to being as important and difficult as the one she had had to make when I was half my present age, when she dressed me in long pants.

Panicking, I phoned Uncle Lazar, who now represented for me all that was left of family authority. "Uncle," I said, "get yourself over here; I need you."

"I can't," he said.

"You must," I said. "I think I'm getting married."

A long silence at the other end of the line, then a voice choking with emotion and tears: "Are you sure you know what you're doing?"

"No," I said. "I mean, yes . . ."

And things acquired a momentum that could not be arrested. The same day I drove out to the MGM studios to see Larry Weingarten, and between shots of Frank Sinatra and Debbie Reynolds, with whom he was making *The Tender Trap,* I formally asked him for his daughter's hand in marriage.

We were married by the Chief Rabbi of Los Angeles, with a few witnesses. Jessie, miraculously cured, was out of bed. Uncle Lazar arrived and was pleased with what he found: "A wonderful girl, wonderful people."

He stayed for several more days, watching his nephew's happiness with a whole ready-made family. As he was leaving for the airport, he took me aside and cautioned, "Remember, it is not easy to be both a son-in-law and a son at the same time."

Norma enrolled at Brandeis University and we left Los Angeles, setting up house in a two-room apartment in Cambridge.

For my doctoral dissertation, I had chosen a subject which, in the tense political climate that prevailed at the time, seemed devoid of any practical application for the foreseeable future, but which was, in my mind, intimately bound up with the issue of war and peace. I would explore the legal aspects of trade between communist and capitalist countries. It was a field that had never been deeply explored.

Intellectually, I was certain that the free-enterprise societies of the West and the state-enterprise societies of the East would continue for the indefinite future. Certainly, neither side would voluntarily dismantle its institutions or drop its beliefs; nor would either overwhelm the other with thermonuclear force. Whether they liked it or not, the two antagonistic systems were condemned either to perish or to learn to live together. My political feelings that East and West would have to learn to get along, moving their hostile confrontation from the brink of atomic holocaust to the arena of peaceful cooperation, had been, however, a matter of instinct as well.

Given the militant atmosphere at the university's Russian Research Center, I had not been able to quiet a certain personal discomfort over the heretical thrust of my ideas. Yet neither could I alienate my beliefs from my life experience. I owed my survival to the Soviets, no less than to the Americans. The Americans liberated me, but if it had not been for the Russian effort that hastened Germany's defeat, I would not have survived long enough to be liberated by Americans.

In all events, one thing was clear as crystal to me: relations between the two superpowers, whether good or bad, would dominate the future of this planet for a very long time to come.

My thesis was awarded Harvard's Addison Brown Prize for 1956 for the "best essay by one of the students in the law school on some designated subject of Maritime or Private International Law." With the prize came a substantial check. But much more important, the work would be published in the most authoritative law journal in the world — the *Harvard Law Review*.

I was dazed. I had sweated it out in the stacks at Widener Library, but I had thought that my subject was too marginal to win any attention. To have two articles of close to 100 pages each, both drawn from my doctoral dissertation, with their copious, multilingual footnotes, in the *Harvard Law Review,* alongside one paper written by Judge Irving Kaufman who had tried Ethel and Julius Rosenberg, and another by that marvelous intellect and conscience, Professor Archibald Cox, later the chief prosecutor in the Watergate scandal! — "Now, Dr. Pisar," I said to myself, "you can be sure that you are more than a quick-thinking buttonhole maker. You survived the Holocaust, and that took luck and a lot of nerve. Now you've survived Harvard, and with flying colors. That's not just luck and nerve; *that* takes the real thing. You are, there is no doubt about it, a scholar."

And what did that mean? I should become a professor. And offers of teaching posts did come in, from Stanford and other universities. In the end I passed them by. When squarely confronted with it, I was forced to admit that a life of teaching seemed too tame. I craved action.

Having been exposed to it in New York, the institution that attracted me most was the United Nations. In what other forum could the old and the newly independent nations, or even East and West, meet so congenially? Where else could the tempering role of go-between be brought to bear more effectively? What better sounding board was there for the emerging principles of federalism and coexistence that pressed on the future of our time?

❖ ❖ ❖

In late 1956, I was offered the post of legal officer in the cabinet of the Director General of UNESCO, in Paris. Norma was intrigued; Jessie perplexed.

"Why can't you be a lawyer in Los Angeles or New York? Don't you see how much you can contribute here? I realize you don't like swimming pools and Cadillacs. But why must you take that girl to a strange faraway city, when she's expecting her first child? Haven't you struggled enough in your life?"

The sudden desire to return to the continent where I had so narrowly escaped annihilation did seem a little absurd — especially at a time when doors were opening to me in America. But I was adamant. Without wanting to deprecate Hollywood, I felt I had more important things to do.

My generation was being carried on waves of idealism and confidence in an emerging new international order. As did many of my fellow students and scholars I believed that, after the latest bloodbath, the greatest of all, we would now succeed in building a new world based on universal respect for human rights. Verily, the major concepts we had lived with were on the way to capturing and transforming society! I was impatient to put to use the marvelous tools Harvard had given me. I had a wonderful sense of belonging to the momentum of our time. The UNESCO job was just what I wanted. To help direct the governments' resources toward the advancement of education, science, and culture in the newly decolonized parts of the world seemed absolutely essential to the creation of a new international climate.

I was twenty-seven; I had a lovely wife; I would soon be a father.

At UNESCO, in Paris, I would have a sufficient income, and all the qualifications for the good life of an international civil servant.

"Mother," I said to Jessie, amazed that I had managed to say that word, the rights to which had been reserved for so long, "both Hollywood *and* Wall Street will survive without me. Norma and I could do worse than to start life in one of the most beautiful and interesting places in the world."

We booked a passage on the *Liberté* and found ourselves at the captain's table in what was then, without doubt, the best restaurant afloat. Later, Leo Sauvage admitted that he had alerted the French Line through the press wires that an important young diplomat was on board. He also admitted that this ruse had come right out of my old bag of Landsberg tricks.

✤✤✤

In Paris I felt immediately fulfilled, exhilarated. The international meetings in which I participated burst with ambitious ideas and programs. In UNESCO's multicolored Tower of Babel where Westerners rubbed shoulders with the first representatives of an evolving Third World, new friendships were being developed and grand new principles elaborated.

After Helaina was born, in Los Angeles, Norma enrolled at the Sorbonne.

I gave myself completely over to my work. It was true the organization appeared a little slow, heavy, even passive, but these difficulties were no doubt unavoidable — perfectly natural adjustments between the reality and the ideal. All would soon fall naturally into place. . . .

✤✤✤

After I had been in Europe several months, I took advantage of my new position to do something that had been on my mind for a long time — to seek traces of Niko, who, with Ben, had been more than a friend, more than a brother. His casual, elegant silhouette, his carefree face, his extraordinary energy were souvenirs which went back more than ten years now. Maybe I could locate him wherever he was. I felt that by trying to relink the trio severed by time, I would reaffirm my own identity. I wanted to stay faithful to my past.

My Dutch colleagues at UNESCO got their government to start an investigation. The trail began at Landsberg. He was, of course, no longer there. But in little more than a week, I was given a written official report, with the address of one Nathan Waterman, who appeared to have been living for some years in a poorer section of Amsterdam. I was taken aback when I read for the first time Niko's full name; it seemed so alien, the name of a stranger. And the precise details furnished in the report drove home an unmistakable reality: the world had become normal and orderly again. Niko had been demobilized for times of peace and prosperity . . . Niko?

I took a plane. The section near the old port was indeed poor, the houses old, sad, scaly. I climbed a dark stairway and, with the help of a match, found the right door. I knocked. A tightness gripped my throat.

The girl who opened the door looked at me with evident surprise.

"Is Mr. Waterman home?"

"At this time? Of course not. He's at work."

She answered my questions with the submissiveness that the poor show before an official inquiry. She was Niko's daughter, she said, and married to a sailor, who was away.

Niko with a grown-up daughter . . . ?

The depressing alleys through which her directions led brought me to a tiny store. Niko here? Impossible! I told myself that in a few minutes I would discover that this was one of those old tricks he liked to play on Ben and me.

I checked the number she had written down. Yes, this was the one. I pressed against the shop window. In the gloomy interior, I could make out a figure in a soiled white apron behind a counter, cutting slices of sausage for a bent old woman holding out a newspaper to wrap them in.

Niko — this? The scoffing, sparkling Niko, the Humphrey Bogart I used to know, in his dark blue overcoat and white silk scarf, now reduced to a stooping servitor at a kosher delicatessen in the Amsterdam slums?

My mind began to race. It was all so silly, grotesque. Niko had fought so hard for his survival. Niko deserved better than this.

For a second, I didn't know if I wanted to go in. It was an affront to justice — to my memories, damnit!

I looked closer. He had not changed all that much. His movements were still lively, precise, even if they served now only to wrap the purchases of poor old neighborhood ladies.

I went inside. It smelled of rancid herring. He looked up challengingly at me. He had trouble recognizing me, too. By my appearance I could not be a customer. Then, frowning slightly, in a hesitant, disbelieving voice, half saying it and half asking, he called out:

"Mula?"

I nodded, without a sound, choked by tears.

He came out from behind the counter and we embraced. A long, tight embrace. He seemed to have forgotten his customers, who observed the strange reunion silently. Niko took a step back to examine me from head to toe, his eyes lingering a brief instant on my well-cut clothes.

The old woman he had been serving whined, and he wrapped up the sausage, took her money, and pieced out the change.

"Look at you," he said when we were alone. "Things haven't gone badly for you, eh, you rascal? What are you doing with yourself?"

"I work for UNESCO."

He nodded. "Fine. What's that?"

"United Nations."

"Ah, yes." He made an effort to remember. Then he gave a dry laugh. "Those jokers you got to spring us from the Landsberg jail."

Not quite, I acknowledged with a smile, but his words pierced me to the quick. I realized suddenly that he had remained in the past, that he had neither seen nor felt the evolution of the postwar world. Unable to grasp the great changes around him, he had simply withdrawn into indifference.

"Come on, Niko," I said, "let's go somewhere."

"Are you crazy? What'll the boss say?"

"Where is he?"

"Behind there."

I fixed it up with the boss. My hero was granted a brief respite from his daily chores. He insisted on going home first to change. It was a hovel. The girl was gone. She was from a prewar marriage, he said — still in Rotterdam when he returned, though her mother had gone off with someone.

Things were obviously going badly for him, and he knew that I noticed it. But his pride was still intact. His behavior permitted no one to pity him.

We walked along the canals. I put my arm around his shoulder. Niko, my Niko. He seemed so fragile, so vulnerable.

"Do you remember?"

Impossible to recall who said it first. Immediately a flood of memories, one after the other, interrupted by bursts of laughter, anecdotes long forgotten, details that had vanished, the entire past, everything — except the horrors.

I took him to a restaurant in a better section of town. I tried to find one that would be cheerful but not too stiff. He squared his shoulders and looked around the room with something of his old impudence.

"Just look at you," he said again. "And how did you learn to speak English like one of them Americans?"

But I am one of them, I wanted to say, and couldn't. I told him about my wanderings to the other half of the world, where I had been, what I had done. He listened with interest, with disbelief.

"Tell me again about Ben," he said. "You write to him often?"

"Benjamin Kaufman has become a prosperous businessman in Melbourne."

"No kidding. So I didn't train you so badly with the secondhand Brazilian coffee after all."

"Look," I said, "we've got to get you to Australia, too."

"No, Mula. Too late."

"We'll try."

He shook his head. "You will only be wasting your time. But if you wish, why not?"

I was sent around the world for UNESCO, with long stopovers in Turkey, Iran, Afghanistan, Japan, and other regions I had never seen. I traveled the length and breadth of India and discussed with the untouchables of Calcutta as well as the exquisitely elegant members of the Bombay Cricket Club, all disciples of Mahatma Ghandi and Pundit Nehru, the seemingly insurmountable problems of that vast democracy. But when I returned to Paris I felt in a rut. The top-heaviness of the international bureaucracy got me down. Enough time had passed, surely, for me to see with accuracy how often the opportunity for accomplishment was lost in a maze of minutiae, opportunism, and indifference.

I wondered again if my restlessness had anything to do with Niko. He had now come to Paris at my insistence, smiling indulgently at my efforts to process his Australian visa application, and, when difficulties came up, saying gently, "You see, Mula, it's no use." I kept trying, and got a polite but firmly worded letter from the Australian embassy. The "problems raised by Mr. Waterman's record ruled him out as an immigrant."

Niko said, "Mula, I have been a guest in your house. You are a good friend. But now I must return to Amsterdam." He would not accept financial assistance and went back to work in the delicatessen.

We corresponded.

Nine months later, he was dead. His death, like Uncle Nachman's, was untimely — he was also only forty-eight — and it had been brought on also by a massive heart attack. What made it worse was that he died as he lived, in his awful room, practically alone.

I suppose someone else, seeing that figure with its frayed, ill-fitting garments, might shrug his shoulders and give a pitying smile. But to conclude that Niko's life had been a failure was to miss the point. Most people are molded to live in normal times, times marked by calm and stability. Then they can entertain illusions of grandeur about themselves and the world around them, make good impressions on others, and even become great men. But in conditions of crisis and danger, how many outstanding personalities would show themselves cowards and weaklings.

Ah, Niko. He was marvelously fashioned for times of disaster, when there are no limits and no rules, when no holds are barred. Then he could dig deeply inside himself and find all the mental resources and physical strength needed to fight and overcome. An authentic hero.

He was undone by the return of normal life; his reflexes became stunted, his muscles atrophied, because there was no further need for his special powers to survive. How unjust and puzzling that in the same gruesome struggle he, drained of his last reserves, should have been rewarded by a life of misery, while I, envigorated, should now be living among the elite.

The example of this rebel against the commonplace made me feel stodgy and bourgeois. I was afraid I might settle, at twenty-eight, for the career of an armchair bureaucrat.

Not only at the United Nations in New York and at UNESCO in Paris, but throughout the widespread family of major international institutions of the U.N., demagoguery seemed to be subverting the dreams, the hopes, the plans of their founders, and of me and my colleagues.

I soon saw cynicism and corruption in the behavior of UNESCO's member states, large as well as small, conditions that were completely out of place in my scheme for the future.

As I think back to those years, I feel confirmed that my impressions were correct. I recall how in our graduate days, Zulfikar Ali Bhutto, who later became President of Pakistan, would be in and out of Norma's parents' home — he courted her adopted Iranian sister, Lailee Bakhtiar — with his radical ideas. "Zulfi," as we used to call him, was determined one day to help consolidate the threatened independence and fragile democratic system of his newly sovereign country. Twenty-five years later he was hanged at the behest of a crude military dictatorship.

I recall also my long, emotional discussions about aid to the Third World with my thoughtful and talented UNESCO colleague, Ambassador Fereydoun Hoveida; and later with his brother, Amir Abbas Hoveida, Prime Minister of Iran — imprisoned by the Shah and executed by a firing squad of Ayatollah Khomeini's, without even the pretense of a fair trial.

"The nice thing about UNESCO is that, having no real power, while it can never do much good, it can never harm anyone. How many national governments or business corporations can make that claim?" said Edward de Grazia, a young Washington lawyer, who, like me, had joined UNESCO for idealistic reasons. Ed had brought to the organization a conception of cultural exchange that paralleled my views of the role of trade. While his belief in UNESCO's harmlessness at that time seemed right, recent events have proved him wrong. UNESCO can do harm, and the ouster of Israel from its important committees on the indecent ground that it was a racist state was not its only pernicious action.

The collapse of UNESCO, and the U.N. for that matter, as a responsible body occurred because the United States and the Soviet Union effectively canceled out each other's power and influence, allowing a cabal of Third World diplomats to play successfully one against the other.

And since then I have followed the increasingly Kafkaesque atmosphere and the slow moral decay of international diplomacy as practiced throughout the U.N.; the emergence of an automatic majority ready to vote for almost any demagogic resolution.

I was, of course, emotionally committed to Israel's search for security. The agony of the trains that moved through the night of my childhood was the agony that gave Israel birth. "If only all Arabs were like you," I used to say at Harvard to my shy and idealistic classmate Sheikh Ahmed Zaki Yamani, today the powerful petroleum minister of Saudi Arabia — believing, as I joshed him and other Arab friends, and as they joshed me back with "If all Jews were like you," that my concept of Soviet-American conciliation via a network of commerce could be applied as well to Israel and the Arabs; hoping, in any event, that the folly of uncompromising enmity would soon become evident to both sides. But, with the years, that enmity had only waxed; and with its penetration of the international institutions for which I worked, I was forced to choose: if the life that had been spared by so many miracles was to have real meaning, I would have to break new ground.

Me and Ben departing for Paris

Uncle Nachman at Raffles Hotel in Singapore

Uncle Lazar in his Australian army uniform

Ben and me in Australia

Getting my doctorate at Harvard

Barrister-at-Law of Gray's Inn, London

Norma

With friends from Boston

III

Journey of Hope

To be both a speaker of words and a doer of deeds.

— Homer

9

LIKE many young Americans, like many young Europeans, I was strongly attracted by the presidential candidacy of John F. Kennedy.

I had met the junior Senator from Massachusetts when he was a member of the Board of Overseers of Harvard University. When I was awarded my doctorate of law — two more were awarded at the same time, to Cardinal Cushing of Boston and to Douglas Dillon, later Secretary of the Treasury — the Senator pointed out with his typical humor that I was the only one who had worked for it; the others received honorary degrees.

Everything about Kennedy appealed to me — his style, his tone, his youth, and most of all, his openness to people and ideas. After the moribund conservatism of Eisenhower's last years, America was ready for a change. A new generation, which had been in its teens and twenties when the war broke out, seemed eager to support and be led by the first of its members who could seriously aspire to political power. I identified strongly with the hopes of this generation and felt, I didn't know by what title, that a part of their America was in me as well, as though my ancestors too had arrived on the *Mayflower,* or with the great immigration waves long ago.

It was in the midst of this political climate that two of my good friends — Thomas Finney, one of Kennedy's campaign coordinators, and David Busby, a leading Washington attorney — recommended to the Committee on Foreign Commerce of the U.S. Senate that I be brought to Washington to testify before it as an expert witness. The committee was exploring ambitious policy initiatives for the decade of the sixties on which Washington had not focused before and about which, from my research at Harvard and my European experience, I knew more than most others.

I felt strongly that new foreign-policy options ought to be placed on the national agenda. I was convinced that it was shortsighted and unworthy for a great democracy endlessly to accumulate ballistic missiles and nuclear weapons, and ignore the need to mobilize its immense human capacities toward positive and constructive approaches to the goal of a peaceful world. The communist bloc was not as monolithic as it had been viewed at the start of the cold war, but the long years of brinkmanship diplomacy on the part of the United States had worked mainly to weld the fissures. Although America continued to undertake creative and innovative economic measures, in the sphere of political thought, it was laggard.

In my presentation to the Senate committee, and my subsequent exchange with individual senators, I proposed a charter of ground rules for expanded East-West trade. My views must have struck a responsive chord at the height of the presidential campaign because I was immediately invited by the committee chairman, Senator Warren Magnuson, to join his staff as an adviser. I eagerly accepted.

In the early summer of 1960 Norma and I rented a beautiful, three-story brick house in Georgetown. The rent was more than we could afford, but we could not resist its colonial charm, its flowering garden and its magnificent cherry blossoms. Our daughter, Helaina, was then three years old and we needed the room. Besides, the political and social life of Washington was all of a piece and we had searched for a home that would serve to enroll us as members of this energetic community of New Frontiersmen.

My spirits were buoyed by the excitement all around me. That is the effect the movers and shakers of American society have had on many foreigners of my acquaintance and that is the effect Washington now had on me. More than ever, I felt an important part of me wedded to the United States.

From my modest but strategic vantage point on Capitol Hill I could request information and research from government departments, universities, and the splendid Library of Congress. I could exchange views and give opinions to political figures who were the lifeblood of the Kennedy campaign and who constantly were in search of new ideas and policies to incorporate into his public statements and positions.

As soon as Kennedy was elected, I was recruited to join a team of advisers who helped formulate the President-elect's future White House policies. It seemed to me sheer luck that I found myself assisting, however marginally, in what turned out to be a far-reaching reassessment of national strategies, for the Congress and the new Chief Executive of the United States. It was a little unreal, but it made me feel very good to be alive. The unfashionable studies I had carried out at Harvard all of a sudden acquired political importance.

I was a member of the President's task force on foreign economic policy headed by George Ball, a close friend of Jean Monnet, the "Father of Europe" and the European I admired most. Ball was, like Monnet, a champion of European integration and of a close partnership between Western Europe and the United States. I found him surprisingly open to my ideas on the future of America's relations with the communist world, which must have appeared rather heretical in the political context of that time. The new policies we helped to hammer out for the Kennedy Administration were dubbed by Joe Kraft, the columnist of the *Washington Post,* "the grand design."

Tom Finney, Mike Rashish, and Richard Gardner were young lawyers and economists known for their intellectual brilliance and Washington know-how. They, and others like them — Myer Feldman, for example, who worked much more closely with the President, and who later also would become one of my most intimate friends — occasionally joined by older men such as Dean Acheson and Averell Harriman, worked in a happy confusion of typewriters, skull sessions, note taking, and speech writing. In the evenings the enthusiasm that had to be curbed in the position papers would spiral off into the blue, over drinks at social gatherings.

It was exhilarating to be part of that group, to be a spectator and an actor, where rank or seniority were of no consequence and everything seemed possible. When I listened to the new President deliver his first speech on the White House lawn, I had the heady experience of hearing whole sentences taken from one of the papers I had just prepared.

I, the speck of dust blown in from the trashcans of Europe, was putting words into the mouth of the American President. Our optimism in those euphoric days must have compared favorably to that of the early pioneers, including a definite tendency to underestimate the immense obstacles that lay ahead.

The Best and the Brightest, the book by David Halberstam on the Kennedy-Johnson era, has since lent an ironic meaning to those words, but for us, at that moment, there was nothing ironic in them. We did believe, even those who, like myself, did not work in close proximity to the President, that we were charged with the same sort of inspiring mission that our teachers had helped accomplish under the leadership of Franklin Delano Roosevelt — to put America on a new and better road. To me, that earlier mission signified something almost sacred, for it had brought not only justice and prosperity to America, but the strength and cohesion needed to save my own and Europe's neck.

It was because of that mission, and the miracle it produced, that America was able, starting from zero at the tragic moment of Pearl Harbor, to deploy mighty armadas against the two most powerful military machines the world has ever known. Because of the reconstruction of the New Deal, Roosevelt, Marshall, Eisenhower, MacArthur and Truman were able to command vast Allied armies to final victory.

It was on the beaches of the Atlantic and the islands of the Pacific that the American century began and the magnificent demonstration was made that democracy and freedom can be stronger than autocracy and repression.

The challenge for the Kennedy generation seemed equally great, the goals equally ambitious, particularly in the international arena. In his eloquent inaugural address the President defined that challenge and announced a search for new concepts needed to meet it, in terms which were ringing echos from my past and which coincided perfectly with my own aspirations and my own concerns. ". . . For man holds in his mortal hands the power to abolish all forms of human poverty and all forms of human life."

History seemed to be dashing off in a new direction. At long last we would be able to address ourselves to the real problems of the future and not the old, tired, and possibly false issues of the past. Big wars seemed impossible in the shadow of an atomic holocaust. Man would have to shift his energy from military conquest to more sophisticated, more productive, forms of competition, with science and technology harnessed for peace.

Education — a thing which had transformed me from a primitive savage amid the ruins of postwar Europe into a valuable member of

Washington society — would perform similar miracles for those millions of others still crawling about in misery and degradation. The unbounded energy and idealism of youth would be released to build rather than destroy. Young men, who for centuries had been drafted to learn little more than how to fight bravely on the battlefields, and young women, who had been taught to become little more than good housewives, would now be given the opportunity, the mission, to draw out from their souls, from their minds, from their nervous systems, all the latent talent and resources needed for a future of peaceful competition and mutual progress among human societies. In this competition, America's best weapons would reign supreme.

To be so close to such power and excitement at the age of thirty was seductive. But I was increasingly uncomfortable with what seemed to me to be a glaring anomaly: privy to the processes of American governmental decision-making and cleared to read some of the secret information, the classified documents that entered into those processes, I was, nonetheless, a citizen of a foreign country. The FBI had gone over my background with its proverbial fine-toothed comb, but the ambiguity in my personal status bothered me more and more.

Who was I? The question that had arisen for me in the U.S. Army camp near Munich on the day of Germany's surrender haunted me again. Was I a European? Yes: for that continent had marked me indelibly in my flesh since birth. Was I an Australian? Yes, again: for that continent had picked me up and reshaped me and instilled in me the outlook and manner of an English gentleman at a time when half the world's map was still scarlet and the British Empire was a proud thing for an illiterate young European castoff to call his own. And yet I had to admit that however adaptable I had proved to be, I had always felt somewhat on the edge of things, a kind of marginal man — in Europe, and in Australia as well. Somehow, it seemed to me that only in the United States was I completely accepted and completely at home, completely sure that I would be permitted, even encouraged, to develop my aspirations to the full.

I was, it seemed, American at heart, but not in the eyes of the law. I was married to an American citizen, I had an American-born child, and I had lived long enough in the United States to fulfill the residency requirements of naturalization, but I had not entered the country under the immigration quota.

Senator Mike Monroney of Oklahoma had introduced a private bill to make me an American citizen. After it was voted by both Houses in June 1961, President Kennedy sent me a facsimile of the act of Congress and the pen with which he signed the resolution into law.

Our friends gathered at our Georgetown house to congratulate me. I moved among them flushed like a boy at his bar mitzvah. They were from California and Georgia and Massachusetts and Virginia. Outwardly, nothing set me apart from them. But, they were Americans born to the traditions of a great republic, reared in the certainties of lasting and stable freedom. I was an American from the slaughterhouse of history, forged by the fires of the greatest political earthquake humanity had ever known.

Deep within myself I knew I would be their fellow citizen, wholeheartedly and forever, that my future was inextricably tied up with them and this generous, open country, which, like no other ever could, has given me the opportunity to find my place and play my part. But I also stayed wrapped in the secret knowledge that I was inextricably tied to my past. My naturalization had, in fact, taken place long before, when I was barely sixteen years old — when a black GI climbed out of a tank with a white star to liberate me. In that moment he made me into an American, like himself. Congress, with its formal and solemn decision, had done no more than to legitimize that event.

Raising a glass to thank my guests for their help in the enactment of what they fondly called the "Pisar Act," I found myself incapable of expressing what lay in my heart. Instead, I wisecracked, not quite managing to hide the deep emotion within me. "You, my friends, are American citizens by the mere accident of birth; I am American by the declared will of the people."

Few of my Washington acquaintances really knew about my past. Yet surviving that past had, I believed, enabled me to see more clearly than most of them what their — our! — country needed desperately for its own survival: a radically new policy that would banish the danger of nuclear holocaust and — if that ultimate disaster were indeed fended off — fortify a world, America included, too threatened for democracy to be sustained.

I had glimpsed the vulnerability of the communist system firsthand during my childhood, and I had perceived that vulnerability more objectively in the course of my research at Harvard. I also owed the Russian people an emotional debt of the sort that one cannot fail owing to those who, dying, save your life. Not surprisingly, I had a less inflexible and more concrete view of the Soviet system than most of my colleagues. Despite the bellicose policies of the Kremlin, my conviction that Moscow's braggadocio proceeded more from economic weakness than from military strength kept me faithful to my belief in the softening effect of economic and technological cooperation.

When German lightning struck Poland in September 1939 and the Red Army rolled ponderously over the eastern half of the country to claim Stalin's share of the spoils, I was ten years old. With my family I stood on the balcony of our home and watched the Soviet cavalry clatter by — an exotic mixture of Slavic, Mongol, and Islamic horsemen. I remember how relieved my father and my mother had been. The Molotov-Ribbentrop pact between the two sworn enemies was a bitter surprise and a moral outrage, but at least it promised ten years of peace. The Russians were occupiers, but we had known them as such before. It is true that they were communists now, and that made one apprehensive, but the revolution that established Soviet power had its roots in cities like Bialystok, so there was curiosity about them too.

Above all, the Russians were our saviors from submission to Nazi rule. For many families, the salvation exacted a certain price. All heads of household were issued new identity cards; if the card was stamped with the word *bourgeois,* the family was often told to exchange its house or apartment with the more deserving working class. The move would be enforced within a matter of days. As a rule, the evicted family had to leave its furniture and most other belongings behind.

That was not the worst of it. All shops and factories were immediately nationalized. Rationing of food and clothing was instituted. My mother and grandmother would spend long hours queuing up for a pound of meat or butter, items which were more readily available in the thriving black market, a ubiquitous feature of communist life.

Bialystok also came to know the midnight knock on the door. Thousands of Jewish families, including many of our relatives, were surreptitiously exiled to Siberia, as "undesirable from a class standpoint." What a bitter twist on the old Jewish joke — "That's bad?" . . . "No, that's good" — that suggests that misfortune can prove to be a lucky break! Little did the despairing deportees know that in the fastness of some Siberian labor camp they would have an immeasurably better chance of survival than the rest of us, marked by Hitler for a fate no one foresaw.

My own family was left alone. The Soviet authorities came upon my father while he was fixing an automobile engine; he stood before them with greasy hands. That was enough to have his identity card stamped with the word *worker*. And that made us members of the newly privileged class. Their failure to discover that we were propertied, landlords even, may have derived in part from my father's shrewdness, but it provides an overall reflection of their inherent bureaucratic ineptitude; and we were grateful for that.

In school, my education underwent a radical change for the better. It would be a mistake to regard Soviet schooling, even in Stalin's day, merely as crude indoctrination. There was plenty of that but the quality of the teaching compared well with what we had known before. I acquired a liking for study, for there was strong moral tone to it now — the product of the revolutionary ideals that were still taught in the schools even as they were betrayed by the Stalinist regime elsewhere. That last circumstance was not something we children could know about, and, as the newest citizens of the Worker's State, we responded ardently to the political courtship that was inherent in the Soviet educational process.

We were stirred by our Soviet teachers' recital of the indignities heaped upon the Jews under the czarist government: the pogroms of the "Black Hundreds"; the denial of basic civil rights and higher education; the kidnapping, from the streets, of six- or seven-year-old Jewish boys to fill army recruitment quotas — the so-called Czar Nicholas soldiers, who served for twenty-five years, losing all sense of identity.

We followed, as in an exciting bedtime story, the exploits of the giants, Marx, Lenin, and Stalin, who came into the world to rid it of all injustice and oppression. We thrilled to the Great October Revolution that was the outcome of their heroic deeds. A new man, "Soviet Man," had stepped onto the stage of history. To Russian, Pole, or Jew, his was a life of freedom and dignity. He was meant to serve as our model.

For me, the world acquired a perfect clarity. The Soviet Union was progressive; the rest of the world was antiquated, still subject to the hateful forms of exploitation of man by man that were characteristic of the czarist era. Russian was declared to be the official language at my school, with German replacing Hebrew as the second language; Polish was abolished altogether.

With great solemnity I announced to my parents that when I grew up, I wanted to be a general of the Soviet Air Force. Meanwhile, I joined the Pioneers and the Cadets, and by the age of twelve had risen to junior officer rank. My favorite music was martial and I still remember some of the songs we sang, marching in parades to celebrate the anniversary of the Great October Revolution while the red flag, with the hammer and sickle, fluttered above: "If tomorrow be war, if tomorrow we march, be ready for battle today," or, "He was ordered to the Western front, she to the one in the east."

Hitler took Denmark, Norway, Holland, Belgium, Luxembourg, then Yugoslavia and Greece. We heard in the summer of 1940 that he had occupied Paris and we saw pictures of helmeted Nazis goose-stepping toward the same Arch of Triumph that I had seen on postcards Aunt Barbara had sent us, before the war. Nearly all of Europe was now under Hitler's heel, but he had not dared — and would not dare — to march against the unmatched, mighty Red Army.

I saw that my parents were not exactly enchanted by my conversion. That troubled me, but I assumed they were too much a part of the old world to accept the new. I am sure, thinking back on it now, that they had probably decided it would be wiser not to apply the weight of parental authority against what I was being taught in school. To have done so would have been to create an unbearable conflict in my mind and might have brought danger to them. We children were told by our teachers to report any "deviations" we noticed at home, and, given the prevailing environment and my exalted state, there is no telling what I might have done. In any event, before long, any deprogramming my parents could not undertake was brought about by the Nazis, abruptly and with gale force.

The total collapse of the Soviet defenses at the first German blow, early on Sunday, June 22, 1941, when I was twelve shook my new set of beliefs as nothing else could. Where was the unconquerable spirit of the new Soviet Man? As wave after wave of Messerschmidt bombers emptied their payloads over the city's railway junction, the people who represented Soviet civil and military authority in Bialystok dropped everything and ran. Where was the unmatchable might of the Red Army? When we fled east in a truck "requisitioned" by my father, we saw that vaunted Soviet force decimated — reduced to columns of ragged, beaten, hungry prisoners of war who had been cut off by the German advance. So were we. Within several days we found ourselves headed back, part of a horde of refugees resigned to the inevitable.

More even than the Russians' early defeat, it was the way their zeal evaporated that astonished me. I saw my Soviet teachers and other Soviet officials behave in a manner that signaled a profound loss of faith in their cause. Many of them, Ukrainian, Lithuanian, White Russian deserters, collaborated openly with the enemy, and even joined the killer battalions of the SS, as though they had been liberated rather than enslaved. Although I was too young to put it into words, I was not too young to understand it: the zeal, the faith, could not have been very deep to start with. A system that was so brittle could not be such a great system. The glorious virtues, the solid foundations — all those ideas and songs and poems that had been pumped into my mind — were sham.

I remember sneaking a look at my father, sitting at the wheel of the truck, with our family and belongings piled on top, and thinking how solid, how strong, how dependable he was.

⁂

Having served as a member of President Kennedy's early task force, I now became a consultant to the State Department and an adviser to the Joint Economic Committee of Congress as well. Never again was I likely to be in a better position to influence American policy. I devoted myself to that aim.

As East-West tensions over Berlin were culminating in the construction of the Wall, I submitted to the committee a special report it had invited me to prepare, on which I had worked for many months. The political climate was far from ideal for my purposes, but I had learned in America not to fear to swim against the current of established ideas.

I confess feeling a thrill when I opened the 103-page booklet published by the Government Printing Office. I respected the powers lodged in the legislative branch even more than I admired the sweep of the presidency, recognizing in the former a wise check on the arbitrary — the edicts, the orders, the commands of my guards . . . the nightmare of my life. And here was a document of Congress entitled "A New Look at Trade Policy Toward the Communist Bloc — The Elements of a Common Strategy for the West," and, under the title, my name. In the introduction I had written: "Our recent policies and practices have been marked by a notable lack of vigor, clarity and consistency. At home as well as abroad, the dominant impression created has been one of drift in several directions at the same time. As a consequence, U.S. economic policy toward the U.S.S.R. and its satellites has become isolated from that of the other members of the Atlantic Alliance. . . ."

To my surprise and pleasure, on the day of the report's release, a detailed story on it appeared on the front page of the *Washington Post,* and similar stories were carried by wire services, throughout the world.

It seemed to me absurd that more than one-third of the population of the planet — Russia, Eastern Europe, China — should be practically excluded from international economic exchange; and dangerous, too, because Western Europe and Japan would refuse to be held to such a policy. I felt it was urgent to construct a framework of ground rules that would make it possible to integrate the immense natural resources and potentially huge markets of the communist countries into the world economy; and to accept the bet that human freedom would progressively benefit from this process.

What I had proposed was a series of small but concrete steps that would send Moscow a signal of American willingness to consider a new relationship. For example, Washington would relax somewhat its list of "strategic" goods that could not be sold to the Soviet Union, and it would lift the American embargo on the importation of Kamchatka crabmeat, which had been banned on suspicion that it was produced by "slave labor." The gulag system that Alexander Solzhenitsyn brought home to the Western public in such overpowering detail was then on the way to being dismantled, and it seemed to me that Nikita Khrushchev's anti-Stalinist reforms would not be encouraged by embargoes stemming from the Stalin era. I felt something positive should be done to steer the Soviets in the direction of further liberalization.

My report was written in careful language, with ample bows in the direction of the ruling cold-war mentality; I wanted to persuade, not polemicize. Nevertheless, its controversial nature was enough to bring the political right down on my head, notably a blistering attack by Congressman John Dent of Pennsylvania, one of the country's foremost Protectionists.

Someone outside of government, whom I liked and respected, chided me in sorrow more than anger.

''Listen, my boy,'' said General Sarnoff, still a dominant figure of the international communication establishment in terms of his economic power and the potential impact of his views on public opinion, ''your ideas are all wet.'' This fabulous immigrant, so proud of the military rank he received when he organized the armed forces communications network for Eisenhower during World War II, was now an open admirer of Richard Nixon. He fixed me with his lively eyes. ''You can't coexist with the Russians and the Chinese. You can only fight them with their own methods.''

''But then won't we become like them? How will you explain to future generations that our way of life is worth fighting for?''

I don't know if he himself understood where the worldwide clandestine methods and the tampering with America's basic values he had in mind would lead the country; I certainly did not understand it at the time. He only shook his head. He was sorry to see a promising young fellow waste himself on foolishness.

Sarnoff resembled another of my favorite cold warriors, Louis B. Mayer. He, who made and unmade some of the greatest Hollywood stars, had wanted, immediately after my graduation from Harvard, to give my career a different direction from the ''intellectual foolishness'' I was interested in. He saw me as a big-time studio lawyer, and when he set his mind on something he was difficult to resist. I told Norma that if a man like Mayer was going to get behind me and push, I'd better get out of his way fast.

It was, I suppose, a sour joke, considering the pull that Norma's parents exerted trying to get us back to Los Angeles. It also was an omen of what was to strain our happiness. But I was too wrapped up in my work to be sensitive to omens.

In November 1961 I accompanied Senator Javits of New York, who was chairman of the Economic Committee of NATO Parliamentarians and with whom I had established a deep rapport, on a trip to Moscow and other European capitals. The purpose of our visit was to investigate the prospects of increased East-West trade. During the trip, which included discussions with high government officials, I found that the Soviets responded suspiciously to my approach. That, I decided, was probably the consequence of their continuing fears of anything that might open up their system to Western influence. It was a fear that could yield only to experience and time.

Similar resistance had built up in Washington as well, based on concern that we were "building up the Soviets at our own expense." The burst of energy that had marked the launching of the Kennedy Administration had petered out. The Iron Curtain was still down.

Both in the White House and in the Cabinet, the President had been surrounded by modern, gifted, and well-meaning men, just as Roosevelt had been; but unlike Roosevelt, Kennedy was unable to weld them into an effective operational team.

Robert Kennedy, McGeorge Bundy, Robert McNamara, and many other remarkable minds were receptive, as was the President himself, to completely new ideas, including mine, for a new approach on East-West relations. They all understood that these relations would in one way or another impinge on America's relations with the increasingly restless Third World and importantly affect many other vital problems at the global and at the domestic levels.

But they found themselves more and more hamstrung by the powerful, almost autonomous, entrenched bureaucracies in the Pentagon, the CIA, and the State Department. They underestimated the powerful reach of the military-industrial complex against which even Eisenhower had warned when he left the White House. It was tragic to see the blunders, the oversimplifications, and the perversion of priorities that diverted the intelligence and energies of these men into dead ends. One mistake of strategy seemed to lead to another. The 1961 Vienna Summit, during which, by his own admission, the President had been too polite and too timid, emboldened Khrushchev to test the mettle of the "inexperienced young man." The Cuban missile crisis, the Bay of Pigs disaster, the commitment of more and more manpower, lives, and equipment to Vietnam soon brought the two superpowers to a new phase of brinkmanship diplomacy.

In this climate, enthusiasm for bold policy initiatives in the East-West area quickly evaporated. The more moderate, sophisticated, and politically more courageous proposals for managing Soviet-American relations, which had been put forward by my task force, were shelved. Irony of ironies, they would be revived some ten years later, by Richard Nixon.

10

WAS it echoes of Landsberg I was hearing? I looked at my Washington friends. Most of them had settled down in the government for the long haul. In a way I envied them, but I knew that was not for me. The nation's capital had enough bureaucrats; it could not have been for this that my life had been spared. Of course, I wanted to maintain my ties to the government, to serve my country, but I could effectively do that from the outside, through special jobs for the Administration and the Congress as a recognized expert on international affairs. I decided, in the spring of 1962, that it was time for me to go out and practice my profession.

For years I had worked under the umbrella of protective institutions — as a scholarship student in academia, as an international civil servant, and just now as a functionary in Washington. I had not tried to earn my living in the harsh competitive world since I was sixteen, in Landsberg.

My idea was to specialize in international law — a field that was developing rapidly with the unprecedented expansion of trade and investments between the United States and Western Europe. When I made known to friends and colleagues the decision I had made, several offers came in from some of the largest Wall Street law firms, including that of then Under Secretary of State George Ball. Although I was sorely tempted, I felt even more strongly that I should create my own law office and, most of all, be my own boss.

In the midst of a brief family vacation in California, I met an attorney, Leon Kaplan, whose human warmth and professional reputation made a deep impression on me. The firm he headed was comparatively small, but dynamic, efficient, and open to new ideas. Before many more meetings, we agreed that I would join him and open a European office to practice law along the lines I had in mind.

Paris seemed the perfect place for such an office. After the signing of the Treaty of Rome, Europe was taking its first steps toward federalism. And, federalism was in my professional bones. In my view, the fundamental idea behind the Common Market charter, with its hundreds of clauses, was no different from, and basically a derivative of, that one brief clause of the U.S. Constitution which provided "the Congress shall have power to regulate Commerce . . . among the several States."

As it developed, the European Common Market system would surely resemble that which the American Congress and the federal courts, through a long process of trial and error, had provided over the course of two centuries. Moreover, the European Community's High Court of Justice, which was given the task of watching over that charter, appeared analogous to the U.S. Supreme Court, before Chief Justice John Marshall came on the bench and implanted that remarkably important and fertile idea, in the case of *Marbury* v. *Madison,* that the federal judiciary had the right to strike down any act of an executive or legislative organ that appeared to them to contradict the Constitution.

I set out for Europe, stopping first in Lausanne, where I had some of my first professional business to attend to. There, I had the stroke of good luck to chat with British financier Loel Guinness. "Tell me," he said in his low, Oxford-accented voice, "what are your plans, now that you have Washington behind you?" When I told him that I was on the way to Paris to scout for an apartment and office space, he said, "I've got just the place for you. I can rent you an empty floor in my building on the Place de la Madeleine."

How could I tell this friendly Croesus that my budget was impossibly tight, that I did not have any clients, and that it was all a question of "how much"?

"Thank you, but, you know, I'll only need two rooms, for me and a secretary."

Guinness said, regally, "I'm going to Paris tomorrow in my plane. Come with me and take a look for yourself."

Ten days later, I had fourteen rooms on the third floor of a splendid building overlooking the flower market at the foot of the Madeleine

Church, for a rent impossible to improve upon. The first thing I did was to block off all but two rooms, so my prospective clients would not see in what solitude I conducted my business.

It was not long before I could stop worrying about all the money running out and no money coming in. My first major client was brought to me by my friend and former UNESCO colleague, Edward de Grazia, who had now become legal counsel for International General Electric. GE was a large American designer and manufacturer of nuclear energy plants. I was asked by Ed to advise on how the company could limit its potentially catastrophic liabilities under European law in case of an atomic accident.

From then on my clientele expanded rapidly and came to include heads of large corporations and banks, authors, inventors, and so forth. Gradually, my staff and office equipment expanded to fill all the empty rooms — and the rooms on two more floors as well. What with tariff walls falling within the Common Market, capital and technology moving on a new scale across national borders, and American investments pouring into Europe, my work had a novel, pleasing variety. It even lent me a touch of glamour.

Those were the big years for movies shot in Europe by American companies, often in partnership with European producers, and the legal complexities of the ventures involved brought executives, directors, and ultimately movie stars to my door. In a way, the law business I had evaded in Hollywood followed me to Paris. This time, I was more susceptible.

I found it intriguing to meet Ava Gardner for breakfast in Madrid in order to discuss her next movie contract, and then take the morning flight to London in time for a luncheon conference at the Rothschild Bank; to help negotiate the purchase of an enormous diamond or yacht by Richard Burton for Elizabeth Taylor at the same time that I was preparing the papers for a hundred-million-dollar bank loan to a major multinational corporation; to help straighten out Catherine Deneuve's or Jane Fonda's studio problems while assisting in the establishment of American and Japanese banks in Europe, English and Dutch firms in France, or French and German corporations in the United States.

My affairs prospered and the dollar everywhere was at the peak of its strength.

Uncle Nachman's daughter, Ethel, from Melbourne, and Aunt Barbara's son, Pierre, from New York, came to live with us and continue their studies at the Sorbonne. I was heading up a multinational and multilingual family and a multinational and multilingual practice.

I was a member of the Washington, D.C., and California bars, and I was admitted to practice as a Barrister-at-Law in London and as a Counselor at Law in Paris. I was on the boards of banks and companies all over Europe.

Still, in one area, I had guessed wrong. East-West trade did not develop as I had hoped. The decade of the sixties was passing under the ambiguous signs of an abatement in U.S.-Soviet military confrontation and a virtual freeze in the superpowers' relations, owing to the American preoccupation with Vietnam.

There were some pioneering international business deals in which I served as chief legal counsel, notably the construction of Pan American Airway's Intercontinental hotels in Eastern Europe. But the vast potential for profitable exchange of the Soviet Union's raw materials and consumer needs for the grain, equipment, and advanced technology of the United States had gone largely untapped. My opportunities for contributing to the weaving of mutual interests between those two countries were disappointingly scant.

The entertainment law side of my practice, which largely emanated from the Kaplan office in Los Angeles, was also taking much more of my time and energy than I was willing to give it.

❖ ❖ ❖

My intensely cosmopolitan activity was very rewarding, attractive, even seductive. But a new client knocked on my door and demonstrated to me in the most unexpected way that this type of life had limits. He was a young boy with a shaved head, pale skin tightly drawn over his face, and an almost broken body. I had nearly forgotten him. He viewed his successful lawyer from deep-set, sunken eyes with a touch of irony, verging on disapproval. He did not pay fees. The number of his file was B-1713.

The government of Chancellor Konrad Adenauer had passed a law offering monetary compensation to Jews who had suffered under the Nazis. I was indignant. What gall, to think that money could wipe clean the slate. Never, I remember writing to Ben, would *I* apply. When Israel adopted a contrary position, working out a reparations agreement with the West German regime, I was shaken; I decided the inconsistency in our positions was to be explained by Israel's dire economic needs. I had no such necessity.

And what value could I place on what I had lost? What price could I put on my stolen adolescence, my mother's engagement ring ripped off her finger under threat of bayonet, my father's gold watch exchanged for a drink of water, the bouquet of artificial white flowers thrown into the fireplace of our home? To think that a few marks could wipe out the greatest crime in history. Never!

Ben wrote back that I was a self-righteous fool. If I had no need for the money, I could turn it over to charity. Then I met David Ben-Gurion and I talked with Nahum Goldman, who had negotiated the reparations accord with Germany and who presented Ben's view in more diplomatic terms; and I was even more confused. Was I a better Jew than the founder of the State of Israel or the head of the World Jewish Congress? But the more I argued with myself the angrier I got at the Germans. Make *them* pay!

I remembered how, after the war had ended, when we learned the Americans had dropped atomic bombs on Japan, I had exclaimed instinctively: "Why didn't they drop a couple on Germany?" This thirst for vengeance welled up again and again in many of us. And it occurred to me that the money was not meant as a payoff — that it was the only way the Germans knew of saying they were sorry. Expiation was impossible, repentance was all that could be asked.

I reached my decision and filed my claim just before the reparations law ran out. The litigation was lengthy and Germanically thorough. I had to prove that I was in Bialystok when the SS moved us into the ghetto, that my father had been executed by the Gestapo, and that I had been through the death camps, although the witnesses and the evidence that had not been destroyed by the Nazis were hard to come by. When I was finally awarded the compensation under the relevant statutes — so much for being orphaned at an early age, so much for being deprived of an education, so much for damage to health, so much for loss of property — it came to no more than a few thousand dollars. That, I calculated wryly, was less than my firm's bill for a week of my counseling a large company doing business in Germany.

I never touched the reparation money I received. I do not say it bitterly, but it is all I ever got in exchange for my father, my mother, and my sister. As such, it is sacred to me. One day I will use it to honor their memory. I must wait until I find the right way.

✣✣✣

This brief excursion into my past convinced me that it was time to take stock. It was a difficult time.

The assassination of John Kennedy, followed by that of Martin Luther King, had hit me, like most Americans, hard. Now, when Robert Kennedy fell in his turn, I began to wonder what sinister forces were at work within American society. Just as I had concluded, upon my arrival at Harvard, that American democracy had a way of permanently secreting the germs needed for its own cure, I began to suspect that America was also capable of sowing the seeds of its own destruction.

In my private life too, there was cause for concern. Our second daughter, Alexandra, was born in 1965. But Norma was out of her element. She had bridled a bit at the intellectual assertiveness of Harvard, she hadn't been impressed by the diplomatic rounds of my two years with UNESCO, and while Washington had proved a stimulating interlude, my hopes that she would adjust to a comfortable and cosmopolitan life in Paris were, I could see, misplaced. Norma was a child of Hollywood. She missed her family and she missed the effervescence and artistic creativity of that unique world. More, she wanted to be someone in her own right. She had always flirted with the notion of becoming an actress or singer. She thought she'd start now.

Our life acquired a tacit duality. She studied music and lieder. I worked for another doctorate, at the Sorbonne.

I felt that I needed renewal, that my intellectual batteries had to be recharged, as they had been once before during my bout with tuberculosis and the literary voyage on which it had taken me.

I was also preoccupied with my love-hate relationship with the culture of Eastern Europe, where my ancestors had sunk their roots centuries ago when they moved to that part of the world — a culture that had now risen to challenge America's.

The two greatest tyrants of the century had crisscrossed my life. Over one I had triumphed completely, both physically and spiritually.

Over the other, I had triumphed to the extent that I had cast out the poisonous seeds of Stalinist indoctrination planted in my mind at a tender age. But the system that tyrant had established was still very much alive. I knew that it could not be destroyed with force of arms, that this time there could be no physical triumph. A new way had to be found. My early life, my academic research, my work in Washington, and my recent experience as a negotiator in the hard-nosed, practical world of business gave me good reasons, I thought, to help find a way to render harmless Stalin's grim legacy to his own people and to the world.

I felt more keenly than most the impatience with which the gulag victims viewed the prudent calculations of Western statesmen in their dealings with the U.S.S.R. Their agony, their anger, I had experienced myself when, locked up with my comrades for what seemed like an eternity, I waited and waited for the arrival of the Allies. General Patton's and Field Marshal Montgomery's troops were held back too long by their interminable tactical differences and vain personal quarrels, while life was ebbing out of us in the camps.

From a human standpoint, I approved wholeheartedly the moral position of the Russian dissidents. But I could not overcome my belief that to run the risk of permanent nuclear confrontation would be a policy of madness and would accomplish nothing in the field of human rights. I could not admit to myself that caught between two disasters — having to coexist with a totalitarian society and running the risk of atomic annihilation — the human mind must give up. My visceral instincts from other times rejected such defeatism.

Although the views I had managed to put across in Washington had produced some results, they had fallen short of a real breakthrough. I had to demonstrate to the skeptical policymakers that my thesis was not utopian, but practical, achievable — even essential. Driven by this determination I withdrew from all social life, other than that which was indispensable to my professional responsibilities, in order to write a book; it would be a massive, technically detailed and documented work.

I realize now that the project became at least in part a deep and solitary refuge from an impending family crisis that I could not face.

I turned inward. I told myself that, apart from being scholastic in content and hence intended primarily for experts, the book would be too out of step with contemporary thinking to be acceptable to the public at large. I packed everything I could into it: my conviction that the conventional methods of diplomacy could never drain the poison from Soviet-American relations; that only the growth of living commercial and human tissue between the two societies could accomplish this aim; that only by engaging the Soviets economically could we begin to ease open their society; that only through this patient process could we persuade the Russian rulers to relax their grip and permit the Eastern European countries to restore their natural ties with the West; that only a bold initiative on the part of the United States, as the strongest and most vital power on earth, could get this indispensable project under way. I concluded with a charter of eighty theses on how to establish, maintain, and further East-West coexistence.

I wrote in the evening; I wrote while traveling in planes and trains and waiting at airports; I scribbled notes to myself at the office during the day. I worked most of all during weekends and holidays at Authon, in the Loire Valley, where I had rented a château property from the then Minister of Finance, Valery Giscard d'Estaing. It took me five years.

When I sent the manuscript of more than 1,500 pages to my New York publisher, McGraw-Hill, their reply fulfilled my worst fears: "Your manuscript is too long and too technical. Simplify, condense." I started all over again.

❖ ❖ ❖

Coexistence and Commerce came out in the fall of 1970 to astounding — to me — critical acclaim. Though I had expected it to be of interest to a very limited number of people — economists, politicians, businessmen, students perhaps — its publication stimulated debate and controversy among an ever-widening audience.

What was particularly gratifying, after the knocks from the political right for my 1961 report, was the acceptance, in the most diverse quarters, of my central thesis. In the United States Congress, Senator Edward Kennedy welcomed it as "an enlightened course for the future of American and Western policy." In the business world, Henry Ford II said it "cuts through the fog of emotionalism, ideology and misunderstanding." Among scholars and experts, Professor Arthur Schlesinger called it a "fresh and astute inquiry," and David Schoenbrun praised it as "massive in its documentation and impressive in its quiet and even humble tone."

Even in Moscow, *Pravda* and *Izvestia* gave the book favorable write-ups — a distinct advance, I thought, on the hostile reaction of the Soviet leaders to those same ideas in 1961.

Time magazine declared that the book "could hardly have been better timed." That compliment I did not deserve. I knew how little thought of "timing" had been involved. I had not realized, during the years I struggled with the manuscript, that, behind the facade of immobility, a new mood, receptive to some such proposal, had been germinating in the West.

I was called to testify before congressional committees and was asked to address the New York Council on Foreign Relations. The then Secretary of State, William Rogers, told me at his office that a special report on my policy recommendations had been prepared by the National Security Council for the President's personal attention. The then Secretary of Commerce, Peter Peterson, asked me to help in the drafting of a new commercial treaty he was about to negotiate with the U.S.S.R. — the first in forty years.

In Europe, under the title *Weapons of Peace,* the book caused debate in the House of Commons, the Spanish Cortes, and the National Assembly of France; Giscard d'Estaing hailed it publicly as "the bible on East-West economic relations." New worlds were once again opening up before me.

I am aware that I am in danger of making these lines read like a celebration of myself. That is not my intention. I wanted to write the present book because of a mounting presentiment that we live at a time when military, political, and economic forces of unimaginable destructiveness are building up around the world, a world that on a quiet summer afternoon can be rent apart by unforeseen storms. I also felt I had some special insights to offer on the dangers that people prefer not to think about, insights based on the premises of past tragedy and the tragedies that may lie ahead.

But to speak of your insights means to speak of what gave them to you, and once you tell of one important event you must go on and tell about them all. My accomplishments, such as they are, are the milestones of my road from death — both physical and spiritual — to life, and I must speak of them if I am to give a true account of my odd journey. *Coexistence and Commerce* was the apex of my intellectual achievement in the things I hold real.

I dedicated the German edition of the book to Niko and Ben. I thought Niko especially would have appreciated the private joke. It would have reminded him of the "coexistence and commerce" between the victors and the vanquished that the three of us had practiced in Landsberg. Imagine the surprise and amazement of all those distinguished critics who had reviewed it so favorably, had they known that the deepest wellspring of this unemotional book, containing not the least allusion to my life, was our trade in recycled Brazilian coffee between the extravagantly rich Americans and the desperately poor Germans of 1945.

Ben arrived from Melbourne to spend the 1970 holidays in the country, at Authon. He was now a well-to-do businessman and a little rounder than when I had last seen him. But he was the same warm, spontaneous Ben, simple and direct. Despite my recent celebrity, I was still not able to impress him; not in the least.

His plain Bialystok manner, his abrupt gestures, his Yiddish accent, provided a lively contrast to the somewhat stuffy atmosphere of château life in the Loire Valley. He shook the hand of Giscard d'Estaing in a matter-of-fact fashion and engaged in casual disagreement over something or other with a couple of the titled families of the region, at whose tables he dined. I found myself enjoying his plain speaking. My own words sounded guarded by contrast. I wondered if he found me more changed than I found him.

As always, he inspected the nooks and crannies of the house to make sure that the doors opened and closed smoothly, that the electric switches worked properly, and that the TV antenna did not need adjustment.

Shortly after his arrival, he asked me to go with him for a long walk in the woods. I took along our dog, a King Charles Cavalier whom the children called Balalaika and who was in dire need of training. For obvious reasons, neither Ben nor I liked overtrained dogs.

I looked at the stocky figure, bundled up in a fur coat, trudging along beside me in the deep snow and trying, fruitlessly, to keep the carefree animal at heel. Suddenly, apropos of nothing, he stopped and looked at me sternly: "How are you, Mula?" he said, "All right?"

"Of course," I answered uneasily, wondering whether he was referring to my marital situation or my life in general. "Why do you ask?"

"Don't you think you ought to calm down a little?"

"What do you mean? Have you ever known me not to be calm?"

"I mean, you are running around like a chicken with its head cut off."

I was annoyed. "Benek, what I'm doing is quite important. I have a lot of responsibility, I have got . . ."

He stopped, looking up as though importuning heaven to shed some light on my head.

"My poor friend," he said, "are you sure they need you all that much?"

His question took me by surprise. I felt my annoyance — and arguments — evaporating. All these dignitaries, all these meetings: did they need me or did I need them?

No use ducking it, I thought. I am with the only person in the world who knows me through and through, maybe better than I know myself.

He now looked almost angry. "What are you doing with all of these people, these ministers, these society types, these movie stars, in America, here, all over the place? I can hardly recognize you. You act like them, you eat like them, you speak like them, you even look like them. Why don't you pay a little more attention to your health, to your family. That's what's important."

I looked away from his stare. We seemed so different, worlds apart, yet I felt so close to him. Ever since our reunion in Blizin, our friendship had remained so complete, so irreplaceable, despite the enormous geographical distances that separated us, and although years would go by without our seeing each other. Each of us had, of course, made new friends. But what did the word "friendship" really mean in today's culture? The more celebrated and important the friends I had acquired over the years, the more inclined I was to ask myself, "How would they have behaved amid the horrors, humiliations, and hardships of those days? How closely would they have measured up to Niko and Ben?" Very few passed this acid test in my mind.

We walked on and on through the cold, in step as always — an unshakable habit from the past. A long silence set in between us. His face was serious, his eyes distant. Then he came back, as if he had been waiting till the end to say what concerned him most.

"Mula, you know, your ideas about expanded contacts with the Russians and the Chinese and the Arabs and the Germans, it's all pretty doubtful you know, it's all . . ."

"I know, Benek, but do we have a choice? Any other policy . . ."

He cut me short. "You know, I am not well informed about all these matters, but where are the limits? In Germany, for example, when you were advising those bankers in Frankfurt, all the hands you shook. . . . How do you know that some of them were not former Nazis, or even SS guards from the camps . . . ?"

"You can never know for sure, Benek, but do we always have to live in the past?"

He turned toward me and poked my chest with his index finger. His face was white.

"We may not have to live in the past, but the past lives in us. Take heed, Sam. The most important thing about you is your past. There is nothing stronger or more true than that. If you go on the way you are going, someday you, like most of the people you knock around with, will lose sight of the things that really count."

As in the camp at Blizin, when he shook me out of my fantasies of suicide, as in Melbourne, when he scoffed me out of giving up my chance for continuing my education, we faced each other as though the future turned on a moment of decision. Only this time I struggled to understand what he meant.

Suddenly Ben smiled at me awkwardly, almost apologetically, grabbed Balalaika by the collar, and walked off toward the house.

11

WHEN I arrived at the elegant New York apartment where I was a guest for dinner that night, I could not take my eyes off her.

Brazilian? Greek? Yemenite? There was something indefinable about her beauty.

In the midst of what promised to be a conventional social evening, this young woman, with her copper-hued skin and slim, refined silhouette, radiated a mixture of lightheartedness and reserve that riveted me.

Her first words, in French because she knew I had just arrived from Paris, told me nothing about her origin. Continuing the conversation in English, I discovered that Judith was a native New Yorker.

Her world was far removed from mine. She spoke of the avant-garde canvases of Mark Rothko, the electronic music of John Cage, the experimental theater of Peter Brook and Bob Wilson, and the Merce Cunningham dance company, which she administered. I was faced with one of those situations where a man feels out of his depth.

I was, at that time, a very unhappy man. Norma and I had made one last try at saving our marriage, and both of us saw now that it was no use. Writing my book had become more and more the escape from the thoughts that opened up a void under my feet. Norma kept making frequent trips to Los Angeles. I, too, traveled a good deal, on business.

My encounter with Judith created havoc in both our lives. She had married at twenty and her own family situation suffered from a burden of incompatibility not unlike mine. While we both retained great affection and respect for our spouses, we felt an immediate attraction for each other that we would not long be able to resist.

I began to time my business trips to be near her. When the Merce Cunningham dance company flew to Mexico or to Rome, I would find a reason to go there too. And it was wonderful how she happened to be in Chicago, Montreal, or London at the same time as I.

The situation could not last. We were, at the same time, happy and acutely distressed. We felt our family responsibilities keenly. Her son, Antony Blinken, was eight; my eldest daughter, Helaina, was entering her teens, and Alexandra was ready to begin school. We knew we had to stop seeing each other or join our lives forever.

I was afraid, afraid as never before in my life. Had I misread, that fateful day in Beverly Hills, my mother's silence from the tomb?

It was not the fear of rupturing my ties of friendship with Norma, or even with her family, which had become my family too; I knew that would never happen.

I was afraid for my children: I knew what it meant for a child to say goodbye to a father one morning and not to know when he would be seen again.

I was afraid of the brutality that says ''women and children go this way and men the other way.''

I was afraid of the memory of a family that had had to stand up one day in its home for the last time, lift its suitcases, and walk out into the street.

I was afraid because this time the mayhem would be voluntarily, not the violence applied by a vicious enemy. And yet I knew and Norma knew, and even the children suspected, that our marriage was over.

How I wished that the Second World War had never broken out, that Bialystok had never been destoyed, that I had lived peacefully in my own hometown, married, perhaps, to the girl next door, leading a normal, uneventful life, a life where children could hold on to their parents, grandparents, uncles, aunts, cousins, and school friends.

Yes, your life has been a fascinating journey, Sam Pisar. All in all, fate has rewarded you more than most others. You have accomplished much — intellectually, professionally, and socially. Bravo! But where it really counted, the resurrection of loved ones, the departed that had motivated and propelled you all these years, there you have failed, there you are brankrupt, unable to meet the debts you have incurred to your blood and to your past.

Bitter separations are painful, but they have certain advantages. Jealousy, hatred, fights over property, alimony, and child support act as anesthetics. Amicable separations can be even more painful, and the pain never goes away. This is the way it has been for Norma and for me. I am conscious of how much we shared during our formative years in Cambridge, Washington, and Paris, before our marriage went bad. And I, at that time still unaccustomed to living among the sensitive and fragile, with my rage to live too many lives, must have proved unable to share enough.

Norma went back to Los Angeles to resume her studies and to start a new career, taking Helaina and Alexandra with her. Our divorce became final at the end of 1970, after fifteen years of marriage; Judith's, a little later. We were married in Yonkers, New York, in the presence of our three children, by Rabbi Abraham Klausner, who, twenty-five years earlier, as chaplain to the U.S. Army in Munich, had compiled the list of death camp survivors on which the name Samuel Pisar had appeared for the first time.

Antony came to live with us in Paris. Helaina and Alexandra spend almost as much time with us as with their mother in California. And Leah was born in September 1972. It is the miracle of Judith that she has been able, with sensitivity, determination, and love, to weave together, from all these seemingly broken threads, a happy and harmonious home.

As I write these lines, Leah, who seems to have taken the best from Judith and from me, is the same age as Frieda was when the bombs began to fall. Her grandparents, Beatrice and Sol Frehm of New York, break out in laughter over the pearls of wisdom that come out of her mouth at breakfast, as Frieda's grandparents used to do.

Alexandra is of the age when I entered Maidanek. Her school report card — straight A's — and tennis backhand are better than mine were at that time; and in a long dress she also passes easily, too easily, for an adult.

Antony is at my Landsberg age. He outskis me without difficulty now. But he has agreed to pass up the motorcycle he always wanted and wait for the car that he will surely get now that he has been accepted for admission to Harvard.

Helaina, my most astute critic, is about to graduate from the University of California. Her great love is literature, which she reads with equal ease in English, French, and Russian. She finds Thomas Mann a little obtuse, but she is enchanted by Flaubert and Turgenev and likes Hawthorne and Faulkner.

Through these children I now live my childhood and my adolescence and my youth more fully and more richly than I ever had a chance to myself.

In the summer of 1971, Judith accompanied me to the Soviet Union. The occasion was the annual Dartmouth Conference — so called because the first of its kind had been held at Dartmouth College — between a group of Americans and a group of Russians who were in a position to exchange views, in a private capacity, with greater candor than would have been possible on an official level. The stature of the delegation — which included David Rockefeller, Milton Eisenhower, General James Gavin, Senator Frank Church, and Patricia Harris — insured that both governments would give careful consideration to whatever consensus developed.

One year the conference would be held in the United States, the next year in the Soviet Union. In 1971 it took place in Kiev. The agenda included nuclear arms control, pollution of the oceans and the atmosphere, and expansion of scientific, industrial, and economic relations between the two countries. Organizing the American delegation's views on this last subject was my job.

We arrived in Moscow in an expectant mood. After two decades of cold war, the United States and the Soviet Union seemed ready for a better relationship.

Judith and I promptly gave notice to the Soviet interpreter-guide, a minion of the KGB who had been assigned to us, that my Russian was more than adequate to get us around. We spent several days taking in the museums, the Bolshoi and the treasures of the Kremlin, and visiting the studios of some underground artists. One evening, at a restaurant, I joined a balalaika orchestra in singing some old Russian lullabies that my grandmother used to sing. Judith didn't think we could get as close as we were to Leningrad with its Kirov ballet, Hermitage Museum, and the fortress where Dostoevski was held prisoner, without going there, too. So we went everywhere and found a feast of history, music, and poetry.

The night trip from Moscow to Kiev was in a special wood-paneled railway car that was equipped with a steaming samovar and buffet that included the obligatory vodka and caviar; it all heightened the optimism of the American delegates.

But when the two delegations seated themselves across a table from each other, in the Palace of Culture of the Ukrainian capital, the smiles on our side faded. Instead of settling down to the matters at hand, the Soviets launched into repeated tirades on issues that were not on the agenda.

For some time, in the Soviet Union, the pendulum that had swung between liberalization and crackdown ever since Stalin's death was once more moving in the direction of repression. The immediate cause was the growing pressure on the part of many Soviet Jews for permission to emigrate to Israel, and, more particularly, the uproar that had occurred after an attempted aircraft hijacking by several Leningrad Jews had resulted in their being sentenced to ten years hard labor. The Zionist cause had became enmeshed in the bold demands of a small but vocal part of the Soviet intelligentsia, for greater respect of fundamental human rights.

We understood the sensitivity of the Soviet leaders to a form of dissidence that signified a serious threat to their authoritarian rule and were not surprised to see the regime lashing out with its time-honored tactic of wholesale vituperation — this time against the "handful of traitors who had sold out" to the capitalist West. But we were not prepared to experience this propaganda barrage unleashed at us. We had come to Russia in hope of a dialogue that would rise above official rhetoric.

Like the campaigns I had read about in the Soviet press, the speeches contained an anti-Semitic undertone. The United States was pictured as the agent of an unscrupulous Zionist plot designed to weaken the Soviet Union and whip up war hysteria in the West. References to the "Jewish Nazis of New York" and the "Israeli Fascists of Tel Aviv" cut through me like a knife. Between the headphones of the simultaneous-translation system, the faces on the American side became increasingly glum.

With blood rising to my head, I stared at the faces across the table. They stared back — bumptious, disdainful, hard. The Soviet cochairman, Alexander Korneichuk, president of the Ukrainian parliament, looked angry, as though accusing me personally of the offenses being elucidated by one of the lesser Soviet lights.

I knew that face. Not exactly that one, of course, but one like it, a face multiplied many times over, bearing that hard moralistic look that arrogated to itself all virtue, leaving you with no hope of clemency. It was the look that knew everything, judged everything, and settled everything. It was the copy and projection of the face that had reigned in the Kremlin and before whom all Russia quailed. Stalin was dead; yet Stalin lived.

Alone of all the Americans in that room, I had known from firsthand experience what it was to live under the power of that look — its dynamism, its sorcery, and its lie.

❖ ❖ ❖

On the afternoon of the second day, the sightseeing bus with the American delegates stopped in front of an enormous statute in the center of Kiev — a warrior in full armor, sword outstretched, atop a prancing horse. "What is it?" someone asked.

"Bogdan Khmelnitsky," said our Soviet guide. "One of our great national heroes, a seventeenth-century liberator from the invaders of the West."

On hearing that name I instinctively dug my fingernails into Judith's arm.

The guide's English was pat, memorized from a textbook. It was not the text in use during the two years I had spent under Soviet rule. Khmelnitsky was a Cossack hetman, or chieftain, whose revolt against Polish overlordship in the Ukraine was an interlude in a career of bloody raids on Jewish villages in his domain. For two centuries, observant Jews would not pronounce his name without adding: "May it be obliterated." When the Bolsheviks came to power in 1917, they cast him into obloquy. But, in 1941, Stalin rehabilitated him as part of an effort meant to remedy the desperate situation created by his systematic execution of the country's best officers in bloody purges: the army was not willing to fight for communism. It was Stalin's stratagem to rally the country against its German invaders by evoking the memory of every national figure since Ivan the Terrible. Bogdan Khmelnitsky was rediscovered at that time as a great Ukrainian nationalist.

Out of the vast reserves of Russian courage, endurance, and patriotism, the country drew the stuff of resistance, counteroffensive, and final triumph; they were able to drop the baggage of Leninist-Stalinist ideology until victory was won, when it was loaded on them once again. But for Jews the world over, the glorification of Khmelnitsky was too much.

My uncle Lazar learned that the Soviet government had minted a medal in the hetman's honor — and that the first Soviet soldier to receive the award was, of all people, a Jew — and fired off a polemic to the Melbourne press. The war was still on, and the Australian papers refused to print his letter on the grounds that it would be offensive to an Allied power and inimical to the war effort. So Uncle Lazar secured a week's furlough from the Australian Army, wrote a pamphlet, printed it at his own expense, and distributed it by bicycle from door to door. "We are proud," he wrote, "of the Jewish officer who was honored for his valor in battle. But we reject the Khmelnitsky medal in disgust."

When the conference resumed the next day, our Soviet hosts picked up where they had left off, inveighing against Jews and anyone else in the West who dared to intrude in Soviet internal affairs, throwing in Vietnam for good measure. I found it increasingly difficult to keep still.

From the stony expressions on my side of the table, I could tell that my colleagues felt subjected to a shocking display of bad manners, if not something worse — some essence of the Soviet system that made honest discourse with these people extremely difficult, perhaps impossible. But that was just it. What we were experiencing represented the worst of that system — its counterfeit zealousness, its fervid hypocrisy, its tendency to reflex action that was the more bombastic the greater the unavowed and unavowable knowledge of the brittleness of Soviet power.

Behind the false front lay a human reality, to be sure — men who still sized things up for themselves, who were afraid when there was cause for fear, who stood fast when it made sense to stand fast, who were as capable of comprehension and reasonableness and bravery and sacrifice as any people on the face of the earth, and whose emotionalism at that meeting owed something to their core of sincere belief in a different kind of social ideal. But, due to the nature of the system, none of that reality had percolated to the surface. Soon, the conference was in danger of collapsing in the breach that had formed between the Soviets' gratuitous assault and the Americans' offended silence.

I caught General Gavin's eye. On the spur of the moment I rose and edged over to his chair. "Jim," I whispered, "could we step outside for a minute?" Senator Frank Church came with us.

"Don't you think," I asked when we had closed the door behind us, "it's about time someone talked back to them?"

Gavin shrugged. "Oh, it'll blow over."

"Don't be so sure," I said.

I drew a deep breath, suddenly feeling afraid I was going too far. "Listen! I think I know a thing or two about the Russians, and at this rate they're going to walk all over us and that's not going to do the conference any good."

I tried to read Gavin's deep-green eyes. He had never been a cold-war enthusiast, but neither was he a man to yield a position unnecessarily. He had told me, one day, that if he and General George Patton had received the green light from Washington, in early 1945, the U.S. Army could have beaten the Russians to Berlin. A special brigade of parachutists had trained for that purpose under his command. Now, however, as the leader of the American delegation and cochairman of this conference, his job was to smooth over any problem that arose. My suggestion entailed risks.

Frank Church, who until then hadn't said a word, broke in. "Sam is right, we should answer them. I'm sick of listening to their endless barrage on Vietnam, too. I have been on public record on this issue for a long time and we certainly don't need any lessons from them."

"Jim," I added, after a brief silence, "I'd like to answer them."

The general grew thoughtful, concerned. Then he said calmly, putting his hand on my shoulder, "Okay, let them have it. Good luck."

I had always felt a special affection for General Gavin, whom I got to know when he became President Kennedy's ambassador to France. I had the sentimental idea that when he had "jumped" on St. Mère Deux Eglises on June 6, 1944, as the commander of the 82nd Airborne Division, he had singlehandedly accelerated my deliverance by many days, maybe crucial ones.

Having retaken my seat, I waited for the latest Soviet harangue to end. Then I raised my hand.

"*Gospodin Predsyedatyel,*" I said, as firmly as I could. There was a stir from the Soviets at the sound of Russian from our side. I continued, in Russian, addressing Korneichuk. "Mr. Chairman, may I have the floor?"

Surprised as he was, he could not very well deny it to me. I was on my feet but what was I going to say? — that we return to our agenda? I glanced at Judith, sitting in the row behind us. She gave me a heartening smile.

"Mr. Chairman," I began, in English, "ladies and gentlemen." The Soviets fidgeted with their headphones. "The hospitality is warm, the company is good, the city is beautiful, but the conference is off course. I feel compelled to stray outside my own proper sphere, the future of economic relations between the Soviet Union and the United States, and to express a highly personal point of view. Our distinguished Soviet colleagues have seen fit to move very far from the agreed-upon agenda and to lecture us on America's support for Israel, the Jewish protests in New York, the tragic events in Vietnam, and other painful subjects. In such a free-for-all, there must be room to mention additional matters some of us have in our minds and our hearts."

Later, when I got the transcripts of some of the speeches at the conference, I was surprised at how deliberate this one sounded. When it had happened, I had felt awkward, that I had overstepped my bounds, for I did not, at the time, have a very clear idea what I was going to say.

I went on to state the obvious — that the meeting would have squandered a great opportunity if it bogged down in sterile polemics — and then, realizing that I would have to do much better than that if my interruption was to have any effect at all, I asked the delegates to forgive "an allusion to my personal background."

"Although I am here as a representative of American public opinion," I continued, "I am not a native-born American. That I have been included in so eminent a group of Americans is a tribute more to my adopted country than to myself. What we have come to discuss here relates to the subject of peace. A childhood spent in Nazi concentration camps has made me into something of a specialist on this subject.''

I paused. Milton Eisenhower had his elbows on the table, his head between his hands — was it an attitude of attentiveness or of dismay? Professor Harrison Brown doodled on the pad in front of him. On the other side, Georgi Arbatov, the top Kremlin adviser on relations with the United States, studied me coldly. But the writer Boris Polevoy thoughtfully stroked his long mustache. I had not meant to refer to my childhood. But once the words were out, they tapped a wellspring of emotion in me. Whatever the effect, I was going to go on.

I made a passing reference to the Soviet delegates' excoriation of Israel's policy vis-à-vis the Arabs, suggesting that a problem of such magnitude demanded greater modesty from us all. This brought me to the main topic. I could still stop. But I plunged ahead. I had, I said, a few comments to make on the ''Jewish question'' in Russia.

''Like all of us here, I do not admire the militant behavior of some extremist Jews in New York. But if we are to deal with this problem effectively, we must understand the memories of genocide, the fears and the traumas expressed in the desperate cry, 'Never Again!' After the Holocaust and all the slaughters and pogroms that came before, whenever the remnants of the Jewish people feel threatened, they react with emotion. In a society such as America's, which tolerates few limits to freedom of expression, popular reactions to all emotional issues tend to be strong and loud. When they please you in the Soviet Union, you applaud. When they disturb you, you curse. But you would be well advised to bear in mind that these are the ways of American public opinion.''

I felt the tension in the room, but I had gone too far to stop.

''Why are these reactions so extreme? Misled as the people involved may be, they are conscious of the ancient roots of anti-Semitism in Russian history. I know that you are not racists, and that those who made the October Revolution were determined to eradicate these roots, but you have not yet fully succeeded.

''Yesterday you showed us the wonderful sights of Kiev. Among them was a heroic statue of Bogdan Khmelnitsky. But to me, that statue is not so heroic. We have a famous musical play in the U.S. called *Fiddler on the Roof*. It depicts, with the soft simplicity of a

Chagall canvas, the Jewish life that used to exist in this area of the Ukraine. It also depicts the pogroms that were carried out periodically against innocent people. In times past, Bogdan Khmelnitsky was a leader of such pogroms, a killer of defenseless women and children.

"Several years ago, the American writer Bernard Malamud published a book, *The Fixer,* that described the trial of a number of Jews in this city for alleged ritual murder of Christian children. The Soviet government later exposed the libel as a fabrication of the Czar's secret police. But over the centuries, episodes of this type have become deeply ingrained in the psyche of your people and have been passed on, as a form of religious and racial hatred, from father to son. There is much work left to be done before you can effect a full cure.

"Consequently, I would suggest that if Jews in Russia attempt to commandeer an airplane, in order to flee from your country, they should be brought to justice, because they have broken the law. But their crime and punishment should not be broadcast with quite so much fanfare, because this tends to awaken old animosities and feed the defamatory image of the Jew as troublemaker. I would further suggest that it is unnecessary to put the word *Jew* on your citizens' identity cards to denote the bearer's nationality, because there is no Jewish national republic among the republics of the Soviet Union. Finally, I would suggest that if some Jews wish to leave the Soviet Union because they do not feel comfortable here, for religious or cultural reasons, they should be allowed to go."

I was almost finished, and after delivering myself of a few observations about the United States — that it was a more original and revolutionary society, with more curative powers against its own excesses, then our Soviet hosts perhaps realized — I was ready to sit down. But something pushed me on.

"On the outskirts of Kiev, there is a hole in the ground. It is called Babi Yar. Almost one hundred thousand Jews were massacred and buried there by the Nazis. Your poet Evgeni Yevtushenko wrote a poem that begins with the heartbreaking line: 'There is no monument at Babi Yar. . . .' "

How often I had read that poem, how well I knew it. Snatches came disjointedly to my mind, including a line that seemed to evoke so peculiarly and so precisely my own fate:

There is no monument at Babi Yar. . . .
I am frightened.
Today I am as old as the Jewish race . . .
Wandering in Egypt. . . .
Dreyfus — I am he. . . .
I feel that I am Anne Frank. . . .
I am a small boy from Bialystok,
My blood dripping on the floor drop by drop . . .

Suddenly, I was dissatisfied with myself. Compared with these electrifying images, what had I said? I had rebuked our hosts for lecturing us — and I had lectured them in turn. It was just another speech. Something more was needed to jar this conference out of its deadly rut. A poet's words — yes, but I was no poet. Wasn't there something, something beyond words, an act . . . ?

"Comrades," I said, "yesterday, you gave us an opportunity of seeing the memorials to your Great Patriotic War against the Nazis. Permit me to say that, today, it would be worth our while to pay a visit to Babi Yar."

I sat down, and for what seemed like a full minute there was uncomfortable silence. I thought: "The poem is proscribed, the site is deliberately ignored — the Soviets expressly don't want a shrine to the Jewish dead. They don't want to heighten Jewish consciousness — and here you have prodded them in one of their most sensitive spots, practically proposing a reversal of policy. You have asked publicly, on Soviet soil, for freedom of Jewish emigration — *Let my people go.* You are no Moses and they are no pharaohs. They'll make you persona non grata. Say goodbye to any influence you might have had in the furthering of coexistence and commerce, in the betterment of relations between East and West."

Without really intending to, without really knowing what I was doing, I had knotted together the two crucial issues of the era of détente — improved economic relations and respect for human rights. The French author Jean François Revel would later call it, in an article in the French weekly *L'Express,* the "Gordian knot of Kiev."

Korneichuk cleared his throat. He began to call for a recess when Senator Mark Hatfield was on his feet.

"Comrades, may I make a brief statement," Hatfield began in the sonorous voice of a Protestant preacher. "As Sam has just said, we have all come here to discuss the issue of peace. Only one word, in one language, conveys the full meaning of that issue. The language is Hebrew, and the word is *shalom*. I therefore say to all of you, comrades: *Shalom.*"

No one seemed to have anything to add. There was a scraping of chairs and everyone was standing. I found myself in a circle of young people — Frank Church's son Chase, Gavin's teenage daughters, Lina and Chloe, and Rockefeller's son Richard, shepherded across the room by Frank's wife, Bethine, who was saying something complimentary. I spotted Judith in the crowd and she was nodding at me and beaming. Lina, Gavin, and Chase Church said, "Dr. Pisar, we want to go with you to Babi Yar."

The Americans caucused. Some of them thought it would be better to leave well enough alone. Babi Yar was officially a nonplace. To go there would seem like a provocation.

Patricia Harris, the only black member of our delegation — later to be a member of President Carter's Cabinet — spoke up. "Sam said we should go to Babi Yar. I am going with him."

Mark Hatfield would give his impressions of that day's meeting in an extension of remarks printed in the *Congressional Record:* "Up to that point, we had nothing but charge and countercharge. Then came Sam. At first it was pretty horrifying. He was like the living embodiment of the Holocaust. We weren't sure that the Russians wouldn't get up and troop out. But they didn't. No one could have mistaken the spontaneity of that speech. No one could have rehearsed it, either. It moved us all profoundly."

We asked for a bus, and we got one. We arrived at the edge of a wood — the entire American delegation — and walked across a clearing. As Yevtushenko has written, there was no monument at Babi Yar, no plaque, nothing to tell of the infamous mass grave under the newly planted birch trees. Yet the Soviet guide faltered and dabbed at her eyes as she recounted what the Soviet government preferred to hush up — how tens of thousands of men, women, and children (there were

Ukrainians, Gypsies, and others among them, but the vast majority were Jews) were taken to this place by the Nazis, made to dig their own graves, and shot.

The guide was still talking when another bus drove up and stopped, and out piled the Soviet delegation. My heart leaped. Without a word, like late arrivals at a funeral service, they hurried across the clearing and joined our line. There was Korneichuk, bareheaded. There was Polevy, of the long mustache. I caught his eye and thought I detected a hint of — what? I could not tell, but I was sure it was not hostility. There was Arbatov, the Americanist, and Yuri Zhukov, the editorialist of *Pravda,* and the scientist Fedorov, and the others, every single one of them standing with head bowed, hat in hand, listening in respectful silence while the Soviet guide continued with her story.

I have observed that the events in people's lives that seem to affect them most strongly on the spur of the moment are not the truly elemental ones — marriage, birth of children, death of loved ones — but turns of happenstance, which take them by surprise. That, at any rate, is how it has been with me. I was overcome when I fell at the feet of the black GI on a battlefield in Germany; it was then, and only then, that I knew I had survived. I was shaken up by the inclusion of my doctoral thesis in the *Harvard Law Review;* I knew then, and only then, that I could produce original work. The episode at Babi Yar was another such moment.

The Russians' unexpected arrival was deeply moving. Was it possible that an appeal to sentiment and decency could make even these hard-boiled types join us in a pilgrimage that went against the official grain? I knew then that my belief in the moderating power of human commerce — a commerce of poetry and reason as well as of goods — between Americans and Russians, Arabs and Jews, Japanese and Chinese, and other allegedly sworn enemies was not misplaced, and that my work toward that end deserved to be tried.

It would be foolish, I knew, to make too much of one incident. The Soviets were not going to change their system, at least not very fast. But within the Russian character there was enough potential for generous response to make the effort at cooperation, averting the apocalypse, meaningful. The main thing was to speak our minds frankly and not be afraid to step on a few toes. The biggest mistake would be to let the more intractable aspects of the Soviet approach, stemming at least in part from their sense of insecurity, discourage us from pressing on with the dialogue. We never could know which of our positions would produce results beyond our expectations. The sources of inspiration are secret.

I don't remember much about the remainder of our stay in Kiev. The conference, cleansed of invective, made good progress. But I do remember, after our return from Babi Yar — with the Russians still somewhat stiff and very much on their dignity — how Judith broke the ice at a boating excursion on the Dnieper river; she took the arm of the daughter of a Soviet minister and drew her into a Russian folk dance. We formed a circle around them, clapping in time to their dancing, and the Russians began to relax. I watched Judith, who made everything so simple and so marvelous, and thought I was the luckiest man in the world.

Helaina in the Bois de Boulogne

Antony and Alexandra on St. Peter's Square in Rome

Leah feeding the pigeons

With Helaina, Alexandra and Balalaika in the Loire Valley

Boating on the Dneiper River with David Rockefeller and Senator Frank Church, after the visit to Babi Yar

Judith and me

12

THE Mercedes sedan glided along the avenue that stretched emptily in the early morning light all the way to the Brandenburg Gate. In the cold November drizzle one had the impression that the Second World War had somehow remained suspended here. Roadblocks, dead-end streets, and no-trespassing signs made the atmosphere tense and uncertain.

We got out in front of a wooden platform. Before me stretched one of the most repulsive symbols of the postwar era, the Berlin Wall.

It was my first visit to the former capital of the Third Reich except for a brief stay thirty years earlier at a nearby concentration camp on my way from Auschwitz to Kaufering. This time I came to address a conference that included members of the West German government. But first there was this ritual that had become de rigueur.

As we stood on the elevation, my hosts seemed to expect me to say something, anything that would give them a sign of moral support, that would indicate my choice; perhaps declare *"Ich bin ein Berliner,"* as John F. Kennedy had done so eloquently when he visited the site in 1961.

Perversely, the barbed wire, the watchtowers, the police with their restive dogs — all of them standing there, on the other side, as part of a monstrous, organized design to bar the way to freedom — reminded me much too vividly of the tragedies and absurdities of the past.

I thought of the German martyrs who had scaled this indecent wall of hate, and they too reminded me of the extenuated human beings who, in despair, sought their ultimate freedom by throwing themselves against electrified barbed wire . . . in other places and at other times.

My feelings were too confused, too ambivalent. Along with a deep sadness, there was an unsatisfying sensation of bitter triumph. Now the Germans also had a wailing wall, almost like the one they erected around the Bialystok ghetto to separate my people from the rest of the world, almost like the one in Jerusalem that had reduced me to sobs when I saw my people praying at its base again.

My history was unextricably the German's history, the other side of the same sorrowful coin. The lament *Never Again* was theirs as much as mine. Chancellor Willy Brandt had made that clear when on a visit to the Warsaw Ghetto memorial he sank to his knees and silently asked forgiveness in the name of the German people — the same Willy Brandt who during the war had chosen exile and a Norwegian army uniform to fight his own maddened country.

Let my hosts sort all of this out among themselves and explain it all to their children if they cared to, and if they could. It was not for me to remind them of their past. In my mind, the only benefit of doubt I was able to give them was that, while my mother put me in long pants to keep me out of their ovens, some of the German mothers put their sons in short pants to keep them out of the SS, perhaps. . . . .

No, I was decidedly the wrong man for this particular ceremony. After a few minutes I turned around, walked down the steps, and got into the car.

The next day I went to the Berlin Wall again, alone.

Meditating in solitude, I recalled how, as a twelve-year-old boy, momentarily forced into Soviet citizenship and brainwashed by its ideology, I had dreamed of becoming a general in the Red Army. Had that dream come true I would now be on the other side, defending dogmas that today I despise . . . perhaps . . . endless reveries on the hazards that determine the commitments and loyalties of men. Not just reveries; two of my own cousins, who had been deported by the Soviets east of Bialystok, ended up fighting — and losing limbs — in the defense of Stalingrad.

I remembered a young Russian prisoner of war at Auschwitz sentenced to be hanged for attempting to escape. When he was led up the improvised scaffold, his hands tied behind his back and the rope placed around his neck, he raised his head high and cried out: "Stalin and freedom will be victorious!"

I remember the tremor that ran up my spine at his piercing cry as I stood at attention with my comrades, our caps off. It was a scream of defiance such as had rarely been heard in that orderly kingdom of the damned.

His gesture was as moving as it was futile. An SS man immediately set upon him with a knife and slashed at his tongue. The unimaginable then happened. As the stool was about to be kicked from under his feet, the man — his body mutilated, blood gushing from his disfigured face — mustered all his remaining strength, lunged forward, swung on the rope, and in a last gasp smashed the SS man's jaw with his clogs. Unbelievably, the German fell as we heard the crack of wood against bone. After it was over, teeth were lying on the ground. We scrambled for them later as keepsakes.

The young Russian's act showed a courage that could come only from deep faith. But faith in what? Did he know the truth about Stalin? He knew no more than the hundreds of thousands of his comrades who fell heroically during the battle of Stalingrad, a city that now no longer even bears Stalin's name. Whatever his faith may have been, it helped him to die. But, my God, for what cause? Must it always be this way? Must every commitment to an ideal end as an illusion, a self-deception, an act, in the end, against oneself?

The black American soldier who, near Dachau, pulled me to safety from the machine guns that were barking around us had come to save freedom in Europe. Twenty years later his son was sent to Vietnam, also to defend freedom, only to return a broken man, his life stained forever by a dirty war.

When the battle-weary Russian and American soldiers met near Berlin in 1945, they could hardly contain their emotions. Unable to speak to each other, they embraced, slapped one another on the back, and yelled "Russki — Americanski, okay!"

Together they were going to bring peace to the blood-drenched European continent, once and for all. Yet somehow it was not "okay," somehow they failed. Somehow, Europe had become once again the refuge of all the nightmares and psychoses of history.

Few Americans realize how vulnerable, how divided, Europe really is, and how much the fate of European democracy is tied up with America's own freedom. And, for that matter, how much the political health of each is dependent on that of the other.

I had returned from a trip to Washington and stopped at my office on the way home after a tiring overnight flight. Carla Lewis, my secretary, told me I had just had a phone call from Jean-Jacques Servan-Schreiber, the founder and publisher of *L'Express*.

I had always wanted to meet Servan-Schreiber, whose notorious and at times provocative contempt for conventional politics fascinated me. I admired his writings, particularly his powerful book *The American Challenge,* a call for European rebirth through the adoption of American methods in industry and management, and his earlier classic, *Lieutenant in Algeria,* a courageous and prophetic warning against the evils that France was bringing down on her head by trying to retain her North African colonies. I returned the call at once. A minute later I almost wished I hadn't.

He wanted me to go to Athens. The Greek colonels, whose despicable regime was already six years old, had demanded the death penalty for thirty-four political dissidents.

Among the condemned was Mikis Theodorakis, who had composed the music for *Zorba the Greek,* a symbol of opposition to the junta's rule; and Manolis Glezos, a hero to Greek youth, who, during the German occupation, had climbed the Acropolis in broad daylight and torn down the Nazi flag.

Servan-Schreiber was flying to Athens with a group of former French Resistance leaders. They would try to negotiate with the colonels for the prisoners' lives.

"As an American and as a lawyer, there are certain representations you would doubtless be able to make," he began.

I wasn't sure what kind of representations he had in mind or what connections he thought I had in Washington that might be useful to his cause, but it was an appeal I did not feel I could turn down cavalierly. In retrospect, I assume he meant that, given the American involvement in propping up their regime, the colonels would be less likely to ignore an American than a Frenchman, regardless of his distinction.

"If I switched around a few appointments" — I looked at my calendar — "I could leave at the end of next week."

"You don't understand. A group of Greek students came to see me this morning. The situation is urgent. We have a plane ready to take off in an hour and a half."

"An hour and a half! Look, I've been out of the country for two weeks — I've just come back. I haven't even been home yet."

"I'll pick you up in an hour."

I rushed home to repack my suitcase and waited for him downstairs. We shook hands on the sidewalk in front of my house and he swung my suitcase into the trunk. On the way to Le Bourget airfield, I sat silently next to this determined man, asking myself what I was doing, going off on a Greek adventure, with people about whom and about whose purposes I knew next to nothing. Could it be the old Landsberg craving for action again, I wondered?

On the small private jet, I met the other three members of the group — France's foremost atomic scientist, an eminent professor of medicine, and a much-decorated general who had been one of de Gaulle's closest associates during the war. I understood why they were taking part in this mission. But did they know why I had agreed to go along? They probably thought that for me it was a job like any other, to offer counsel and assistance in a complex diplomatic situation.

While we waited in our hotel suite in Athens for a phone call from the Prime Minister, Colonel Papadopoulos, my companions talked laconically about the Nazi occupation of Greece and the Greek civil war of 1947.

"I suppose" — the professor turned to me — "that these events did not make much of an impact on you, far away in America?"

I then did something I had never deliberately done before: I rolled up my sleeve so that they could see the number tattooed on my arm.

They stared in disbelief. Servan-Schreiber closed his eyes, then broke the silence: "Messieurs, from this moment on we are all members of the Greek Resistance. We have a lot of work to do."

We negotiated day and night with several members of the junta. It was an impetuous mission, but it worked. The colonels at first were adamant: all thirty-four men would be shot. But, they didn't want any adverse publicity while their military aid requests were pending before the U.S. Congress. So, with the capriciousness common to all tyrants, great or petty, they suddenly reversed themselves.

Theodorakis, who had fallen ill with tuberculosis, was released first and permitted to leave the country. His wife and two children, however, would have to remain — hostages to ensure his silence.

This was a condition we could not accept. I found the Frenchmen studying me speculatively. It seemed that the time for "American representations" had arrived.

Servan-Schreiber's idea was to call Jacqueline Onassis. Certainly she was not without friends in Washington. And her new husband clearly was not without friends in Athens.

We reached Jacqueline in Paris just as she and Aristotle Onassis were leaving for his island, Skorpios. She suggested we join them there.

A plane was sent for us, an amphibious craft that picked us up at Corfu and deposited us in the bay of Skorpios. The luxurious yacht *Christina* was riding at anchor. The famous couple waited for us at the dock, the gateway to their kingdom. Onassis took my companions with him in one jeep; Jacqueline and I took the other.

Speaking in English, now that we were alone, she asked me to drive.

I looked at the landscape. In the glare of the setting sun, Skorpios seemed to be the unreal setting of absolute egoism, a parody of Greek mythology.

"Jackie," I said, unable to call her "Mrs. Onassis." I had not seen her since my early Washington days and I could not get used to seeing her other than as she had been when I saw her for the first time, with John F. Kennedy at the inauguration ball, at the Washington Armory.

Without makeup, badly coiffed, she was still stunning and majestic. I knew that contrary to legend, she had been more than an ornament at the White House. She had a definite personality and a definite point of view on issues of substance, and as an adviser to the President, to Bob Kennedy, and to Ted Kennedy, she was to be reckoned with.

She immediately agreed that keeping Theodorakis' family hostage was outrageous.

"What if you called the White House. You still remember the number, don't you?" I said, and instantly regretted it. "Richard Nixon could get a message to the colonels. So could Melvin Laird at the Pentagon. He's shipping them military equipment by the ton. They'd listen to him."

She gave me a wan smile. "I don't think I've got much influence in either place, Sam."

"We must do something," I said, not even trying to hide my impatience. "It's too embarrassing for you, a mother of two children, to stay in this country as long as that woman and those two kids are not allowed to leave."

"Don't worry. Ari will think of something."

She drew her husband aside when we got to the house and spoke to him animatedly. The Greek tycoon, who had welcomed us in an almost playful mood, listened morosely and shrugged his massive shoulders. Interceding on behalf of political prisoners was somehow inappropriate to his scheme of things. He had too many other interests at stake.

Jackie stood there, tense and expressionless, acquiescing silently to her husband's evasive answers.

I remember that brief visit not for anything it accomplished — Ari, she had to report, felt he ought to stay neutral in this affair — but for the glimpse it gave me of Jacqueline Kennedy, adrift and powerless. It wrung my heart. She had once represented America to me. I remembered that resplendent dinner at Versailles when the President of the United States mockingly introduced himself to Charles de Gaulle as the husband of Jacqueline Kennedy. She now stood alone and frustrated: associated with power, married to power, unable to help an innocent woman and her two children.

At another time, in another place, nothing could be done for my mother and my sister and me, either.

The secret part of the American government had played its role in installing the colonels; the open part of the government now supported them with arms. All in the name of military solidarity. The preservation, safety, and happiness of a mother and her babies could not interfere with such arrangements.

All the Kennedy strength and charm, which I first encountered in 1960, was now distant and irrelevant. Once again, but this time sadly and forlornly, Jacqueline represented America to me.

In the end, we accomplished our objective in a manner that took the know-how and daring of a Servan-Schreiber–Niko Waterman combination to envisage and bring off. Mrs. Theodorakis and her two children were smuggled out of the country by a commando raid in a fast boat through Greek and Turkish waters, brilliantly executed by a young Frenchwoman, Marie Bernadette Raimbault, herself the mother of two children.

When civilized and diplomatic methods fail, one has to fall back on primitive instincts and actions common to authentic resistance fighters.

There were two fundamentally irreconcilable types of regime on the European continent at that time — an advanced form of social democracy in the north, stretching toward the Scandinavian countries; and three oppressive dictatorships in the south — Franco's Spain, Salazar's Portugal, and the colonels' Greece. No meaningful dialogue between these two extremes, and no forward movement toward West European unity, was possible as long as this state of affairs persisted.

Many well-meaning people, including some highly respected intellectuals in the United States and Europe, expressed their disapproval of these regimes, but for the most part only by signing their names to eloquent petitions that ended up in the wastebaskets of their embassies abroad. Although I had no mandate from anyone, and found myself involved by coincidence, I came to feel that it was not a bad thing for a U.S. citizen to lend a hand in this humanitarian effort. That America had found it necessary to go to such lengths, with military and financial aid, to prop up a clique of illiterate dictators was difficult to grasp and to stomach.

It was clear that the planners in Washington, by backing the colonels, believed that militarty expedience was more important than the political and economic unification of a democratic Europe.

Small wonder that there is worried talk about the demoralized state of NATO's divisions; and that in Holland a young politician has won a respectable following for the proposition that, in case of Soviet attack, the Dutch population should offer no resistance and the Dutch troops should lay down their arms.

Seldom in modern history have the younger people of country after country been so consistent in their alienation from what — with the exaggerated clarity of the young — they see as a society that has lost its way. In the United States, at least, they had their moment of glory, when they helped awaken the country in opposition to the Vietnam War. In Europe their attempt to influence government attitudes had been rebuffed by an establishment wedded to the notion that the young should know their place.

All of this added up to a pervasive feeling of weakness, irresolution, self-doubt, a feeling that no array of production statistics or NATO missiles could remove. It was as though some miasmic vapor from the ruins of the postwar years was taking its revenge on the progress that had followed, obscuring true accomplishments with imaginary ills.

But what the planners in Washington failed to realize was that whatever effects demoralization, drugs, or long hair might have on NATO's battle-readiness, they were more than offset by the ambivalent loyalties of the Eastern European divisions of the Warsaw Pact.

The Russians are far from sure that young Czechs, Poles, Hungarians, Rumanians, or even East Germans, if it ever came to an armed trial of strength, would obediently aim their weapons west rather than east. In the last war, even the bestiality of the Nazis did not keep some Soviet ethnic groups from the temptation of treason.

Any realistic assessment of present-day Soviet society indicates that the Russians are not likely to invade Western Europe, even if they could bank on an unopposed march to the English Channel; the occupation of a vast area filled with diverse, disaffected peoples is not something the tense Soviet regime would relish. But a semblance of debility can determine national policies just as surely as actual weakness, and so long as Western Europe feels weak, gigantic military programs undertaken to protect it from Soviet attack will remain in force — generating countermeasures in the Soviet Union, where every "defensive" action by the West is seen as aggressive in motive. And so the Berlin Wall will remain in place, along with the stalemate between the ever-growing Russian and American arsenals.

The Greek episode was my baptism in European politics.

A few years later I was invited back to Athens. The Greek colonels had been overthrown. In the ancient amphitheater of Herodes Atticus, at the foot of the Acropolis, a platform had been erected for a debate on "The Future of Democracy."

With me were Professor John Kenneth Galbraith, Séan MacBride, founder of Amnesty International, Vladimir Bacarič, Marshal Tito's second in command, and Mário Soares, who, after years of imprisonment and torture under Salazar's dictatorship, was now Prime Minister of Portugal. At last, Portugal, Greece, and Spain had regained their freedom and had begun to negotiate with the other European democracies their admission into the Common Market. The traffic toward totalitarianism was not moving along a one-way street after all. But, out of the 155-odd countries that were officially members of the United Nations, only about twenty were still practicing what an American might consider democracy, and the number seemed to be diminishing.

From our tragic century, which has yet to find its Sophocles, the Auschwitz kid looked up in awe at the sun-sculpted columns of the Parthenon, the age of Pericles, the cradle of democracy. In 2500 years of history Europe seemed to have learned nothing. Auschwitz had brought it back to the times of the barbarian Huns.

Europe, land of my birth, that has branded my flesh and my soul for life, blessed land of enlightenment and culture, accursed land of fire and darkness, must you always excite the highest hopes and counter them with the bleakest disappointments? Are you always to suffer the deepest wounds in the eternal contest between the best and the worst? Are you to be blighted again now, when you are at the point of achieving your most noble ambition?

The age-old dream of Western European unification, somewhere between the faith of the fifties and the disenchantment of the seventies, had suffered a possibly fatal blow. The sense of purpose and solidarity that was needed to invest the new supranational institutions with real power was everywhere giving way to resurgent national rivalry and domestic discord. Without the vision of progress toward an all-European union, internal politics were going bad, assuming the shape of a fear-ridden stalemate between left and right, shaken here and there by spasms of anarchic terrorism.

Having observed the easy relationship that existed between politicians of opposing parties in the United States, in England, in Australia, I was dismayed to see how fiercely disagreements on the political plane cut through the heart of European countries, just as the ugly scar of the Berlin Wall cut across the continent's heart. In France, for example, it appeared almost treasonous for two political rivals, whose differences to an outsider seemed a question of emphasis, to be seen chatting amicably at a public affair.

Ultimately, I came to the conclusion that a commitment either toward the political left or the political right amounted to the same thing — two different ways of clinging to the past. For my part, I maintained the best personal relations with representatives of the various currents of European democratic opinion.

Judith, meanwhile, had been elected to chair the Board of the American Center for Students and Artists, a long-established American institution, partly financed by the Rockefeller Foundation, that plays an important role in the artistic life of Paris and in cultural relations between the United States and Europe. Together, we began experimenting with guest lists that deliberately mixed people from enemy camps, whenever a member of the U.S. government or friends from the U.S. Senate were at our home. They readily accepted our invitations and seemed to enjoy each other's company. To some degree we and our local guests were joined in a wordless complicity: we were the naïve Americans who broke the rules without knowing it, and they were the worldly French who were too polite to point it out to us. The columnist Ivan Levai wrote, tongue in cheek, in the principal Sunday paper, that, with the possible exception of the National Assembly, "Chez Pisar" seemed to be the only place in France where political opponents considered it proper to speak to one another.

It pleased me, I admit, to see two sworn foes like prime ministers Pierre Mendès-France and Michel Debré converse amiably in my living room, or to observe Senator Russell Long practice his quaint Louisiana French on a fascinated member of the French legislature. But what pleased me even more was to see the two most promising French leaders find common ground under my roof.

Valery Giscard d'Estaing and Jean-Jacques Servan-Schreiber had each written a preface to one of the two volumes of *Coexistence and Commerce* published in France.

Giscard I knew well. His family château at Authon in the Loire Valley was for seven years my country home and I felt privileged to have the powerful Minister of Finance as a neighbor and interlocutor on the economic and political issues of the day. Ours was an unlikely friendship between two individuals whose backgrounds could not have been more different. His philosophy of life came from a fine intellect and an experience derived largely from public service. Mine came essentially from prolonged confrontation with brutality and death. Still, during our leisurely weekends on those enchanted acres of central France I grew to feel an intellectual, even a personal, affinity with him.

In our conversations, he showed particular interest in my Washington experiences with Congress and the Kennedy Administration. I became privy to his views on the future of the Common Market, on Europe's relationship with the United States, and on East-West issues that became relevant to my book, much of which I wrote on his property, as he pointed out with a touch of pride in his warmly worded preface.

While Giscard d'Estaing had a neatly ordered outlook on the world, Servan-Schreiber, with whom my acquaintance was much more recent, struck me instead as a brilliant improviser of concepts and ideas. They were dissimilar in temperament — the first perhaps a shade too cautious, the second perhaps a shade too impulsive. After their student days together at the Ecole Polytechnique, the French M.I.T., they had parted ways politically. Giscard allied himself with General de Gaulle's return to power in 1958. Servan-Schreiber, a fighter pilot with de Gaulle's Free French during the war, pitted himself against the Gaullist system from a lonely position on the center-left. Yet fundamentally, I thought, their hopes for France were the same — that she break out of the constricting attitudes of the past and become a truly modern democracy, with greater economic and social opportunity.

To make this compatibility as clear to them as it was to me would be a service I could render to France, a country for which I had strong feelings of concern and affection. It was thus a source of great satisfaction to me that when Giscard decided to run for President, a race he barely won, Servan-Schreiber gave him his full support. I happened to play a role in that connection.

In early 1974 President Georges Pompidou was at the end of his fight against leukemia. I was certain that Giscard would announce his candidacy for the presidency once it became vacant. Servan-Schreiber, as an influential member of parliament and head of the pivotal radical party, could be a crucial ally or difficult opponent for Giscard.

I reasoned optimistically, and as a friend, that if both could find common ground by putting their names on the covers of my books, why could not common political ground between them also be found? To test my hypothesis, someone had to take the initiative, because with Giscard inside the government and Servan-Schreiber in the opposition, the two men were not on the best of terms.

I asked Judith to invite them both for dinner and they accepted with an alacrity that could not be explained only by the charm of their hostess. The test was conducted at our home and in a serious exchange of views on all the vital issues likely to arise in the forthcoming contest between left and right, the two men reestablished the friendly relationship that they used to enjoy before de Gaulle came to power.

I will not be so bumptious as to suggest that my good offices influenced the outcome of the French presidential elections of 1974. But, this much is certain: had Servan-Schreiber not thrown his political weight into the balance, mobilizing the radical and left-of-center factions, Giscard would not have achieved his narrow victory, which hung on less than one percent; and the socialist-communist coalition led by François Mitterand, whose offer of alliance Servan-Schreiber had rejected, would today be in power at the very heart of Western Europe.

In the 1978 parliamentary elections the future of France hung once again in the balance and was decided by a razor-thin margin of less than one-half percent of the vote. Had the left won, France, Italy, and much of the rest of Europe would probably have moved toward a nationalized, state-operated economy, and away from a free Europe, allied with the United States.

Dr. Henry Kissinger was one of the few in the United States who tried to alert the public to the danger of Euro-communism. As someone well placed to assess that danger on the spot, I visited with him several times in 1977, first at Pocantico Hills, the magnificent Rockefeller property in New York State where he had started to write his memoirs, and then at my home in Paris.

I gathered around Kissinger and his former under secretary William D. Rogers a group of personalities devoted to the concept of an integrated Europe, who ranged from Simone Veil, the highly admired French Minister of Health who as a young girl had been interned with me at Auschwitz and who is today the president of the first popularly elected Parliament of Europe, to Pierre Uri, a socialist who had helped draft the Treaty of Rome, as well as a number of ministers and members of parliament from the right and the left of the political spectrum. The event demonstrated that the political dialogue between these opponents was not entirely dead. After he had said goodbye to my guests, Kissinger said to me, "What I heard tonight offers some hope that this country will not plunge into chaos in the forthcoming election and take the rest of Europe with it. If France were to fall to the socialist-communist alliance," he added, "the tide in Italy could not be stemmed, Spain would immediately become shaky, Germany would become politically polarized down the middle, and the consequent seismic waves would reach as far as Washington."

Hearing Kissinger — a man I have admired, but whose views I have frequently disagreed with — brought home to me the intense intellectual and highly personal vision I have of Europe. It is both the source of our civilization and the matrix of our destruction. No longer the most powerful continent, it still remains the most pivotal. United, it can be a true and equal partner with America. Fragmented, Europe will continue to vascillate between the stark extremes of war and appeasement and likely invite once again global catastrophe.

The end of Europe as a world power would mean that China and the rest of Asia would have to stand alone to face the Soviet arsenal: state of seige.

The end of Europe as a center of economic and political influence would transform the continent of Africa into a jungle and render the Middle East even more vulnerable than it is.

The disintegration of Europe's power would have an immediate and critical effect upon America, turning it into a receding democratic ghetto: state of seige.

Everything had tended in the direction of European union and stability when Jean Monnet was the trailblazer of that aspiration; now, even though the outward formalities of integration are following each other more or less on schedule, the lifeblood of union is draining out.

The great design of the "Father of Europe" was tragically interrupted by General de Gaulle in the name of French nationalism almost from the moment he returned to power in 1958. Twenty-one years later, the first Europe-wide election in history demonstrated that progress toward union was stunted for a long time to come. Twenty-one years lost.

Today, with huge economic clouds gathering once again on the horizon, it is difficult to see how the small, fragmented, divided nations of that continent, with almost no oil, without meaningful material resources, with rapidly contracting export markets, without an effective system of defense, will be able to face up to the dangers of the future.

Even though in our conversations I never managed to convince him that weaning the smaller Eastern European countries economically away from Moscow had as high a priority as Common Market integration, Jean Monnet has remained in my mind one of the towering figures of the century, the antithesis of Charlemagne, Napoleon, Hitler, and all the other European warriors with whom our history books are filled.

If Western Europe fails to realize that divided, and separated from America, it cannot stand, it may lose its freedom again, this time forever. The Berlin Wall remains the central symbol of its vulnerability. Germany must be more firmly anchored to the Atlantic Alliance, lest it succumb one day to the Russian siren song of reunification with its eastern provinces in return for neutrality.

These concerns had invaded my mind when I addressed a gathering of NATO Parliamentarians at the German Bundestag in Bonn in 1972.

There was something surrealistic about that appearance before the representatives of the people who once treated me as a subhuman earmarked for liquidation. It was very difficult to keep this tiny irony of history to myself. How I wished Niko and Ben could have been there with me. For I could not avoid recalling, as I spoke, the almost prehistoric times when our only "dialogue" with an earlier incarnation of those representatives was a one-sided "*Caaps* off, *caaaps* on!"

IV
The Storm Ahead

O human race, born to soar,
wherefore at a slight wind dost
thou so fall?
— Dante

13

ONCE I'd delivered myself of the book, with its eighty theses on coexistence and commerce, I was anxious to come out of my scholastic shell. I would open myself to some of the new things that Judith had brought into my life — modern art, experimental music, avant-garde theater. That thought did not last long.

The world's economy was in commotion. Goods, technology, capital, and labor were crossing national frontiers as never before, and in unprecedented directions. Substantial trade was beginning to flow across ideological frontiers as well. Since my ideas were germane to this trend, I was called upon to consult and advise business and political leaders. I was also invited to debate my views with corporate managers, with academicians, and with students around the world.

At times, I would ask myself with what credentials, by what mandate, was I waging my one-man campaign? Worse, I had to deal with Ben's criticism that I had become a busybody, concerned with issues that were not my affair. Was it simply a grand conceit that, because I had been spared, I owed a duty to my fellows that transcended the obligations of profession, friendship, and family? Or, did I — an ex-Polish Jew who had started life in Bialystok and almost finished it in Auschwitz — have as much right as, say, a Kennedy, or a Giscard, or any other scion of prized heritage and tradition to be concerned with the future of the human race? Was my constituency — the six million — irrelevant?

Ben, Niko, my comrades, my brothers, with whom I shared everything, endured everything, survived everything, how I wish you could have accompanied me on this long and winding journey. But death separated me from you, Niko, after long years during which I did not dare to explore to the full the silence that fell between us. Life separated me from you, Ben, when I moved away, following what I believed to be my destiny. And now I must go on. As I look back, I understand for the first time that whatever takes you far and gives you much also makes you leave much behind.

Most of my new political friends, compared with my earlier companions, did not have the same awareness of danger or of the crude realities of life. Their horizons were limited by the exigencies of the next election: they were followers rather than leaders of public opinion. My own hope was to generate new currents of thought in influential quarters. A decade earlier, I had stimulated policy discussions in Washington, and some of my proposals had found their way into American legislation. If there was a chance to influence policy again, I told myself, it was my job to do so.

I saw in my work, and in the ideas on which it was based, an opportunity to persuade leaders in business, government, and academic life that economic integration could replace political confrontation as a stabilizing and constructive force in international affairs. All other approaches had proved sterile. I argued that the maintenance of "atomic parity" entailed wholly unacceptable costs, in arms and in the risks of catastrophe, without guaranteeing security. I insisted that solemn diplomatic commitments by nations not to make war were at best pipe dreams, at worst, death-dealing traps. The idea that peace could be assured by the waving of diplomatic wands was a dangerous delusion; the cynical Nazi-Soviet nonaggression pact of 1939 was a hideous example of the sort of peace that diplomats could arrange — it had brought the world down on my head. Something radically different had to be tried.

The businessmen who retained me were interested in more than just my expertise on the legal and institutional problems of dealing with state-operated economies. Time and again, I found hardheaded executives veering away from immediate problems of contract negotiation, payment terms, and disputed settlement, toward matters that I had thought were the concern only of statesmen and sociologists.

Take the talks I had with Henry Ford II during a long weekend at his home in Grosse Pointe, Michigan. Sometime earlier, he had been invited to participate in the construction of a large truck plant in the Soviet Union. This venture would have meant a resumption of his company's role in the industrialization of Russia, a role that his grandfather had inaugurated in the 1920s with the establishment of a Ford automobile assembly line there. Henry II had to drop the project under pressure from Washington: the Pentagon, already over its head in Vietnam, expressed the fear that Ford trucks might show up on the Ho Chi Minh trail.

I expected him to talk about his disappointment over the government's short-sighted veto of that important undertaking and about his prospects for similar agreements in the future — and he did. But he also talked about something that seemed to worry him a good deal more.

"You know, Sam, we used to send our recruitment people over to Harvard, M.I.T., all the best universities, around graduation time, and they'd sign on the brightest kids of the campus. Young people in those days were proud to work for Ford. It was just assumed. Now they say, 'No, we don't want to work for you. We don't agree with your business philosophy. We don't like what you are doing and what you represent.' "

Ford, whom I found surprisingly open and unpretentious, seemed truly disheartened. "What are we coming to? Not just this company — our whole society."

I found a similar bewilderment, again and again, in conversations with the executives of other industries, a prodigious lowering of morale — a sense of being unfairly maligned by current public attitudes toward business, by no means confined to the young. What was so bad about profit? What was wrong with individual initiative? Granted, the ideals of a free-market economy weren't always reflected in the quality of the end products or the degree of competitiveness in certain industries, but, with all its faults, hadn't private enterprise brought about a better and more stable society, with more social justice, than any other in modern times? What would happen to that society if a whole generation of the young rejected the economic system — and the American businessmen — as morally bankrupt, but without anything or anyone better to put in its place?

Another ego-shattering fact of the postwar economic world was the loss of suzerainty by American enterprise to the enterprises of its wartime enemies. Ford, like its big domestic rivals, General Motors and Chrysler, had failed to achieve any significant technological breakthroughs for twenty-five years. The only innovations that had come out of Detroit were larger bumpers and shinier wheel rims. Meanwhile, the same German inventiveness and efficiency that had once nearly cost me my life led Volkswagen to the "Beetle," the car that was to the postwar world what Ford's Model "A" had been in America's industrial heyday.

Throughout American industry, top managers, despite their much-touted creativity, had not found the time, talent, or inclination necessary to strengthen their perspectives and maintain their industrial leadership. The lack of vision and new direction became more and more apparent as other industrious and imaginative nations made ever-deeper inroads into U.S. markets, beating Americans at their own game.

The "American challenge," which Jean-Jacques Servan-Schreiber had defined in the late sixties with the perception of a modern de Tocqueville, was met with special effectiveness by West Germany and Japan. Starting from heaps of rubble, these two countries created the most thriving economies on earth. In particular, Japan's astonishing ability to invent, organize, manage, and set new standards of quality and price presented the world with possibly one of the most important economic phenomena of our time. Within a brief period, a country without material resources, totally defeated in war, became an industrial giant, on a global scale, whose irresistible force was increasingly felt in all markets. Other Asian economies successfully copied Japan's example.

American and European entrepreneurs could take small comfort in the notion that this competition was directed toward traditional industries, such as textiles, shipbuilding, steel, and electrical appliances; the idea of Western superiority no longer had a basis in fact. It has become apparent that there is no branch of technology immune from domination by the colossal industrial and commercial machines being constructed in Asia, nor from those which will be constructed in due course in Africa and South America as well.

The American captains of industry and finance I have dealt with have come to feel vulnerable on still another front: perhaps the most painful failure of all came in the form of rejection by their own sons and daughters. Frequently, the most fathers hoped for when the family was gathered around the breakfast table in the morning — if, in fact, the children still lived at home and had not become addicted to drugs, cults, or violent protest movements — was a tense, silent truce.

In the late sixties the rebellion of youth gripped the entire globe in a chain reaction that shook up governments as different from one another as those of neo-liberal Mexico, socialist Yugoslavia, Western-oriented Senegal, de Gaulle's France, and Brandt's Germany. In Chicago, they took over the sidewalks in front of the Democratic Party Convention, to condemn the war in Vietnam and the political establishment they deemed responsible. In Prague, they chased through the streets politicians who were collaborating with Soviet occupation forces. In Paris they provoked a general strike and nearly brought down the regime. The Patty Hearst who was seen attending a bank holdup with a submachine gun in her arms symbolized the awful dimensions of the gulf between Western business tycoons and their children.

Everywhere, and as never before, societies that had produced fascism, communism, colonialism, imperialism, and the religion of the atom bomb seemed to lose all appeal to young people. In effect, their message to the generation in power was: "You will never jerk us around again. We are going on the alert. Our enemy may be you."

If the industrial establishment felt wounded by the complaints of the young, so forcefully registered by leaders like Ralph Nader, it was because in large measure it deserved to be. But wasn't it possible that the New Left vogue of blanket condemnation of corporate capitalism owed its spread largely to a worldwide popular feeling of anxiety over uncontrollable forces of pollution, inflation, overpopulation, starvation, and the threatened atomization of all human life — an anxiety that clamored for a scapegoat?

I wondered if conscientious businessmen could not find a release from the scapegoat role, and their new image as exploiters and despoilers of the world, were they to turn their genius, their energies, and their great enterprises to the reconstruction of the Third World. Since leaving the death camps, I have never met a man who, in his heart of hearts, was not more concerned with his concept of himself than with the immediate practicalities. Businessmen have consciences which do not leave them alone; I found most of the industrialists and entrepreneurs who engaged my services eager to explore with me the moral and political implications of what might become their new frontier — a global frontier of the late twentieth century.

I pointed out to them that if Western industrialists would open new markets in the East, and, for example, help exploit the natural resources of areas like Siberia, China, the rain forests of the Amazon, the Sinai peninsula, and the African continent, the jaded world image of business would be revitalized; and businessmen could perhaps regain the allegiance of alienated youth. I argued that a fusing of the idealism of the young with the energy of industrial managers would generate a stabilizing counterweight to that new militarism which was sweeping across vast areas of the world. At every opportunity, I tried to promote this view of a new economic order in the business and political and intellectual circles in which I moved. And that kept me as busy as I had ever been in my life, and forced me to neglect my own loved ones.

As my public speaking engagements, television appearances, and newspaper articles multiplied, my family retaliated and I suffered a perceptible loss of credibility at my own breakfast table. My children reproached me for postponing family vacations and they ironically talked behind my back about that "modern Luther nailing his theses to the cathedral of peace," or "the Pied Piper leading his corporate troops in search of coexistence and profits."

Judith, with her special blend of encouragement for my enterprise and vexation over my absences, now addressed me as "Guru." Although she still traveled with me whenever possible, to the most distant parts of Africa, Asia, and South America, I felt there was a good deal of truth to her chaffing.

During this period of my life and career, my greatest satisfaction seemed to come out of discussions with students, especially, perhaps, with German students where hostility toward parents unable to justify their wartime past ran deepest. I was sometimes myself taken violently to task for expressing the idea that industry and commerce could be forces for peace, not merely exploitation. But I could read in the earnest young faces of those who accused me a deep disenchantment with the ideological illusions that had fueled the faith of my own generation. All such ideologies were discredited in their eyes, morally and intellectually.

I found ground for elation in the otherwise disconcerting fact that the new generation had rejected the dogmas that had entranced their elders. Today's youth were on the alert against ready-made systems of ideas, no matter where they came from. I knew quite well where such ideas could lead the young, where they had led young Nazis and young communists, and where they might have led me following the brainwashing I underwent during the Soviet occupation of my homeland.

In the contemporary world, Marxism, the last of the great ideologies, was hardly more relevant to the resolution of the world's real problems than any of the others. Marxism in action was the Soviet Union, and after the disclosures of Solzhenitsyn and the other Soviet dissidents, the Russian model was no longer tenable; to young as well as old, it seemed to lead, inexorably, to the violence of the gulag.

As one who had lived through the nightmares that the young feared, I spoke with them about the need not only to demolish, but to build; and about the obligation to mobilize their energies for a thrust toward new aspirations. "You should know that in Moscow, Peking, Havana, and the other cities that many of you still regard as the spiritual capitals of the world, the heirs of Lenin are no longer struggling for revolution. What they crave are efficient managers, technicians, bankers, farmers. Their heroes are the same people you despise — your own fathers."

When Khrushchev or Brezhnev made a speech on Red Square, he, of course, paraded before the people the dogmas of Marx and Lenin. But I had firsthand knowledge that when a Soviet manager had to meet a production quota, build a factory, grow corn, or open a coal mine, nothing was further from his mind than the litanies of the communist faith. What interested him far more was a pragmatic arrangement with his Western partner, that promised to circumvent the ideological scriptures and get the job done. The same held true for the Chinese manager: he knew perfectly well that his steel production would not rise if he relied upon Mao Tse-tung's absurd assertion, during the "great leap forward," that the people should take to building blast furnaces in their backyards.

I participated in negotiation after negotiation on behalf of American business firms. I took part in countless meetings, large and small, formal and informal, tough and friendly, intended to smooth the way for projects under discussion — trying, for instance, to convince a handful of Soviet economic planners that even if Marx had theorized that, under capitalism, the economic infrastructure determines the political superstructure, they would be misled if they applied such doctrines literally to the United States. There is a threshold that cannot be crossed even by the most influential of American capitalists, if the Congress, youth, and other powerful segments of the American people express their disapproval. The United States was run, politically, from Wall Street no more than it was run, economically, from Washington. The decision of Congress to condition the normalization of Soviet-American commercial relations upon greater freedom of emigration for Russian Jews was a good example of this proposition — one which the Soviets found impossible to square with their own pet theories.

By the same token, I argued to an audience of American executives that, while the sale of photocopy technology to the Soviet Union might make it easier for the Communist Party to distribute its propaganda, it would also end up improving the spread of dissenting *samizdat* literature of the Pasternak and Solzhenitsyn variety as well.

I had become chairman of several international conferences in Europe and America. To one of these, in Vienna, I invited the white-haired Professor Nikolai Lubimov, one of Lenin's personal assistants. In welcoming him I quoted Pushkin in Russian. With an urbane smile he responded by quoting Goethe in German. A stir of pleasure rippled through the audience except for the stolid and stiff KGB functionaries who were part of every Soviet delegation. Obviously, they thought the St. Petersburg–born old Bolshevik was being lured back into misguided, bourgeois ways.

To Budapest I invited Senator Abraham Ribicoff, the highly influential chairman of the Senate Subcommittee on Foreign Trade and, no less important, godfather to my youngest daughter, Leah. To insure that the leaders of Hungary and the rest of Eastern Europe understood that nothing could be accomplished in the area of trade without Congress's approval, I asked the Senator to expound on congressional attitudes toward the link between trade and human rights and he laid it on the line.

I was glad to see that the more important the government official or businessman, the clearer his realization that it was in our best, not our worst, interests to help the Eastern countries arrive at a more comfortable standard of living, a permanent stake in maintaining the peace.

As counsel to Paul Austin, chairman of Coca-Cola, I helped to negotiate arrangements for supplying the soft drink the Stalinists had once excoriated as a symbol of the Americanization of the world. With my assistance, William Hewitt of John Deere & Co. agreed to the exchange of know-how for the construction of tractors and earth-moving equipment; Edgar Bronfman of Seagram agreed to swap the joys of American bourbon and Canadian whiskey for those of genuine Russian vodka; and Robert Armstrong of Revlon offered to upgrade the Soviet cosmetics industry and thereby to unleash the long-neglected Russian female on a male population that for more than half a century had been kept under the spell of more martial involvements.

With Armand Hammer of Occidental Petroleum I participated in a signing ceremony at the Kremlin that was more like the conclusion of a treaty between heads of state; both the American and the Soviet flags were unfurled on the dais. Hammer's consortium would help build ammonia plants in the U.S.S.R., complete with pipelines and port facilities for shipping the output to the United States. In return, the Russians would buy phosphate fertilizer from the coast of Florida for their chronically inefficient government farms. It was one of the largest transactions ever concluded, with an anticipated turnover of twenty billion dollars over a span of twenty years.

I grew more ambitious. At the Dartmouth Conference of 1974, which was held in Tbilisi, Soviet Georgia, and was attended by Senator Edward Kennedy, I pained our Soviet hosts with new ideas for cooperation in the economic development of impoverished countries. The implications of such cooperation could be breathtakingly wide. The Soviet bloc and the West could teach these desperate peoples how "to fish." The present export drive in conventional arms, which piles up modern weapons in the Third World in rival bids for political influence, could be diverted to urgently needed programs of health, education, medical aid, and agriculture. Together, East and West could do something effective about the dangers of overpopulation and drought and famine that stare half of humanity in the face. They could also start dealing with the planetary dangers of pollution of the seas, the atmosphere, and space, and with energy and raw-material shortages that threaten to overwhelm us all.

I reminded the participants that both powers had sunk untold wealth in the Third World without anyone having gained anything of lasting value. On the other hand, East-West cooperation, on the basis of what I called "transideological enterprise," could be not only economically advantageous for all concerned, but could also modulate the competing political interference in the internal affairs of the host country, that each side was accused of.

I invited both sides to consider the Aswan Dam. The bidding for its construction was accompanied by a spectacular propaganda contest between the United States and the Soviet Union. And, the Russians won out. But in addition, they won the privilege of sinking some twenty billion dollars in military aid in Nasser's regime before Soviet influence was abruptly ended by President Sadat. Both powers would have lost less, I claimed, and Egypt would have gained far more, had the project been undertaken on a trilateral basis. I wondered aloud: Did the same mistake have to be repeated in India and Bangladesh, where the sterile game of power politics was achieving absolutely nothing for anyone, while hundreds of millions of people barely subsisted in conditions of perpetual famine? The same sort of questions could be directed later to the American involvement in Iran, where the world's fourth largest army, equipped with the most up-to-date American weapon systems, would capitulate, almost without firing a shot, to a turbaned religious fanatic sitting in a small town near Paris.

Any transideological approach of the sort I had in mind necessarily presumed an ideological truce in the very regions where, under official Kremlin doctrine, it was the communists' duty to range themselves with the "forces of national liberation" against the "forces of neocolonialism." The Soviet delegation spotted the heresy in my remarks and froze into silence. But later, in Moscow, David Rockefeller told me that when he repeated my proposal to Prime Minister Alexei Kosygin, the latter, far from blanching, suggested that a high-level Soviet-American group be constituted to explore the matter. Secretary of State Henry Kissinger also cautiously endorsed the proposal and Rockefeller invited me to chair the group. I was tempted but, as I feared, that was too much for the Soviets and they vetoed it, preferring a docile American business executive; they were not interested in losing control over a sensitive political issue.

As we were flying back home, and my thoughts turned to Washington and the testimony on East-West trade that I was expected to present, the next week, to the Senate Subcommittee on Antitrust and Monopoly, my eyes were glued to the window of the small Gulfstream jet. Somewhere below, west of Minsk, lay the remains of my native city. The ghostly world of my childhood was so near and yet, somehow, so many light-years away.

I thought about how Russian officialdom had just treated David Rockefeller, with all the protocol due a head of state, and I remembered how David's family had been presented in the schoolbooks I was required to read during the Soviet occupation of the town now almost directly below us. Bulky, in top hats, and, ironically, with huge *Cuban* cigars between their teeth, the Rockefellers were caricatured as the ultimate symbols of bloodthirsty capitalism, the enemies-in-chief of the world's people. During our week-long stay in the Soviet Union, the only image of the Chase Manhattan Bank's chairman which *Pravda* and *Izvestia* chose to convey to its readers was one of a peace-loving partner in economic cooperation. How strange and how sad that "peaceful coexistence" was a Russian, not an American, phrase.

Everything seemed upside down. I began to wonder if my children did not have a point. It was time for a respite from my frenetic activities, time to stand back, time to reflect.

Ben paid us a visit. He was now in the import business, traveling regularly to America and Europe. He barely knew Judith or Leah and I suspect it was an inspection tour; out of politeness, he inspected our house first, checking the washer and dryer, all the appliances.

One evening I heard a noise downstairs after everyone had retired and found him standing motionless in front of the open refrigerator door.

"What's the matter, Benek? You want a snack?" I asked.

"No, thanks. I'm on a diet."

"You should be! Thirsty?"

"No. Just looking."

I found the scene a little bizarre, but dropped the subject.

Sometime later his son Paul explained to me that as long as he could remember, Ben was unable to fall asleep without first going into the kitchen to see if the refrigerator was fully stocked with food, and that Paul's mother, Bebka, saw to it every day. Even thirty years after the physical hunger had vanished, the psychological hunger was something he could not shake off.

Soon it was time for our usual walk. We were accompanied by our new dog, a huge shaggy briard whom the children had named Mitzva; Balalaika had moved to California. I was ready for another barrage, but I was taken by surprise.

"Mula, you're doing all right. You have a real home."

"I'm glad you approve. Now knock it off, what's on your mind this time?"

"You're still running around too much."

"You're not doing too bad a job running around yourself."

"Mine's business. What'd you go to Auschwitz with Giscard for? — he's got relatives there too?"

"Benek, for God's sake. . . . You've read the newspapers! You've heard of French-Arab oil diplomacy and the danger it represents for Israel! As long as Giscard was going, I wanted to make sure he said 'Never Again' — loud and clear. Loud and clear to the Poles, to the Russians, to the Arabs, to everybody. And I wanted to say it too, because too many people may be tempted to trade blood for oil."

Ben picked up a stick and threw it. Mitzva chased it, but refused to bring it back.

"Won't you ever train a dog?"

"Forget it," I laughed. "I've got too many other things to do."

"Yeah, that's what worries me."

The world of business, like the world of diplomacy, makes strange bedfellows. In 1939, Stalin didn't hesitate to join hands with Hitler to destroy Poland, thereby becoming an accomplice in the launching of World War II. In 1972, the Kremlin welcomed President Nixon to Moscow only a few days after he had ordered the mining of Haiphong Harbor. In 1979, when they signed the ill-fated Salt II agreement in Vienna, Presidents Carter and Brezhnev kissed before television cameras; less than a year later, after the Soviet intervention in Afghanistan, one called the other a liar.

Moscow never flinched from supplying electric power stations to the colonels' Greece although thousands of communists were at that time rotting in the jails of Athens; proletarian Poland did not hesitate to ship coal to Franco's Spain while that country's coal miners were on strike. And the communist countries in chorus celebrated the aristocrats of corporate capitalism, as if "business is business" were a Marxist slogan.

Examples of similar moral indifference exist as well on our side of the ideological divide. Logically, the corporate enterprise is meant to behave as an impersonal, efficient machine, ruled only by its profit requirements. With varying degrees of intimacy I had observed the operating methods of international business; I grew aware that it became simpler and vastly more attractive with every passing day to negotiate manufacturing and commercial arrangements with authoritarian regimes than with democratic ones. It is the very nature of such regimes to guarantee the generous investor a climate free of political unrest, labor difficulties, youthful agitation, consumer criticism, the nuisance of competition, the intrusions of a legislature concerned with bribery and corruption, or even the excessive zeal of national courts — advantages which democracies are constitutionally unable to provide. I have even heard the chief executive of a major corporation — an upright, God-fearing man and a model husband and father, say only half in jest: "Today, one has to have his head examined to invest in a democratic country."

The young people who criticize corporations so vehemently, often with good reason, and who wish to subject them to massive, even complete, state control, have no idea of the dangers that lurk in the incest of government and business.

Consortiums between those holding economic power and those holding political power can lead, and have led, to unholy alliances in which all ethical considerations vanish. I had learned this lesson as a youngster the hard way and it was driven home to me quite brutally in the course of a debate sponsored in 1974 by the London *Times* and several other leading European newspapers.

My opponent was Charles Levinson, a Canadian economist who

heads the international chemical workers' union, and author of a book, *Vodka-Cola,* that has been described as the antithesis of my views; his attack hit home: "Your clients," he said, "have collaborated with the worst regimes. They were in Pinochet's Chile, in the colonels' Greece, in Franco's Spain. Today, when they are not supplying napalm for use in Vietnam, one finds them thriving in the communist East. Their activities are reminiscent of the heyday of Hitler's Germany, when the I. G. Farben company worked hand in hand with the Nazis."

Levinson could not have known that the object of his diatribe was a survivor of the Holocaust. I refrained from enlightening him, because, personalities aside, the point he raised was a crucial one and I preferred that the debate proceed along unemotional lines. Certainly, I did not need him to remind me of facts to which I could testify from bitter personal experience.

I. G. Farben, a mammoth German chemical cartel created in the early part of this century, had a strong corporate presence throughout Europe and in the United States. Since its inception, its scientists, many of them Nobel Prize–winners, had accumulated an unmatched record of extraordinary inventions in the petrochemical and pharmaceutical fields. It held thousands of patents, registered and licensed throughout the world, that included processes for converting coal into synthetic oil and rubber, for producing explosives, lubricants, fibers, and other products without which the German war effort would have been impossible. It also held the peculiar distinction of having developed poison gases and producing Zyklon B, the crystals used in the gas chambers of Treblinka, Maidanek, and Auschwitz.

The moral degradation of the brilliant and upright men who had created the technological miracle of I. G. Farben went far beyond this and was a subject, certainly as far as I was concerned, that deserved intense scrutiny.

During the Hitler years a complete economic and political partnership between company and regime developed — the foundation of the Reich's military-industrial machine. The first step was to eliminate summarily, despite their precious contributions to its know-how, all Jewish scientists. Then, on the heels of the stunning and repeated success of the Nazi's blitzkrieg, the company embarked on a unique policy of mergers and acquisitions; it simply took over every significant plant in the territories conquered by the Wehrmacht. A serious problem developed in the next phase, but Farben's imaginative managers, always equal to the task, rose to an unprecedented level of business efficiency. The indigenous workforces in wartime Germany were disastrously reduced by manpower requirements on the military front. Logic and efficiency dictated the solution: new giant factories would be built near concentration camps. Thus, a few miles from Auschwitz, a plentiful supply of servile and almost cost-free labor would operate the company's largest synthetic oil and rubber plants. Endless regiments of pitiful subhumans — Ben, Niko, and I among them — would be utilized to the point of exhaustion and death in rapid turnover, to make German-occupied Europe self-sufficient in gasoline and automobile tires.

The joint venture between the company and the SS was baptized the I. G. Auschwitz division. Under its declared corporate policy, "All the inmates would be fed, sheltered and treated in such a way as to exploit them to the highest possible extent, at the lowest conceivable degree of expenditure." Under the terms of the venture, I. G. Farben agreed to pay the SS a daily rate of four marks per skilled worker, two marks per manual worker, and one and a half marks per child worker. Needless to say, the prisoners received nothing.

The business arrangements between the company and the camp included an extraordinary range of transactions. Following are excerpts from I. G. Farben's correspondence with the SS at Auschwitz in 1943, offered in evidence at the Nuremberg war crimes trial of the company's directors:

For the purpose of our experiments with new sleeping pills we would like to be furnished with a certain number of women. . . .

We have duly received your offer, but feel that 200 marks per woman is an excessive price. We do not intend to pay more than 170 marks per head. If this is agreeable, we are ready to enter into possession of the women. We require approximately one hundred and fifty of them. . . .

The shipment of the one hundred and fifty women has been duly received. Despite their emaciated state, we have found their condition adequate. We will keep you advised as our experiments continue. . . .

The experiments have been completed. All the subjects are dead. We will be in touch with you shortly regarding a further shipment. . . .

I had a full taste of the new economic order that was being prepared for the world, not only as an indentured slave at Auschwitz, but also when I worked in the subterranean factory near Stuttgart, riveting, at an inhuman tempo, with practically no sleep, the wings of aircraft for another eminent member of the German corporate establishment. I was too young at the time to understand that a novel chapter was being written in the epic story of mankind. In ancient times, the master treated his slave as a valuable chattel, like a prime work animal, an asset to be prudently maintained and preserved for his profit-making potential. Under the new combination of National Socialism and business enterprise, man was an expendable raw material, without the least risk of depletion. The human mineral, from which all vital force was first extracted, was then treated with Zyklon B gas so that it could yield its secondary products: gold teeth and fillings for the Reichsbank, hair for mattresses, grease for soap, and skin for lampshades.

As I rethought my early experience in the shadow of I. G. Farben, a series of disturbing questions posed themselves in my mind. I also remembered the ironic fact that Niko, Ben, and I had been imprisoned in the Landsberg jail along with the corporate head of the Krupp empire, then held as a Nazi war criminal. How could a group of preeminent professional managers become the eager accomplices of the most monstrous crime in history, accomplices finally called to judgment at Nuremberg? The most painful question of all: Was I, the former slave, today the favored counsel of international corporate enterprises, aiding and abetting the immoral flirtation of modern management with morally corrupt, antidemocratic regimes? Is this where the Harvard thesis, on which I had worked so purely, so scientifically, so unemotionally, had brought me?

It is possible, but difficult, for me to imagine that even in times of economic and political upheaval, managers could again be driven to the type of psychotic behavior that the saga of I. G. Farben, Krupp, and the other revered names of the German corporate establishment so glaringly exemplified.

Theoretically, it is the task of politicians to construct a sturdy framework of government institutions to channel the dynamic energy of industry for the good of society, curbing abuses that accompany the free economic process. In this century, however, business, vigorously exploiting the world's new and ever-accelerating technology, has grown increasingly powerful; politicians and political structures, on the other hand, have clung to the past, addressing old problems with worn-out solutions.

Most contemporary political leaders, despite the vast armies they command, are powerless; by and large they fail dismally in their efforts to govern. Either ignorant of or insensitive to the new and real problems of the world, they merely respond to momentary shifts of public opinion and the whims of the media.

In America, business is subject not only to government regulation, however ineffectual, but also to unhampered competition and to a welter of organizations, interest groups, and the press, who monitor and challenge it on every conceivable front, be its excesses real or imagined. The system of checks and balances elaborated in the Constitution against tyranny by any branch of the government is extended by the richness and diversity of American institutions, which serve as a baffle against the domination of society by any particular group. It was Ralph Nader, not the government, who alerted the public to the dangers of Detroit's products. It was Rachel Carson, not the government, who alerted the world to the devastating hazards of pollution. It was Bernstein and Woodward, not the government, who alerted the public and the Congress to the significance of the break-in at Watergate. The list could be extended indefinitely.

Still, given the lack of hide-bound guarantees against the rise of another I. G. Farben, should we dismantle our free-enterprise system or place it under the close control of state agencies, workers' councils, or consumer associations?

The experience of communist and fascist regimes demonstrates that when business activity is subjugated to a government bureaucracy, the inevitable price is the loss of both economic creativity and individual freedom. Yet in a world faced with so many new and difficult problems — escalating energy prices, raw material shortages, environmental dangers, savage industrial competition — the free-market system cannot be left to cope alone. It could become chaotic, opening the door to domestic tyranny and a global nightmare. If it is not to break, private enterprise must bend, to allow a degree of economic planning as an appropriate technique for the conciliation of individual initiative and overriding public needs. How the youthful critics of corporate life finally respond to these historic challenges will determine the future.

The crucial need is for innovative ideas that will overcome the flagrant failure of contemporary statesmanship throughout the world to forge a common political will and the institutions to deal constructively with the internationalization of the world economy.

In 1971, on the editorial page of the *Wall Street Journal,* I compared the modern conflict between nation states and multinational enterprises to a struggle that took place in twelfth-century England. The outcome of that struggle, between the Church of Rome, a truly multinational force, personified in Thomas à Becket, and the crown of England, a truly national force, personified by Henry II Plantagenet, ended with murder in the cathedral. Today, in the liberal West, politicians who know better how to destroy than how to build, are likely to commit murder again. In the communist East, the murder has already been committed. All creativity in agriculture, industry, and commerce lies prostrate before a blind and brutal political machine.

The professional manager of the modern corporation is no more or less efficient, aggressive, or moral than his predecessors who, fifty years ago, in America brought a cornucopia of wealth to the people, but in Europe contributed to the destruction of a people. Now as then, the means he employs, and the ends to which his products are used, are determined by the legal and institutional environment in which he operates. But today the multinational man operates globally, in a vacuum for which the politician has failed to provide any effective national or international rules that would channel his creativity for the good of mankind and curtail his propensity for abuse.

I know what it means to live in an environment devoid of rules. It is as destructive to oneself as it is to others. In the heady anarchy of Landsberg, Niko, Ben, and I, having barely escaped extinction, nearly destroyed ourselves.

With Henry Kissinger in Mexico City

With Jean-Jacques Servan-Schreiber and Leah on Cape Cod

With my next-door neighbor Artur Rubinstein

With Moshe Dayan in Jerusalem

th my Yiddish-speaking friend Marc Chagall

Judith trying to train Mitzva

With Sheikh Zaki Yamani, my classmate from Harvard

14

It was night when I landed in Moscow. A week of difficult negotiations lay ahead.

You can usually tell the importance the Soviets attach to the business at hand by whether they put you up at the ornate old National, across from Red Square, or at some newer but plainer hotel farther from the center. That night I found myself at the National, in part of a suite that Lenin had used as his office apartment in the days following the October Revolution. The large windows overlooked the Kremlin.

Unable to sleep — it was still day by New York time — I got out of bed long before dawn and stood at the window. Moscow was deathly still. Before me, the spires and domes of czar, commissar, and chairman stood out majestically against the half-light of the crouching sky, casting dark shadows across the square. The ethereal scene conveyed the mystery and power of eternal Russia.

In my time I have acquired many vivid impressions of Moscow. In the company of U.S. Cabinet members and top American business leaders, I have even been entertained by Chairman Leonid Brezhnev in person at banquets that were overwhelming in their archaic magnificence. Receptions on this order are inconceivable in Washington, London, or Paris.

Guests enter the Kremlin Palace by way of the central staircase and proceed into the vast hall of St. George, whose white marble walls display in encrusted golden letters the names of Russia's greatest heroes, fallen in battle. The Secretary General of the Communist Party and his capitalist guests dine peacefully together in the bejeweled Chamber of Facets, decorated wall to wall with motifs of the Orthodox

Church. As I observed Brezhnev and his comrades seated against this background of old illuminated icons, I could not help thinking of Leonardo's fresco, *The Last Supper*.

In this imperial splendor, leaders of party and government mix wine, goodwill, and bluster in an alarming demonstration of autocratic spirit. Once, for openers, a toast to the health of the American delegation ironically informed us that the sanctum sanctorum in which we were then dining had been constructed by Ivan the Terrible, two years before Columbus discovered the New World. Every gesture and every word radiated an aura of pride and power. This was the image they had of themselves and this was how they wanted others to see them.

Snowflakes drifted out of an astonishingly clear Moscow sky, as I reflected on these impressions.

Suddenly something stirred below. A huge shape, a sort of monster fish, detached itself and filled the street as in a dream. I literally rubbed my eyes. It moved slowly, silently, on a soft carpet of snow as though to pass unnoticed; and behind it came another just like it, then a third. They swam out of the darkness, baleful in their symmetry, contemptuous of the human scale, while a thunderous din shook my room.

Of course! I had arrived on the eve of the anniversary of the October Revolution. Colossal trucks carrying the most up-to-date thermonuclear missiles were being wheeled into position on some side street, for the parade in Red Square, now just hours away. The ghostly nocturnal sight below was the ultimate dress rehearsal for an annual theater piece that some profusely decorated field marshals would present to a tense world later in the morning. The show would convey the usual slogans about the invincible might of the Red Army.

Between the ages of ten and twelve I had watched Stalin's tanks roll westward and Hitler's panzers roll eastward. But nothing that I witnessed, then or since, equaled the impact that those intercontinental ballistic missiles, larger than any I had ever imagined, had on me — floating along the ancient crenellated wall across from my window, packed with infernos of death.

A few years earlier, another experience with the military also had affected me profoundly. I had been flying from New York to Washington, for a meeting with Secretary of State William Rogers, when my plane developed trouble in its pressurization system. The pilot made an emergency landing at McGuire Air Force Base in New Jersey, one of the nerve centers of the Strategic Air Command. Since I was curious to see what that giant complex was like, while the plane was being repaired I wandered around the base. I did not enter restricted areas, but I saw enough to give me a sense of the place.

The camp was composed of countless orderly rows of hangars, administrative offices, and living quarters dedicated to — waiting. Its entire population of officers and enlisted men alike did little else than lounge about the grounds, drink beer or Coke, watch old movies on TV, and toss a football around. Some just sat — waiting. In the main mess, to which I was invited for refreshments, colonels and generals sat — waiting — every day of the month, every month of the year. For what? Somehow, in the benign air, under that innocent sky, the question seemed incongruous, out of place, unanswerable.

It was surrealistic or, rather, absurd, the contrast between the demonic technology on this strategic air base — one of a hundred spotted throughout the country, and on submarines and aircraft carriers around the world, ready to spring from the bowels of the earth or the sea for the ultimate act of the nuclear era — and the humdrum, dismal existence of these carefully selected, highly trained men, whose reason for existence was to be ready to perform that ultimate act instantly, unquestioningly, and irrevocably when told to do so. Somewhere, near them, the missiles were poised in their silos. The targets were programmed into their computers. Everything was set for automatic detonation.

What every one of these men seemed to be waiting for was doomsday, or the day he retired. Every one of them was weighed down by the monotony of this eternal waiting, so that in one frightful moment, which I quickly brushed aside, it occurred to me that the unthinkable signal to which everything was geared, and after which everything would end, might come almost as a release.

In the Soviet Union, too, comparable lives, minds, careers, and the weapon systems they serviced were poised for the same alert. Their days were just as sad, just as boring, as those of their American counterparts. They, too, had been conditioned to perform blindly and unhesitatingly the same superior order, aimed at the same goal — the final solution of our time.

At another time and place, another lieutenant-colonel performed his duties with total dedication, without questions. He was the personification of the inhuman cog in the machine; he was the banality of evil. Is it possible that there is an unwitting Eichmann in each and every one of us?

On both sides of the globe, and wherever else countries pride themselves on being atomic powers, everything possible has been done to keep such men from reflecting on the meaning of their lives. They have been taught not to ask themselves why they are there, or what, exactly, is expected of them, other than robotlike obedience. For who among them would remain sane if the answers to the forbidden questions sank fully into his soul?

We live, in some core part of us, amid fear and hope — a fear of nuclear obliteration that we keep well hidden from ourselves because we don't know how to deal with it, and a hope of deliverance that we don't dare examine, lest we realize how precarious it is. Its precariousness was never borne in on me as poignantly as by the juxtaposition of these two scenes — the night missiles of Moscow and the doomsday vigil of McGuire.

You cannot keep piling up weapons of such magnitude and sophistication, so finely calibrated to the vagaries of political crisis and the supposed intentions of the potential enemy, and not have an eventual explosion. Looking at the arms race today, one could say without wandering far from the mark that it is the engines of destruction that command and drive mankind, and not the other way around. Robert McNamara's warning against the "mad momentum" of arms production, in one of his final reports as Secretary of Defense during the mid-1960s, had proved indeed prophetic. What had placed these obscene engines in the driver's seat was that epic mutual misunderstanding known as the cold war.

The origins of that conflict have been the subject of debate between the conventional and the "revisionist" historians for more than a decade now. I do not mean to minimize the importance of scholarly debate when I say that, having experienced the quality of Soviet rule in both triumph and defeat, and having worked at the centers of America's government and business establishments, I feel sure in my bones that the decisions taken in both Washington and Moscow to mobilize for an indefinite political struggle was, for both, the outcome of a misperception of the other's aim.

In Washington, the extraordinary physical force that burst upon central Europe at the close of World War II, blaring its belligerence in the Stalinist style, was mistaken for a military threat to the whole of Europe; instead, the horizon of Moscow's intention and capability at that time actually was to create at the continent's eastern belt a security zone against further invasions.

In Moscow, the American insistence that the Soviets withdraw from Eastern Europe was mistaken for a political-military offensive meant to undermine the Soviet regime; instead its actual source was the American fear that "appeasement" would encourage the communists to extend their dominion still farther, making another war a virtual certainty.

Given the history of successive invasions of Russia from the East and the West, by Mongol horsemen, Polish barons, Teutonic knights, Napoleon's Grand Army, and, most recently and viciously, the Nazis, can one blame the Russians for their determination to ensure that it happens *never again?* Given the lessons of the Anglo-French appeasement of Hitler, stamped on the consciousness of a whole American generation, can one blame the United States for resolving *never again* to seek to purchase peace by appeasing a totalitarian aggressor? The ring of "never again" in both these vows — who could understand it better than a Jew, one who had lived through the Holocaust?

These original misconceptions were translated into dogma, and ossified in military policies that seem impervious to political reassessment. Look at the situation today! The United States and the Soviet Union both have enough missiles on land, at sea, and in space to destroy each other many times over; neither has been content simply to strengthen its nuclear punch. The reasoning that rules the Pentagon's drawing boards is that, somehow, the Russians may gain a technological advantage that would lend them the capacity to destroy all the American land-based missiles in one blow — or enough of them to be able to withstand any American counterblow, with yet enough missiles left to emerge as victor. On this reasoning, it is imperative that the technological lead remain with the United States.

This theory of "preemptive strike" — and we may assume that

similar theorizing goes on in Moscow — has generated a whole series of refinements, including calculations of "how far" the Russians may feel able to go, in provoking "conventional" war, or even "low-yield" nuclear war, without undue risk of a full-scale American retaliation.

I do not say that each of the nuclear options does not have a certain plausibility. But taken together, they are crazy. Who can imagine that any responsible Soviet leader — unless convinced that his country faced total defeat, obliteration — would initiate an attack that, win or lose, would carry an appreciable risk of his country's total destruction, certainly of the historic heart of his country — a de-Russification of the Soviet Union's multinational population?

Taking this arcane logic a step further, anyone who imagines that a war between Russia and America might be kept below a certain "acceptable" nuclear threshold — perhaps through some sort of "gentlemanly" mental telepathy between Moscow and Washington — has lost all touch with reality. To someone who has already witnessed the first scientifically organized destruction of humanity, a better definition of madness is hard to imagine. It is the specter of a crematorium without limits, a thousand Hiroshimas rolled into one.

The people pay their taxes, blink at the dimensions of annual defense budgets that eat up the funds needed for other priorities, and go about their business, praying these billions will not be turned lethally against them. Yet it is only the force of public opinion that might break this spell. We cannot expect the military, in East or West, to wind down the arms race on its own, yet civilian authority seems incapable of producing the fresh ideas and political courage required for any real change in direction.

The years of Soviet-American negotiations on limiting strategic arms had achieved nothing more than numerical ceilings that stay high enough to permit continued buildups on both sides. And the irony may be even wilder. The arms talks have come to serve the military planners of both governments as a mechanism for disguising qualitative improvements in their arsenals behind the benign image of arms control.

During the Cuban missile crisis, the world stared into a fiery pit. The smell of sulfur was lifted only when the Russians, then markedly inferior in strategic capability to the United States, backed down. That humiliating lesson spurred the Russians to an extensive buildup; they cannot be depended on to back down so easily a second time, as the 1979 crisis over the Red Army brigade in Cuba and the 1980 crisis in Afghanistan have shown. While a nuclear attack by the Soviets is demonstratively self-destructive, even insane, it remains a grotesque possibility, should they find themselves squeezed between NATO on one side and a billion Chinese deploying nuclear intermediate-range ballistic missiles on the other. The more predatory Russian generals and ideologues, with their paranoia toward renewed invasion from the East or the West, might then urge their government to act "while there is still time." Let us assume the worst and never let our guard down, but one of our last interests is to exacerbate such fears.

New confrontations with the Soviet Union will prove even more difficult to retreat from, for the United States. Any major crisis could swiftly get out of hand and, without either side wishing it, bring an uncontrollable armed exchange. Added to that danger are constant tensions in Asia, the Middle East, and Africa, where the great powers, having supplied client states with prized conventional arms, have their own prestige at stake.

Diplomacy, as currently practiced, is not dedicated to reducing tensions, but to keeping the trade in arms flourishing. For some supplier states, it is a way of dumping obsolete weapons and forcing a buyer armed to the teeth to become politically dependent for further supplies. For others, it is a way of preserving hundreds of thousands of jobs. The vicious circle is organizing a pattern of international exchange that before long will come to dominate everything else — the economics of death.

There are, to be sure, some perfectly good reasons for the export drive in arms: it is a way to extend political influence, prop up the dollar, and compete in the world's export markets. But taken all in all, they are again crazy. The stockpiling of sophisticated weapons in areas beset with tensions can scarcely avoid engaging the interests of the superpowers and bringing them into perilous collision. What can such other reasons count for if, above all else, they multiply the risk of World War III?

Any petty dictator, any terrorist organization, can acquire modern arms as long as the funds to pay for them can be found. And as insatiable appetites for weapons are fed, at the expense of economic and social development, the poor nations grow even poorer, and vast regions of the world are turned into powder kegs.

The entire planet is being transformed into a chessboard for potential war on an unimaginable scale. The great powers are placing their deadliest pieces on all the strategic squares: land-based and submarine-launched ballistic missiles with multiple, independently targeted nuclear warheads, heavy bombers with cruise missiles; subterranean and movable launching pads, "intelligent" rockets attracted by their own targets, cluster bombs steered by television, and laser beams — the inventory is endless. The next stage in the arms race is a system of satellites with nuclear charges, which circle permanently in space, and killer satellites designed to destroy them, at accelerated production costs that may bring on a fatal economic hemorrhage for both superpowers.

Even these highly sophisticated weapon systems are likely to become obsolete as new means of destruction come off the drawing boards: artificial stimulation of "natural" catastrophes such as huge storms that flood large areas and drown their populations, climatic changes that bring on drought and famine; "new and improved" toxic chemicals, and "nerve gas," a small dose of which is lethal to millions. The early chapters of this book offer ample testimony that the production and use of such weapons are perfectly conceivable.

Science, which was supposed to bring hope to humanity, has brought terror instead. Today, the most gifted researchers and technicians in America, Russia, France, Great Britain, and other developed countries, large or small, are squandering their precious talents on the most sterile activities of all — the production of weapons; while other pressing local and global problems are left smoking on a back burner.

Everything seems poised for the apocalypse. It is as if an Auschwitz fever has taken hold of mankind, pushing it irresistibly toward the precipice, an Auschwitz ideology, characterized by rapid devaluation of the ultimate human right — the right to life. The combination of high technology and high brutality, which I had seen practiced on a pilot scale not so long ago, shows that man is quite capable of resorting to both the ideological premises and the scientific means for wholesale annihilation.

I will not have completed what I set out to recount without expressing my sense of protest against this silent acceptance by the peoples of the East and the West of a fate that is all too likely to destroy our children's world, if it does not destroy ours. If I permit myself to invoke the symbolism of Auschwitz it is because I feel a heavy duty to speak my mind in the doomsday debate that currently sweeps the world, to speak it to my fellow Americans as well as to the Russians, to my fellow Jews as well as to the Arabs, to my fellow whites as well as to those whose color is different.

The events that brought me to Auschwitz taught me the dangers of weakness and unpreparedness that tempt aggressors, and the suicidal tendency democracies have of underestimating their security. Because of this I do not argue for disarmament, or an immediate and unilateral halt in arms production. Nor would such an argument be realistic at a time of global economic decline, when the worldwide weapons industry accounts for more than $500 billion in sales and more than fifty million jobs. But what does seem to me reasonable and imperative is the need to keep on trying to find an alternative way of constructing peace, so that the deceleration of the mad race for arms may one day begin.

It was and is my central conviction that the only sword capable of defending humanity from the risk of self-destruction is the expansion of economic ties and human contacts between East and West, and the progressive conversion of their vast military production capacities to alleviating the desperate plight of the Third World; otherwise, each side is likely to see its civilization swept away, civilizations that have common cultural, religious, and ethnic origins.

My thinking was animated by a peaceful vision of the world. One cannot live what I have lived and reject, even at moments of darkest pessimism, the prospect of a sane human future as pure fantasy. Were reason to prevail, just one project — the opening of Siberia's vast energy resources — would serve the vital interests of America, Russia, and the poverty-stricken regions of the world.

Even an old-guard Bolshevik like Anastas Mikoyan, for many years Minister of Foreign Trade and then Chairman of the Presidium of the

Supreme Soviet, admitted the U.S.S.R.'s dire need for expanded commerce in this sphere. With surprising frankness, in a private conversation at the Kremlin in 1973, he told me that Russia had no choice but to try to sell to America large quantities of natural gas and oil in exchange for products that would help compensate for his country's agricultural and technological backwardness.

"If we are ready to supply you with part of this natural wealth," he said, in Russian spoken with a thick Armenian accent, "it's not out of the goodness of our heart, because the energy problems you are facing today will be ours tomorrow. Our children and grandchildren would not forgive us if we were reckless with our natural resources, for the day will come when they will need all the oil and gas they can find to heat and light our cities." Then he added, with a show of the shrewd flexibility that had helped him survive Stalin's remorseless purges: "But, we need your technical equipment and know-how, and almost every year we need your grain to feed our people. So we must sell, whether we like it or not, in order to be able to pay for the goods we must buy from you."

No one knows how large Russia's oil and gas reserves are, but CIA studies suggest that unless the proven Siberian oil deposits are quickly brought on stream, the Soviet Union and its satellite countries — including Eastern Europe, Cuba, and Vietnam — eighty percent of whose energy is now supplied by the Soviets, will be forced to look to the world market. The added pressure — out of sheer industrial need for oil — on prices, sources, and the political soft spots of the Middle East could critically aggravate economic conditions in the United States, Western Europe, and Japan. Any policy that seeks to reduce the Soviet Union's access to energy at home practically invites the Red Army to the Persian Gulf and constitutes an added danger to our security and our welfare.

A prime objection to any effort to dismantle the ideological foundations of the arms race is that our safety lies not in putting an end to it but, on the contrary, in accelerating its pace. This is the view of those who argue that, given our economic and technological superiority, we can so far outclass and outdistance the Russians in the frenetic competition for ever-more-complex weapon systems, that they will reconcile themselves to a second-class position. Alternatively, they will spend themselves into bankruptcy because their qualitatively inferior means of production make their armaments three or four times costlier than ours. It is a view that can be sustained only through willful ignorance of the historically fueled Soviet paranoia about defense. I saw symptoms of that paranoia at the Kiev gathering in July 1971, on the day of the pilgrimage to the mass grave of Babi Yar. None of our Soviet hosts, not even Georgi Arbatov, the Kremlin's foremost expert on American affairs, could contain his consternation when the news broke, in the middle of one of our sessions, that Henry Kissinger had just completed his first secret mission to Peking.

Russia's gross national product may not be much more than half of America's but it is large enough to enable the Soviet Union to keep up in the nuclear arms race. The experience of the last three decades makes that clear. If it comes to a choice between defense and consumer needs, the masters of the Kremlin will not hesitate to sacrifice the consumer, and will not need to fear that, in consequence, their regime will explode from within. For a people who suffered twenty million dead in the last war, privation for the sake of defense is not that difficult. However meaningful the rhetorical choice of "guns or butter" may be in the West, it carries little weight in the context of Russia's blood-soaked past.

A crucial question I have been unable and unwilling to avoid is the link between the cooperative relationship with the East and the suppression of civil liberties. It is a question that is bound to give great pause for a person who had endured the worse kind of oppression.

I had long ago come to the conclusion that the single most important action that could be taken on behalf of Russia's human rights activists, and on behalf of that incomparably larger elite of plant foremen, industrial managers, agricultural experts, students, educators, scientists, writers, and artists who are their potential allies — because they too, are impatient with the top-heavy system that dooms Russia to lag economically forever behind the West — was to encourage the Soviet Union's integration into the world market.

The vast superiority of American agriculture and technology is not lost on the rising generation of frustrated Soviet and East European planners. I observed the almost hypnotic impact on these people of audiovisual presentations by American experts on how citrus fruit is grown in the swamps of Florida, how lipstick is manufactured in the industrial centers of New Jersey, and how tractors are operated in the prairies of Oklahoma; I saw human beings won over by the process of creation, indifferent to the dogmatic pretensions of Marxism-Leninism, demonstrating that the humanism of this process can, if given a chance, cross ideological boundaries more effectively than armies, churches, or diplomats.

Like many young Americans who feel that we cannot afford both to be an omnipresent gendarme abroad and to address adequately the urgent nonmilitary problems that are neglected at home, many young Russians resent seeing their best resources squandered on a permanent war economy, and their best brains constantly suppressed. They are concerned, albeit more silently, over housing shortages, labor inefficiency, and rampant alcoholism. It can be safely assumed that large numbers of them do not want to sacrifice forever, on the altar of a stale ideology, the hope of more freedom and a better standard of living, much less run the risk of an apocalyptic showdown with the West. Our interest, I have always felt, was to encourage these people, not to show them up as naïve dreamers and thereby push them back into the arms of the ideological hacks who are ever ready to tighten their iron grip in the name of internal and external security. For these people know that if their country is to overcome its chronic agricultural, industrial, and technological shortcomings, it must begin with internal liberalization. No matter how mighty the Red Army may be, to strike at the heart of its problems the Soviet Union will have to experiment with new concepts of research, production, management, and marketing. In the final analysis such experimentation cannot bear fruit except in a climate of greater freedom of expression. For if the intellectual environment is such that writers like Solzhenitsyn cannot write, musicians like Rostropovich cannot play, and scientists like Sakharov cannot work or speak, then the inventor cannot invent, the technician cannot innovate, and the manager cannot manage. There can be no sustained human progress unless minds and ideas are allowed to clash. It is precisely because the Third Reich did not have room within its borders for the likes of Thomas Mann, Willy Brandt, and Albert Einstein that it became the moribund, sinister, and ultimately suicidal society that I knew so painfully well.

In both East and West, bemedaled generals will no doubt continue to stand behind the economic and political managers, ever ready to blow disagreements into crises and confrontations. If those who are searching for a way to forestall the apocalypse become disheartened and give up, then any vision of a saner future would be a fantasy and even this book of testimony on another episode of history when the bemedaled generals had the upper hand is a futile exercise.

We cannot be sure that broadened contacts, even on the widest front, could humanize the Soviet Union at home and restrain its ambitions abroad. But we can say that since political pressure has not worked, and military force cannot work, our best — our only — hope is to catalyze those elements and those movements in Russia whose interests in pursuing economic development and in averting nuclear disaster coincide with our own.

Nothing could stir us out of the hypnotic trance of cold war like the reknitting of the two schismatic halves of the industrialized world. In a more rational atmosphere, Russia and America could yet find it possible to resume existence as two normal nations, rather than two causes in a theological conflict whose sources are clouded and whose lack of resolution gambles with the survival of mankind.

If not this course, what other? The other is at best the continued development of both societies into gigantic and opposing arsenals, ultimately ruled by bellicose metal-eaters, and the escalating risk of a furnace infinitely enlarged — cities and countryside consumed in the fireballs of nuclear damnation, millions of decaying bodies, tens of millions of the half-alive, and radioactive poisoning and epidemics ready to finish the job.

We avert our minds' eyes from such a vision, and as we do so, the quiet, steady, unmalevolent augmentation of power and planning for the nuclear option — the final solution of the cold war — recreates the madness of the Holocaust on a global scale.

Humanity is at a crossroads, and it must make a choice.

✣ ✣ ✣

"But, Mula, you know, your ideas about expanded contacts with the Russians and the Chinese and the Arabs . . . it's all pretty doubtful. . . ." I would be untrue to the rigorous Socratic method inculcated in me at Harvard if I failed to admit that Ben's questioning found an echo in my innermost thoughts. But Ben was not susceptible to the Socratic method. He was all instinct and intuition, as I used to be. My arguments were too intellectual for his needs. He wanted irrefutable proof that if my ideas were followed the Eastern raw materials that would make their way to the Western market would not be extracted by the same sorts of helpless slave workers that we used to be — in some remote labor camps of Siberia, or ideological reeducation centers in China. I could not give him such proof, any more than I could assure him that those who toil to produce export goods in the miserable slums of São Paulo, Islamabad, or Lagos lived at a level superior to slaves; or that the tin mines of Bolivia, the carpet mills of Turkey, and the toy factories of Pakistan were not operated day and night by work-forces that included young children. I could only try to persuade him that short of atomic war, which he found as unimaginable yet as plausible as I, a commitment to take the hysteria out of East-West confrontation offered the only hope of doing away with such practices; otherwise the whole world faced the risk of becoming a vast labor camp, or concentration camp, or gas chamber.

Though we have never met, I feel a strong bond with Alexander Solzhenitsyn. He, from his years in the Stalinist gulag, and I, from my years in the Nazi death camps, share a knowledge of human agony, of human madness that, in one form or another, persists even today, and could engulf the world again.

But the philosophy he has distilled from his suffering cannot be mine. Solzhenitsyn, if I understand him correctly, had pronounced a curse on Western liberalism as well as on the Marxist-Leninist revolution. He wishes a spiritual rebirth for his country, based on the religious tenets of the "true Russia," which can only be found in her past. He simply wants the West, with its democratic corruptions and socialist heresies, to isolate the Soviet regime so as to speed its decay. Expanded East-West intercourse is, naturally, one of the last things he favors.

His outlook represents an interesting revival of the Slavophile spirit, and it appeals to a significant number of people within and without the Soviet dissident movement. But it is a vision that does not, in my view, hold out much hope to the rest of us. Well before a spiritual regeneration of Russia could occur, a Soviet system caught in the grip of Western economic sanctions and internal food shortfalls could generate enough tensions to blow the world apart. Close as I feel to Solzhenitsyn, my fellow victim of oppression who has borne eloquent witness to evil, I do not believe that his position offers constructive solutions. He is too much of a seer, too much a man on the edge of the abyss.

Intellectually, I feel closer to Andrei Sakharov, the calm and humane nuclear scientist and "father" of the Soviet hydrogen bomb, who has spoken out courageously for arms control and human rights. When Sakharov issued his famous manifesto of 1968 — "Progress, Peaceful Coexistence and Intellectual Freedom" — calling for global cooperation between East and West and looking toward an eventual convergence of the two systems that would combine the best of both, I was encouraged. But by 1973, as his appeals for internal reform brought him under official attack, his position began to grow ambivalent and he appeared to oppose any agreements providing Moscow with Western goods, except in return for undertakings to increase human rights within the Soviet Union. He seemed, in short, to have despaired of reform in response to domestic pressure, and to have concluded that the only effective leverage for internal liberalization lay in the West's, especially America's, ability to grant or withhold the economic cooperation sought by the Soviet regime.

I did not think that this kind of pressure would work. For one thing, the level of trade between the two countries was still minuscule, insufficient to offer incentives or inculcate restraints within the Soviet ruling establishment; the tissue of relations that they would find too costly to sunder had never been built. The balance between need and fear of the West was also far too delicate. The host of anxieties — internal and external — that beset the Soviet Union meant that anything as direct and open as a demand for broader human rights tied to specific deals would undoubtedly be seen as an unbearable interference in the Soviet Union's internal affairs; with the same affronted self-righteousness that was the czar's answer to any real or imagined slight to Russia's dignity, any such demand would be rejected.

At the same time, without a clearer idea of Andrei Sakharov's reservations, I felt uncomfortable as an advocate of peace through East-West economic integration. It became a disturbing question of conscience: Was the coexistence toward which I worked being built on the backs of the oppressed? I felt that there was a moral threshold here which my life's experience, my duty to the past, could not allow me lightly to cross.

As someone who knew better than most what the Second World War was like, I decided to put my dilemma, personally and directly, to Sakharov, a man who knew better than most what the Third World War would be like. In an open letter conveyed to him in Moscow by foreign correspondents and published in the principal newspapers of the West, I posed a number of questions. Had he given up hope of a true and lasting détente? Did he contemplate a sort of Western ultimatum to the Soviet government — change your system first, and then we'll talk of coexistence?

The response was transmitted to me by his wife, Yelena Bonner, the next day, again through the medium of the world press: "I am unconditionally against ultimatums of any kind in relations between states. . . . I am in favor of the gradual improvement of the Soviet state within the framework of the existing regime. . . . The danger of nuclear war is the primary preoccupation for the whole of mankind. . . . I also support the strengthening of economic, cultural and scientific ties between East and West."

Sakharov's reply calmed my worst self-doubts. But even though I was emotionally and intellectually on his side, I did not delude myself about the extent of our agreement. Even if he still favored Western economic cooperation with the Soviet Union, he surrounded it with conditions that I was sure would render impractical the whole enterprise. At best, it would require of the West a finely tuned, supremely sophisticated pattern of carrot-and-stick diplomacy.

No country, let alone a free-enterprise one, is capable of operating with such finesse on the body of a foreign power. The U.S. government, which would be the principal agency of such a campaign, is particularly unsuited for this Machiavellian task — and I say it with pride in the decentralized political and economic process that is the genius of the American system. Our attempts thus far to force the Soviet government's hand by open economic pressure have been unproductive, and this not only in regard to its interventions in Central Asia, but to another issue of unsurpassed importance to me — Jewish emigration from the U.S.S.R.

Oddly enough, my exchange with Sakharov brought an unexpected endorsement from Solzhenitsyn. I had prefaced my open letter with the statement that for me "human freedom stands higher than all the commerce of the world." Citing this thought, Solzhenitsyn wrote that "among the partisans of commercial rapprochement with the U.S.S.R., Pisar is one of the few to see clearly." I was grateful for his support and although I knew that we did not see eye to eye on the means to be employed, I took his words as an affirmation of what I felt to be our unspoken pact on some deeper level of commitment to human decency and liberty.

15

OUR limousine sped along the edge of the Dead Sea toward the mighty rock of Masada. We were approaching it from the direction of Jerusalem and the Judean Hills — with their six million newly planted trees, each a living epitaph to the six million who were murdered.

Yaakov, our driver-guide, a veteran of the Israeli-Arab wars of 1948, 1956, 1967, and 1973, was recounting to the children the gory saga of that ancient fortress, a sacred symbol of freedom and resistance.

"Close to a thousand Jewish men, women, and children, armed with little more than their courage and their faith, made a gallant last stand on that rock against an attacking army of fifteen thousand Romans."

"Were the Romans like the Nazis?"

"Not quite, Alexandra," answered Uncle Lazar from the back seat.

The Australian uncle who had helped to resurrect me from the embers of the modern holocaust that had amputated one-third of our people, had chosen to live out his last years in Israel. Now he substituted admirably for all the paternal grandparents, uncles, aunts, and cousins whom my children would never have. His favorite pastime was to discuss with Helaina, with a minimum of religious or Zionist zeal, the Old Testament, the history of the Diaspora, and the modern vision of Israel. Soon the younger ones would be ready too, but would he have time to give them a sense of the prophets — Isaiah, Ezekiel, Jeremiah — the sages of the Torah and the Talmud, the Cabala, the Midrash?

This same man, who when I arrived in Melbourne had helped to reconstruct me, teaching me arithmetic, algebra, geometry, the finer points of the Hebrew alphabet, calming my violence with the discipline of chess, wanted to insure that these children also would be nourished by the ethic of their forefathers.

"After seven long months of siege, when the legionnaires finally reached the citadel, they found that all counterattacks had ceased. Every structure within the fortress was in flames; every defender was dead."

Holding Leah in his lap, his voice choking now and then with stifled emotion, my uncle spoke as if the ancient holocaust of Masada, which had ended the Jewish rebellion against Roman rule at a cost of half a million lives, had happened only yesterday.

"Knowing that the ramparts could not hold out any longer, the leader of the zealots, Elazar, assembled everyone around him and addressed them in words which might have been those of the ghetto fighters: "God has granted us his favor — a chance to die in freedom. . . . Our hands can still hold our swords. Let us leave this world nobly, not as slaves, but as free men, with our wives and our children beside us.' "

A formation of Phantom jets, Stars of David gleaming on their wings, drowned out Elazar's words, as they zoomed across the desert from Galilee and the Golan Heights.

"The families clung together weeping as they kissed for the last time. Acting as if his arm belonged to a stranger, each man killed his loved ones and lay down beside them. Ten men chosen by lot killed all others, then drew lots again to choose the last one who would kill the other nine, and then himself. As fire and smoke engulfed Masada, nine hundred and sixty bodies lay huddled together in the final embrace of death."

The uncle looked at his American nephew, his American niece, their American children. He was pleased. I could almost read his thoughts: "Yes, the world is much changed; but his mother, my sister, would recognize herself in this family, this miracle. True." Worry lines creased his brow. "Mula is so absorbed by other cultures, so absorbed by the problems of the world. Does he have no need to return to the biblical sources, to the laws of Moses on which Judaism, Christianity, and Islam are all based? Perhaps his own experience has been biblical enough, more than enough. He is a source all his own. So much of the past lives on inside him, along with the present. But the children — will the past live on in them, and in their children, or will Hitler have succeeded one day in annihilating yet another Jewish family? God, Hitler's reach is still so long, so endlessly long. . . .''

When we arrived at the cable car that would take us up to the ruins of Masada where every excavated stone cries its sorrow across twenty centuries, Antony, who had just been bar mitzvahed, announced with quiet determination that he would climb. In the blistering desert heat we watched him first from the ground, then from the cable car, and finally from the ramparts, as he doggedly made his way up the steep slope. Climbing down, group after group of Israeli-born Sabras and Jewish boys and girls from all over the world, not much older than he, some with submachine guns slung from their shoulders, stopped to shake hands or offer him water from their flasks.

It was as if these kids were exchanging some kind of unspoken vow that came from the ages — from the slavery in Egypt, the Babylonian captivity, the Roman conquest, the Spanish Inquisition, the Russian pogroms, the Nazi gas ovens, and all the other holocausts of history, large and small — no more Masadas!

I first met Moshe Dayan in Paris shortly after Israel's heady victory of 1967. What has never ceased to surprise me about him is the moderation, even tenderness, with which he speaks about the Palestinians, among whom he was born and grew up. His sensitivity to the human tragedies that have scarred the region belies the image of the daredevil battlefield commander created by popular legend after he led the armored dash to the Suez Canal in the 1956 Sinai campaign, which had added a new chapter to the annals of military strategy.

I believed too firmly in the limitations of any policy based on force of arms to think that military victory would ever bring Israel lasting peace, and I told him so. We were sitting on the flowered patio of his home near Tel Aviv, amidst an extraordinary collection of Egyptian mummies, classical columns, and other ancient relics ferreted out with his own hands from the deserts and mountains.

''You know, General,'' I said, somewhat hesitantly, as one must when giving advice to those who give blood, ''safe borders can neither be deduced from the traditions of the Bible, nor guaranteed by military strength. The only safe borders are in the mind. We must begin by taking the venom out of schoolbooks."

At the far corners of his peaceful orchard I could discern young Israeli sentries with submachine guns at the ready. Inside this private fortress, the man who had lived since childhood in a state of constant military alert confessed to me that during all his adult life he had tried to imagine the contours of a hypothetical peace with the Arabs. I thought I had the answer for him.

"My concept of coexistence and commerce should be given a chance to work in this part of the world. Fantasy, you would say? In the last hundred years France and Germany mercilessly attacked each other three times. Are the contemporary French and Germans genetically different from their parents? Unlikely. But as goods, labor, and capital cross their open borders with increasing intensity, their welfare has become so inextricably bound together that an attack by one country on its antagonist of yesterday would be like stabbing at its own body."

"You are storming at open doors." He smiled. "I should tell you I practiced your theory before ever hearing of it, when I opened the Allenby Bridge across the Jordan River in order to allow the free movement of goods and people between the Arab and the Israeli parts of Palestine. I have always thought this was the best way to calm the sea of violence in this part of the world. We must begin to build a relationship made of the healthy tissue of human contacts — a tissue that comes from working, and trading, and living together."

Then he added, with a roguish smile, "I was once a farmer, you know, then Minister of Agriculture, and that was more satisfying than being Chief of Staff. For example, I believe that developing the industrial fishing potential of this region, given its ready access to the Mediterranean Sea on one side and the Indian Ocean on the other, should be an important priority."

Through the clichés of history, Jews have always been regarded as a people of shopkeepers, moneylenders, and bookworms, who devote every free moment of their lives to the study of the Scriptures. Today, in their own homeland, they have become a nation of farmers by choice and soldiers by necessity in the ancient tradition of the young David, the shepherd and the warrior. This unprecedented transformation of the national character took place within the span of a single generation. It was a transformation that went against the grain, but which had been made inevitable by the martyrdom of the ghettos and the camps. After that, to lay one's head defenselessly on the chopping block of history and hope that some foreign power, governed by the calculus of its own interests, will come mercifully to the rescue would have been criminal folly, a form of deafness and blindness to the obvious lessons of the past.

I have often wondered how the veterans of the Nazi Wehrmacht and SS explain to themselves the strategic genius repeatedly demonstrated by Israeli officers, and the skill and courage shown by Israel's jet pilots and tank crews — the same Jews who, scarcely two decades earlier, had been led to slaughter at Treblinka and Babi Yar.

The full measure of this metamorphosis was brought out in a bittersweet incident related to me by General Ezer Weizman not long after the Six-Day War, in which he demolished the Arab air forces. Weizman speaks Yiddish, and, perhaps because of this, looks at life with a greater sense of humor than most of the Sabras born in Israel. Yiddish reflects a unique brand of laughter through tears, that has made Jewish life in the Diaspora a little easier to bear.

In the mid-1960s, as the commander in chief of Israel's air force, Weizman made an inspection visit to a major West German air base near Munich, a few miles, as it happened, from the place where Niko, Ben, and I escaped from our SS guards during an American fighter strafing raid. Entering the senior officers' mess for dinner, he had been startled to hear a clipped order: *"Achtung — der Herr General!"* The German officers snapped to attention as one man. The Jewish general looked around; the click of the heels, the stiff bearing, all seemed the same; only the uniforms were different. His blue eyes lingering for a long moment, his smile betraying no hint of triumph, he calmly commanded: "At ease!"

Men like Dayan and Weizman, who, much as they detest war, have taken to soldiering, and men like Ben and I, who have chosen other routes, represent two sides of the same fate, the fate of a people molded together by centuries of suffering and persecution. Those of us who agonized in the Nazi death factories have provided additional justification, were any needed, for the existence of men like them in the land of our forefathers, men who are determined to guarantee to Jews, wherever they feel threatened, a place of refuge and of hope, men who brought Eichmann to Jerusalem to be judged.

At times I have asked myself if my childish dream of becoming a general in the Red Army should not, in all logic and duty, have been transferred to the service of Israel. This question plagued me in 1948 when the infant Jewish state was on the verge of annihilation. Today, were the Jewish people again threatened with genocide, I would be no less ready to fight and die for Israel than for America. Come what may, the uncontrollable impulse that pushed me, after I had renamed myself Gerhardt, to abandon the "safe" Aryan column and join Niko and Ben on the way to Dachau will remain with me forever.

I have not felt threatened by anti-Semitism since the end of the war. Nor do I fear another holocaust. Judeo-Christian civilization would go under forever if such things were allowed to occur again. But I know from experience that when a deep economic crisis strikes, a deep political crisis cannot be far behind. Israel and the Jews are, as always, prime candidates for the role of scapegoat, particularly now when the tide of Islam is rising so high and when to many people Arab oil seems thicker than blood.

These dangers are perennial, but when have they not been? I feel serene and confident about the survival of Israel and the Jewish people. What other people has endured such shocks to its body and its soul, and yet lived on? Who could have predicted two thousand years ago, upon the destruction of the Second Temple, that a vigorous Jewish community would flourish in medieval Spain, around Toledo and Córdoba, and that later the epicenter of Jewish culture would shift to Eastern Europe and Russia, and then to America, to return, at last, to the reborn State of Israel.

Despite, or perhaps because of, their suffering since time immemorial, Jews have survived to stand at the graves of all the tyrannical empires that oppressed them. At Auschwitz, rivers of blood have renewed the commitment of the Jews to survival for centuries to come.

"If only all Arabs were like you."

"If only all Jews were like you."

The warm, friendly conversations I used to have with Sheikh Zaki Yamani at Harvard twenty-five years earlier, and with so many other Arab and Israeli friends since then, turn around in my mind like broken records.

Is there really not enough sand in the Middle East to accommodate a few million Jewish and Arab refugees from the holocausts of history, in their joint ancestral homeland? What is this curse that lies so heavily on the descendants of Isaac and Ismaël who, to this day, revere Abraham as the father of their fathers?

It is historic falsehood that Arabs and Jews are sworn enemies unto eternity. Judaism and Islam have coexisted more peacefully with each other than with Christianity or any other creed. In spite of their religious divergence, the productive harmony in which they lived for thousands of years, from the great era of Alexandria to the golden age of Spain, has yielded fertile innovations in mathematics, astronomy, science, medicine, and commerce.

Is it really too utopian to hope that a renewed pattern of coexistence and commerce could help transcend their momentary hatred and defuse the powder keg of the Middle East as well?

For more than three decades, Arabs and Jews have been paying a huge price in human lives and material resources. Their armed conflicts and economic boycotts have resolved nothing. Both sides have remained exposed to the political whims of the great powers, while crushing defense budgets have deepened the misery of their peoples, until President Anwart Sadat's courageous journey to Jerusalem raised a faint ray of hope that they can again live and work together.

The Jewish chemists, physicists, technicians, and engineers who have come to her shores from all over the world have given Israel a scientific and technological potential out of all proportion to her small population, a potential that excels in the rare know-how of desert agriculture, with new methods of land irrigation and the sweetening of seawater. Shimon Peres, for years responsible for Israeli arms procurement, and whom I originally considered a hawk, sketched for me one day his breathtaking ambition to divert this potential from military uses to the development of peaceful goods and ideas for a prosperous common market spanning the entire region. This is what, he expounded, would give Israel the capacity, the means, for the in-gathering of the exiles — particularly the Russian Jews.

But what of the Russian Jews? Remembering the in-gathering at Auschwitz, Golda Meir rated their return to Israel as the highest priority, tied to the very purpose of the state.

The Gordian knot of Russian Jews and Soviet-American trade, to which my emotional outburst at Kiev and my pilgrimage to Babi Yar contributed, need never have been tied. The right to leave one's country has been basic to Western civilization, but not to the centralized Russian state, and under Stalin it became synonymous with treason. I was amazed when this prohibition was relaxed enough during the 1960s to permit even a trickle of Jewish emigration from Eastern Europe. That was a tribute to the policies of de-Stalinization and relaxation of international tensions that had begun under Chairman Khruschchev and President Eisenhower and continued, despite intervening crises — a mounting rebuttal to all those in the West who said that the Eastern countries could never change.

In the early 1970s, when contacts expanded across the East-West boundary, an atmosphere of receding tensions, effervescence, and dissent, of a kind not seen since the early years of the Bolshevik Revolution, was felt in Russia and other parts of the Soviet bloc.

It was unfortunate that these thin but promising developments in the East ran afoul of the Jackson-Vanik Amendment of 1974, which formally tied normalization of American commerce with Russia to freer emigration of Soviet Jews. I realize that the congressional architects of that measure acted out of the best humanitarian concerns. I know that, as a young officer, Senator Henry Jackson was one of the first Americans to see the Bergen-Belsen concentration camp, upon its liberation by the British; and no one understands better than I how such an experience can affect a man's attitudes in later years.

But, stung by what it perceived to be a humiliating interference in its internal affairs, the Kremlin decided to do without the commercial privileges enjoyed by our other trading partners; it abrogated the Soviet-American agreement that had been concluded in 1972. The immediate upshot had been less trade and less emigration.

As hopes for a new era of Soviet-American trade began to go sour under the combined weight of the congressional restrictions, President Carter's ineffectual scolding of the Soviets' record on human rights, and the seemingly irresistible temptation to play with the "China card," the trend toward more tolerant attitudes in Moscow was reversed. The spasm of resistance on our side provoked a corresponding spasm on theirs.

Throughout the ages, minority groups, Jews in particular, have been among the first victims of severe international tensions. It was only the relaxation of those tensions that permitted something like 200,000 Jews to depart from the Soviet Union, and a comparable number to leave Eastern Europe during the 1970s.

Thousands more are clamoring for visas to immigrate to Israel. I would, no doubt, be one of them today if, like my cousins, I had been deported to Siberia by the Russians instead of to Maidanek by the Germans; or if Ben and I had gone back to Bialystok after our liberation by the U.S. Army near Munich.

On occasions, I have intermingled with these people among whose number I could so easily have been counted. When Judith and I have been in Moscow, we would meet, whenever I could break away from my official rounds, with Russian Jews, underground artists, and nonconformist intellectuals. Sometimes these meetings would take place in a modest tenement apartment that contained an astonishing collection of early-twentieth-century Russian art. Chagalls, Malevitches, Kandinskis, Tatlins, Lissitzkys, and others hung cramped on walls and doors in the living room, bathroom, kitchen, and closets, all radiantly beautiful testimony to the optimism that kindled the avant-garde ideas in painting, literature, theater, and film of the new revolutionary state, before they were suppressed by Stalin's conservatism.

Georgii Kostakis, the world's most unlikely collector, made it his life's mission, under unbelievably difficult conditions, to rescue for posterity the best examples of these ideologically contaminated treasures. He would describe how, during the war, after Nazi bombardments had shattered the glass, some Moscovites would nail up their windows with paintings on wood or canvas, to keep out the snow and cold. For a loaf of bread or a piece of sausage, Kostakis would acquire whatever masterpieces his ardent heart and practiced eye could find.

In this eerie refuge, we would listen to recitals of dissident poetry and music and marvel at the eloquent evidence of survival and salvation that hung all around us. In these moving surroundings I would learn — often in Yiddish, a language that establishes instant trust among Jews, even if they had never met before and no matter how different their origins and beliefs — what life in Russia was really like, and why they wished to emigrate to Israel.

The contradictions between the rational and emotional aspects of the trade and emigration question, which I carry within me, came sharply into focus in the course of a dialogue I had with Senator Edward Kennedy, before a congressional committee. We had just returned from the Dartmouth Conference in Tbilisi (and from a surreptitious visit to Kostakis's clandestine museum).

SENATOR KENNEDY: Mr. Pisar, to what extent do you think that politics or ethics should govern our decisions on trade?

SAMUEL PISAR: Senator, your question raises difficult moral problems for me . . . including the issue of emigration. . . . Ever since my law school days it has been drummed into my head that no country can interfere in the internal affairs of another country. The United Nations charter enshrines this principle and our signature as a nation is on it. But the Soviet Union is also inviting our business community, our labor movement, our intellectuals and our minority groups to broadened intercourse. Our public opinion has its legitimate emotions and concerns and cold international law has no bearing on that. My own feelings, on the level of the human being rather than the lawyer, is that in approaching these problems we need more generosity from the Soviet side.

When I answered Senator Kennedy in this way, I was torn in two, my mind from my heart. My mind told me that nothing was more important to the solution of some of the world's most critical problems than a real expansion of U.S.-Soviet contacts, human and commercial. My heart ordered me to say nothing that could give comfort to those in the Soviet Union who were suppressing freedom and stopping Jews from immigrating to the land of their choice.

Again and again, I have wrestled with this dilemma; I concluded that the answer I gave the United States Congress, that time, was incomplete, that my heart had muffled the assertions of my mind.

More generosity from the Soviet side, to be sure, but also more humility from ours. Our well-intentioned trade pressures were not the best way to help ensure a real exodus of Russian Jews to Israel or to further the aspirations of other Russian dissidents; nor were they the best way to restrain the Soviet military. In regard to the Commercial Agreement of 1972, as in regard to the Salt II Agreement of 1979, we have constantly kept one foot on the accelerator and the other foot on the brake.

Western influence can play a liberalizing, restraining role only if it becomes a natural, untrumpeted aspect of working with an adversary for meaningful and mutual economic advantage. The evolving patterns of Jewish emigration in the early 1970s were a start in the right direction, compared with the hermetically sealed borders of the sinister Stalinist era. Nothing was more certain to seal these borders again than a return to the cold war.

16

I FINISHED my lecture and stepped down from the dais. The applause was pleasing, the comments flattering — but I felt discontented with myself.

Here I was at yet another international conference, like the ones in Kyoto, Abidjan, Rio de Janeiro. Only this time it was Stockholm. The auspices — the Nobel Foundation — could hardly have been worthier. The subject — Man, Resources, and the Future — could hardly have been more important. The participants — scientists, scholars, and policymakers gathered from around the world — could not have been more eminent. And the hospitality — of the Swedish Parliament and of King Karl Gustav — could not have been more regal.

But, as I sat in the baronial hall of Hasselby Castle, listening to one after another of those brilliant papers being read, a weariness with the drone of words settled on me like a dead weight.

How abstract all this was, how immaculately removed from the grim reality out of which all these problems grew. We were in a hall of gestures. The definitions were comprehensive, the reasoning was skillful, but the overall meaning seemed to be a ritual of intellectual exorcism. The seminar would end and, like countless others before it, would be preserved in verbatim records — like holy relics on a shelf. Once more, I blasphemed to myself, the conscience of the intellectual elite would feel relief. But in the far reaches of the world, where men grew hungrier and more desperate, or maybe closed their eyes in fear of what they might see, everything would go on as before.

And what about my own words? — as I elaborated on the idea that the problems we were addressing went beyond borders and ideology, which earned for me, from Prime Minister Olof Palme, the soubriquet of "post-national man" — were they any less ceremonial than the words of those who had spoken before me?

You have become like them, my mind said, while my lips read from the paper in my hand. You have adopted their language, this in-house idiom, careful to anticipate some academic objection, mindful of the latest fashion of mainstream thought. This will not move the rulers or the ruled. This will not jar either out of their ruts, force them into those new ways of looking at things that are the only hope of stopping the long slide into the dark. And this will not justify your survival.

I thought of Ben, of how his Bialystok directness of speech had sent a little pleasurable shiver across the mannered dinner table of the aristocrats at Authon, and I wondered just when it was that I had lost this same ability.

Something inside was preparing to rebel. Instead of using the same old code language, couldn't I summon the strength and courage to speak my mind, convey my anxiety about a future which hurled me thirty-five years into the past and made me feel in my joints, like rheumatism, the approach of evil times?

I wanted to resurrect that young buttonhole maker who was able to invent ideas and produce deeds that could drive away despair and triumph over death. I wanted to tell this gathering that life in the raw is nothing but a constant fight to endure, a continuous attempt to overcome danger, humiliation, suffering, and pain.

No, starvation cannot be reduced by conjuring up some facts and figures about the approaching grain shortage.

Yes, behind the problems of overpopulation, environmental pollution, energy shortages, and economic dislocation lurk harsh realities and deadly risks that conventional rhetoric does not even touch.

No. It would not do to disturb this conclave of well-meaning savants like that. But what other audience did I have?

And even if I — if all the good people gathered here — could find the way to lift our discourse to a level where our voices would be heard — would it do any good? So much had gone wrong, in the West as well as in the East, and throughout the Third World.

I recalled that high tide which our democracies had reached by the early 1960s. And now, American self-confidence? — cracked by the needless torments of Vietnam, corroded by the Arab oil embargo, broken by the erosion of the dollar — the rock on which all other plans had been built.

Remember Western Europe's faith in itself, in the Common Market, and in the Atlantic Alliance? — dampened by the American developments and by its own relapse into national bickering, wracked by inflation and unemployment and terrorism, worse even than America's.

And communism? — the communist regimes have not been able to cope with the energy crisis much better than the capitalist countries. They too — Russia, China, Eastern Europe — have been hit by inflation and recession. Now they must pay exorbitant prices for the goods and technology they wish to import, at a time when their raw material exports are decreasing, because of the economic slowdown in the West.

And what of the high-minded expectations of the young? — in country after country, their rebellions against despotism have only installed other despots. The nights of our youth became haunted by reigns of terror and brutality: specters such as Vietnam, just recently admired as "a proud and courageous little nation fighting against imperialism and colonialism," now cowed by an ugly militarism; and the immense human tragedy of Cambodia, where the remnants of a people were dying of starvation and disease, while the rest of the world, as some forty years earlier, stood idly by wringing its hands.

In the West the young turned to violence, or curdled into disillusion, or followed a vulgar careerism that took revenge on their old ideals. In the Soviet empire, youth was stifled by the panicky crackdown of a stale and sterile orthodoxy. In the Third World, they were helpless against a general ebb toward tyranny, stagnation, and strife.

To a degree unparalleled in modern times, the Western mood was to escape to private, even hedonistic, concerns. An occasional piece on the nuclear arms problem on the editorial page of the *New York Times;* an occasional television documentary on those regions of the world where the problem was not even oil, but a dearth of firewood to heat a shabby dwelling or cook a miserable meal, where the problem was not even inflation, but a lack of crops in sufficient amounts to prevent famine. But for most of us these things were too much to think about.

Someone has calculated that over fifteen million human beings starve to death every year. The projections for the next several decades are multiplied, manifold. And all the time we highbrows, at our conferences and seminars, measured out our ineffectualness in the elegant host cities all over the world.

❖❖❖

The events of the 1970s sufficed to destroy the fondest illusions of the industrialized world. In 1969, two men set foot on the moon for the first time. The extraordinary vitality and creativity of our civilization, the boundless possibilities of science and technology, mounted to our heads. For Western man, nothing was impossible. Four years later the oil embargo gave us a bitter demonstration of the fragility of our cherished way of life.

When I observed the industrial democracies scramble for the last drop of oil, I remembered the hopeless crush of half-crazed men fighting over my bottle of water, near the cattle cars at Maidanek; and how they got on their knees to lick the moist ground with their parched tongues.

And while economists and politicians everywhere tore out their hair over the industrial energy crisis, no one seemed to remember that the oil consumption of New York City alone was higher than that of the whole of India, with its 700 million people.

What state, however powerful, can hope to stand aside in splendid isolation from the challenges that assail the world as a whole? A host of planetary problems urgently requires collective planning and action for their solution. Yet national interests continue to diverge, while the once-vaunted international organizations continue to demonstrate their impotence in the absence of a common political will.

I went up and down the list:

The United Nations world conference on the population explosion, in Bucharest — *nothing accomplished*. Even as they sink more and more deeply into poverty, many nations still believe that they will gather in glory and strength in proportion to the size of their populations. Algeria's policymakers swear by the slogan "Nine million inhabitants in 1962; thirty million before the year 2000." At the Bombay airport an enormous poster reminds the startled arrival: "A populous nation is a strong nation."

The world conference on the environment, in Stockholm — *a virtual dead letter*. To compensate for the prohibitive cost of oil we hasten to build nuclear plants, despite the incalculable environmental risks involved. An energy crisis aggravated by waste and self-indulgence leaves us no other option. The blackouts that meant chaos in New York, in 1965 and 1977, are almost daily occurrences in Tehran and Cairo. The traffic jams that bring all cars to a halt in Tokyo's afternoon rush hour are matched a few hours earlier or later on the avenues of Casablanca and Buenos Aires.

Warsaw had been leveled to the ground. Hiroshima had been demolished by the bomb. London had been half-destroyed by air raids. Rotterdam, Dresden, and Budapest lay in ruins. Cities that might have been restored to decent social dimensions instead expanded everywhere into monsters of urban sprawl, congestion, and pollution.

The world conference on the economic development of poor countries, in Nairobi — a hundred solemn speeches about the transfer of know-how — *produced nothing*. The only commerce worth mentioning that flourishes with these countries is the exchange of their raw materials for fighter planes, tanks, and machine guns. Yet the equation, on the scale of a modern Marshall Plan, to draw vast segments of their populations out of misery exists: the advanced technology of America, Western Europe, and Japan; the immense capital resources of the oil-rich Arab states; and the vast, hungry markets of the Third World.

The world food conference in Rome — *a bitter failure*. Its resounding declaration that — by 1985 — no child would go to bed hungry, was a hollow echo of the League of Nations' declaration fifty years before: "The hungry child should be provided with food, the sick child should be provided with medical treatment." Between these two events over a million Jewish children had been exterminated in the gas chambers and medical experimentation barracks, including that handful of starving youngsters with whom I was interned at Auschwitz entrapped by a cynical allotment of white bread and milk. Millions of other children go on dying from malnutrition, year after year after year, while legislatures vote subsidies to farmers as an incentive not to plant surplus crops.

The world conference on the law of the sea, in Caracas — *an endless palaver* about the resources of the oceans as the common heritage of mankind. All attempts to reconcile the competing interests of those who have the necessary capital and technology to mine the seas, and those who have not, ended in failure.

The *Amoco Cadiz* ran aground off the coast of Brittany and poured 220,000 tons of crude oil into the seas, thereby confirming man's capacity for senseless destruction. The next oil plague will probably come from a 400,000-ton vessel, or, perhaps, as in the Gulf of Mexico disaster, from some one of the twenty thousand off-shore wells currently operating all over the world. Aside from the deadly problem of pollution, catastrophes such as these throw light once again on the legal stratagems that permit shipping magnates and oil companies to operate beyond the reach of every responsible international authority and every effective system of international law. A ship flying the Liberian flag, belonging to a Panamanian company, in turn owned by a Liechtenstein firm, whose stateless captain is remotely controlled out of an Athens or Oslo office, is not answerable to anyone.

The failures of political leadership, nationally and internationally, are matched by the moral bankruptcy of the United Nations. The recent resolutions at UNESCO and the U.N., defaming Israel and by implication the Jews, as racist, were for me a bitter symbol of that bankruptcy, and more than I could bear. The international organization, which had been the core of my professional life as a young lawyer, had perversely libeled me as racist, along with the people who had suffered more from racism than any other in the history of the world.

That brutal jolt caused me to search again for the meaning of my survival. It was more and more difficult to chase away the sad, gnawing thought that notwithstanding my aversion to nationalism, in a time of mounting danger to that people I had no right to espouse other causes, to concern myself with universal problems. Maybe there was no way to escape from the mentality of the ghettos and camps after all. Maybe I, too, had to retreat, like those who shout "Heil Stalin" or "Allah Akhbar," into the fundamentalist dogmas of my ancestors' faith. If we are not for ourselves, who will be for us?

The Church of Rome? She truly is a multinational force, but hadn't she likewise failed to use her spiritual authority to inculcate that modicum of moral solidarity needed for effective global action? Her diplomatically phrased encyclicals on thorny international issues have proved to be so many dead letters, like the elegant Latin in which they are written.

During World War II, Pope Pius XII had a moral duty, under the precepts of his own faith, to speak out through the powerful transmitters of the Vatican against the Nazi extermination of Europe's Jews. As apostolic ambassador to Berlin, before the white clouds of smoke from the chimney of the Sistine Chapel announced his election as the Vicar of God on Earth, he had known the truth. Where was the fiery encyclical that might have created a crisis of conscience among the Catholics in the German nation and the German army?

His Holiness was face to face with a challenge that history reserves only once every two thousand years: to pick up the cross on his back and to announce to the tortured skeletons behind the barbed-wire fences: "I'm coming to join you; my place in this world is with you." That challenge he failed to meet, as he maintained a deafening diplomatic silence, the silence of a Pope of indifference.

Now, John Paul II comes from a country on whose living body was inflicted the wound of Auschwitz. He was born and brought up in the vicinity of that wound, and his accession to the throne of Saint Peter was not unrelated to his origins. That he felt the weight of this relationship became clear when he made the heritage of Auschwitz the opening theme of his speech before the United Nations in New York, and when he led the immense crowds on his pilgrimage to the site of the death camp in 1979, calling it the Golgotha of the modern world.

Although I am not of his parish, the knowledge of what he has seen and felt in his youth, albeit from the other side of the barbed wire, gives me hope that he will draw on moral courage, and not mere diplomatic skill, to help develop a global consciousness in a world that is careening toward catastrophe.

❖ ❖ ❖

For centuries the West has dominated a passive world with hardly a trace of guilt. Those days of grace seem to be over. Communism, Islam, and the Third World are rejecting its civilization as the heritage of the rich.

The high moral values that were taken for granted in the relative comfort of recent times, and proposed as a model for more "backward" societies, were products of myopia. For in an environment where countless people are still deprived of the right to work, the right to health, the right to education, and even the right to food, these values do not have the same priority. Those who lack the basic necessities of life are ready to give up their freedom and their civil rights for a crust of bread if this will help them prolong their wretched existence by one more day. That is a naked truth, which I saw with my own eyes.

Destitute, hungry, angry, armed millions, driven by nationalistic or religious fervor and supported by new centers of financial and political power, are asserting sovereignty over the natural wealth in their soil and claiming their just place in the sun. They are beginning to learn, to compare, to invent, to vibrate, to build, and to change all of our previously held assumptions about what we should think and how we should react. We of the advanced Western world have only begun to grasp the implications of all this.

On their current trajectory, our economies are destined to decline, one after another.

Many industries are already beginning to emigrate from Europe, leaving the jobless behind. Understandably, they prefer locations where raw materials are more plentiful, where labor is cheaper and more disciplined, where capital is more readily available, and where the political climate is more stable and propitious.

Under pressure to balance their foreign trade accounts, the industrial democracies will sell turnkey factories to any purchaser able to pay for them in cash or raw materials. These factories will manufacture the products we traditionally export. In time, they will flood our own markets with their considerably cheaper manufactures. And yet, this self-destruction of our industrial establishment is something we cannot prevent. For if one country should refuse to make the sales, another will do so in its place, in hope of alleviating unemployment, even if its future stands to be mortgaged as a result.

The chaotic forces that have swept through the international economy have found a powerful stimulant in the destabilization of currencies. Hundreds of billions of Euro-dollars, Petro-dollars, and other exotic units of account are sloshing around the world, without supervision or control. The major Arab oil producers, unable to find secure, long-term investments, increasingly prefer to keep their wealth — the lifeblood of our industries — in the ground. They feel, understandably, that their children will not forgive them for converting that wealth into worthless paper currencies, like the millions I saw stacked on my father's card table in prewar Bialystok.

These currencies are in turn manipulated by a new breed of speculators whose motives are questioned in too simplistic a way. They are for the most part managers who must anticipate capital market fluctuations, even to the extent of seeking refuge in the barbarous relic of gold, to balance their exposures; otherwise, staggering losses could force their enterprises to fold.

The accumulating debts of the developing countries are also reaching alarming proportions. If some of these countries should publicly declare their inability to repay these debts, an inability which, in many instances, already is an established fact, the entire Western banking system would threaten to collapse.

It is not true, as some assert, that the newly industrialized regions of the world, with their massive populations, are engaged in an economic assault on the hitherto prosperous nations. Those who say so have lost sight of the real problems and have abdicated all possibility of overcoming them. The "aggression" of such countries is little more than a competitive challenge launched in accordance with the rules of a game we ourselves designed; it is only that the "aggressors" today are better at this game than we are.

This time the industrial democracies will be unable to retreat behind protective tariff walls. For the simple truth is that they need the world market more than the world market needs them. To forget that our surplus export earnings enable us to maintain jobs that would otherwise disappear is to prepare for hara-kiri.

The only true defense to the growing competition of other continents is a constant process of adaptation and innovation. At the economic level, this calls for a continuous renewal of our science-based industries, our systems of management, production, and marketing; for a realization that henceforth our human activities must move away from traditional physical types of work, toward endeavors that are the creative fruit of the mind. At the political level it requires a degree of cohesion within our societies to ensure the more equitable sharing — of wealth, which will dwindle, but also of austerity, which will spread. At the human level, it implies a readiness to do without certain creature comforts, a readiness to allow the natural thermostat in the human body to compensate, as it is meant to do, for temperatures in homes and offices that are a few degrees lower in winter and higher in summer, in order to avert dependence on foreign suppliers and possible disaster on the vital energy front. At all levels it entails an ability to perceive danger in time and a will to act upon it before, and not after, the Pearl Harbors of history are upon us.

Our real enemy is the inability to recognize that life is not an uninterrupted feast, but a permanent, painful, precarious struggle for survival. It is the inability to discard the conventional wisdoms derived from a world that exists no longer. It is the inability to develop a common will to deal with an overwhelming combination of problems that are at once local and global and that affect all countries almost indiscriminately. This enemy, whom I learned to recognize early in life, dwells within us.

Survival in the economic arena can no longer be won by force of arms. Let us deny the newcomers from other continents a fairer share of the world's wealth, and we transform them into a hostile and dangerous horde. The only alternative then would be to submit to their domination or destroy them, possibly in accordance with the methods pioneered by Hitler.

There are still some people who think that it was Roosevelt and Churchill who undermined the Western world. By destroying the Third Reich, with its ideology of Aryan superiority, they brought upon the white race all the woes of decolonization. There are others who maintain that peace is not always an ideal state of affairs, that the history of the world has been, and must continue to be, a history of wars.

Those who continue to believe that Western society, the so-called highest form of civilization, is immune from a relapse into this type of mentality and morality have a terminally short memory. When they denounce Marshal Idi Amin Dada's cruelty to hostages in Entebbe and Emperor Bokassa's execution of schoolchildren in Bangui as the lowest form of barbarity, they are using a double yardstick. In the world I knew, these two heads of state would have made only average SS guards and kapos, no more than that. Their ideas and practices have their sources in the proud history of Europe. The death camps were not the creation of some backward tribe run amok. On the contrary, they were a calculated, cold-blooded invention, in the midst of the twentieth century, by one of the crown jewels of Western culture, after it had been overwhelmed by galloping and dire economic and political events.

The shrinking democratic world — Western Europe in first place — is threatened today with the kind of economic collapse that, five decades ago, demolished the Weimar Republic to the sound of goose-stepping boots. A few years later all the unmanageable problems were solved by the Nazis through rearmament, mobilization, the deportation of dissidents to concentration camps, and, in the end, the wholesale annihilation of human beings. It is such dangers, no less than the more visible danger of the Red Army, that we must avert at all cost.

We live for the first time in an age where the crises are almost too numerous to count and where the means exist to demolish the entire planet. But it is not the first time that humanity has been called upon to stand up to the forces of the unknown and the absurd. If man has survived until now, it is only because of his intelligence, his courage, and his effort.

One of the most salient lessons I have brought out of the jungle that waited for me at the end of my cattle-train journey from home is that a human being has a surprising, an infinite, capacity to endure and to invent, even in the most unimaginable conditions, provided he has the will. Neither hunger nor pain, neither horror nor fear has ever shaken me in this belief.

The first precondition of survival in the face of deathly peril is clarity of mind. To avert a holocaust on a universal scale, an awareness is urgently needed that mankind has entered a new historic phase — the dangers it faces in common henceforth eclipse the differences that still divide it: the national chauvinism, religious fanaticism, racial prejudice, and ideological dogmas that cause man to confront man and rob him of his ability to face the challenge of his survival.

My life experience, both personal and professional, informs me that nothing constructive can be undertaken on a global level unless the way is found to defuse the fundamental and unmitigated hostility between East and West, a hostility that exacerbates tensions everywhere and plunges us ever more deeply into a spiraling vortex of armed confrontation, political terrorism, social anarchy, and economic warfare with the diabolical new weapons of oil, grain, and money.

The opposite poles of the East-West struggle — America and Russia — recognizably have fears that the other can allay, needs that the other can satisfy. Each is faced with global hazards that it can, alone, neither overcome nor control. Both are paralyzed by costly and sterile geopolitical war games — they have managed to strike a precarious balance of power which is rapidly becoming a balance of impotence — while the rest of the world disintegrates into a turbulent free-for-all.

Despite its gigantic military might, the Soviet Union is shot through with weaknesses: the restiveness of its manifold ethnic groups, the unreliability of its East European allies, the exposure of its unpopulated Siberian flank to China, the abysmal failure of its agriculture, the backwardness of its nonmilitary industry and technology, the discontent of its consumers, the effervescence of its intellectuals, the dead hand of its bureaucracy that everywhere stifles creativity. Finally, most of its energies are funneled into one sterile goal: countering America in the name of a moribund ideology.

The tragedy of how America — the dominant military and economic power of this century — became reduced to virtual impotence in the space of two decades is even more difficult to comprehend. I recall standing in front of the Capitol on that wintery day in January 1961, listening to the words of John F. Kennedy's inaugural address, entranced by a thousand emotions, visited with a thousand hopes. Here was a young and vigorous new leader, symbol of a rising generation, who would dismiss the old guard along with their taboos, one who would stimulate new energies and talents. Here was an America whose greatness lay in its unique capacity to invent and assimilate change, that distant and aloof symbol of strength and justice that could make each individual feel personally responsible for his own and his country's fate; that America seemed intact. Then, before my bewildered eyes, paraded the adventure of the Bay of Pigs, the quagmire of Indochina, and the entrenched bureaucratic resistance to every innovative policy. The tragic assassination left no time to correct the course. And a new succession of presidents postured as emperors, at a time when the nation needed shepherds.

Despite appearances, America and Russia have a paradoxical affinity for one another. I see this as an affinity of scale. The United

States and the Soviet Union are not ordinary countries. They are continents. Each has a population approaching 250 million people, enormous material resources, a diversity of climates, endless sea coasts, mighty rivers. Each is revolutionary in origin, federal in structure, varied in ethnicity.

For the Soviet Union today the main challenge is how to develop an efficient system of mass production and mass distribution capable of feeding and clothing a vast, long-suffering population, spread over the expanse of a continent. The United States has shown how this challenge can be met. At this point in time, America's historic achievement has never been more relevant to Russia's historic need.

What I commend is not a means of subverting, or converting one society to the ways of the other — it is far too late for that — but rather a rational equation for coexistence and cooperation to steady an increasingly chaotic world tottering at the edge of the nuclear abyss.

As these dangers to our world pressed heavily against my heart and mind, my personal instinct for survival, having served me so well in the past, began to reassert itself. Blood and hope, I thought.

And at precisely the same moment a large part of me, of my past, vanished forever.

Ben is no more. . . .

When Judith phoned me at my New York office, stumbling over words, about a call from Melbourne that Ben was seriously ill, I had an immediate premonition that something irreversible had happened. She was preparing me for the shock, because she knew that he was the last.

The thought that one day I will die has left me fairly indifferent. I have been too long in intimate contact with death to be afraid. What I have never been able to accept without outrage is the relentless departure, one by one, of those who have been dear to me.

My father embraced me one morning and never came back.

My mother, clasping the hand of my little sister, walked off forever into the distance.

My uncle Nachman died quietly in my arms before I even had an opportunity to resume the awkward conversation about the fate of our family which we had begun in Singapore.

Niko was snatched away as soon as I had found him again, after a separation of ten long years.

And now Ben, my last brother, my last milestone, Ben who had tried to bring me back to myself from the great, wide world of success, by poking his finger into my chest and admonishing me with stern authority: "Don't forget that the past is the most important thing that lives within you."

Ben, like Niko, like Nachman, had succumbed to a massive heart attack at the age of forty-eight.

I caught the next plane west. Thirty-six hours of flight. Endless stopovers: Atlanta, San Francisco, Honolulu, Fiji, Sydney, Melbourne. I knew that this voyage to Australia marked another turning point in my life, like the first one thirty years earlier.

Then, I had turned my back on Landsberg, Paris, and Europe and waited for Ben and Niko to follow me. This time, the circle was complete. With them I had learned to survive; and now they survived only as memories in the mind of a man who himself was almost forty-eight years old, a man who had the feeling that he had lived a thousand years, and yet that everything still remained to be done, or at least to be tried.

From the airport I drove to the cemetery. Bebka, his widow, Molly and Paul, his children, were waiting, surrounded by friends and acquaintances who had come to bury Ben, and who knew that Ben could not be buried without Mula.

I looked at the faces, all immigrants or children of immigrants, mostly from Bialystok. They had patiently rebuilt new lives for themselves in a warm and welcoming land. In their hearts was the unbearable pain of the last *shalom* to a survivor, a survivor who had already died six million times with his brothers and sisters in Treblinka, in Maidanek, in Auschwitz.

Ties of blood bound me to him; the blood of the Holocaust, the blood of hope.

When I went hungry, he went hungry. When I was beaten, he felt the pain on his own skin. When we escaped from our hangmen, it was side by side in the same hail of bullets. When we rummaged in the ashes of Europe, it was together. When we discovered again, on this new continent, that life had a meaning, it was still together.

How could I have believed that we were immortal, and that one day, in old age, we would sit in armchairs on a peaceful veranda and relive all that had happened since the day we found each other, with shaved heads and sunken eyes, in the pit of hell? Now I know that this was not meant to be.

I came from the other end of the world to bury him. And as I threw the first shovel of earth upon his coffin, I knew that I was burying part of myself. The part that remains is that which is left for me to do in this world. I have only a vague idea of what that might be, but I know that it is linked to the mission with which my mother entrusted me when she gave me life for a second time, before going off to die. I know that it is linked to the sacred command that millions of martyrs have left to the few who survived — *Never Again*.

This command inhabits me today. It is the command to do whatever I can in the struggle for a victory of hope over hate, destruction, and death, forces that can yet again, if it does not take care, drive mankind to madness.

To you, Ben, I say that the hope which has been nurtured in our blood — your hope — lives on; as does the hope of all those who, out of respect for freedom and life, despise all crusaders, all fanatics, all tyrants, all the phony citadels of indifference and power.

I will express that hope to the world. I will express what we have experienced in our bodies and in our souls: our testament, yours, Niko's, and mine: that man can overcome, if he has the courage not to despair, the courage to confront his fate.

Ben, I will light a candle in the darkness; I am going back to work.

Judith and me at Auschwitz with Giscard d'Estaing and Gierek

Epilogue
Survival

Tell me, Son: Who will change man, who will save him from himself? Tell me, Son: Who will speak on his behalf?

— Elie Wiesel

ONE peaceful summer day history sucked me into its whirlpool and spun me out in bits and pieces far, far away from my native roots. Since then I have lived and thrived in unlikely places and unlikely cultures. When I think back to my childhood, to the anonymous corpse condemned to being worked till exhaustion and then destroyed, I sometimes feel that it belongs to another.

No one seeing me today would have reason to guess my past — lawyer, author, counsellor in the worlds of government and business — I show no visible scars, physical or psychological, of what I have gone through. I am attentive to my family, considerate toward my friends, and effective for my clients. My voice is measured, my suits are well cut, and my manners reflect ease and moderation in the well-appointed universe through which I now move.

All this is on the surface. Within me you will find little resemblance to the conventional man of affairs.

That I managed to elude the cruel monsters and violent events that laid waste to so many millions of others like me, that I have had to measure myself against the extremes of anguish, hunger, disease, and death itself, has simplified my life: things that often burden my acquaintances with worries and complications seem to me much less tragic.

When my mother pushed me away into a brutal adult world, hoping to give me a chance to live, I grasped at that chance. In time, I came to interpret her gift as embodying a sacred trust — to live out my own life and to try to give meaning to the lives of the others who had been so mercilessly cut down.

After the war, even during my initial spate of reckless freedom amid the ashes of Europe, I sensed that my first duty was to serve as a transplant of living tissue between a family that had been virtually wiped out and those still-living branches, scattered over the earth, branches that irresistibly reached out to me, with love and warmth, as part of a process of renewal that has helped my people to survive since the time of Moses.

There really was no doubt about the path I had to take: the long, difficult journey to physical and spiritual rebirth. How else could I undo the mayhem that had been perpetrated upon my kin?

I never felt the least desire to burn down the world in anger and protest over my fate, or to lament publicly for the dead. On the contrary, as one of the few who escaped among so many who perished, I felt impelled to take my place in civilized human society and contribute what I could to the cause of justice and peace, lest the horrors I witnessed revisit our world in some new, unpredictable form.

Wisdom argued that I would do better not to stir up the passions and agonies of the past, once I had gained the satisfactions of a full and creative life. For years, I respected this wisdom, telling myself that I had earned my share of happiness and security, like anyone else, perhaps even a little more.

As I progressed with my studies, made contact with philosophy, literature, and art, and developed into an educated and thoughtful man, I came to believe that the ink of the scholar teaches more than the blood of the martyr. As I write this book, I am no longer so sure.

Today I feel that the instincts and intuitions of a Ben, a Niko, and a Mula, making their way through the inhuman bondage of Auschwitz and the postwar anarchy of Landsberg, offer more valuable insight into the present world than all the learning of the sophisticated, well-adjusted, modern man I have become — the survivor of the survivors.

The gratuitous retelling of the gruesome events of my youth has never appealed to me. Neither do I believe in the value of personal memoirs as a guide for others. But when I think back to the days during which a combination of slogans and bombs tore apart my happy childhood, when I see mankind heading once again toward some hideous collective folly, I feel that I must either lapse into total silence or broadcast to the world my urgent sense of the horrors that threaten to destroy our own and our children's future.

This is why I decided to decipher and transmit some of the lessons that lay concealed in the torrents of blood and hope that had flooded my life. I wanted to convey to as many as I could how, not so long ago, a proud civilization had collapsed physically and morally, before my very eyes — the eyes of a child — and had left behind only cruelty, suffering, and destruction. I wanted to tell it in the raw, which was the way I had lived it and felt it and thought about it; to convey everything that came to preoccupy me later, as reality upon reality imprinted itself on my flesh and on my mind, and made me what I am, and what I think and feel today, and what I see ahead.

I wanted to shed the elegant style of the orator at some important international convention, I wanted to drop the learned jargon of the expert expounding on legal, economic, or political subjects of his competence, embroidered with the science and knowledge of the world's finest thinkers.

If my warning was to be heard, I had to find my own voice, not the voice of Melbourne and Harvard and the Sorbonne, not the voice of Washington and London and Paris, but the voice that Ben feared I had lost when I sank new roots in social environments where nothing is ever straightforward, where the rules of good conduct require that everything be said in muted, sterilized tones, where the dialogue is usually far from the innermost currents of one's emotional life. For even if the diverse identities that had been foisted upon me as I touched the depths and the heights of human experience did not divide my soul, I realized that I had blended far too well, from too many origins, into the cultivated worlds of refined British gentlemen, witty French aristocrats, and dynamic American businessmen and politicians. I had left the subhuman of Bialystok and Maidanek way too far behind.

As I thought about recovering that inner voice, I wondered: Would it be like the scream of the sixteen-year-old convict seeing for the first time the white star of freedom? Or, like the scream of the Russian prisoner of war who refused to submit to his fate on the gallows? Or, like the scream of the small boy in front of the long cattle train, who, in all his outraged innocence, dared to raise his fist to heaven and curse God?

If I was to be heard, I had to do one other thing that Ben had asked of me before he left this earth: to stop, and think, and reexamine myself.

I had to stop and think and tell — tell our story to whoever would listen, like a beggar with an outstretched bowl, asking for the coin of attention under an impassive sky. I had to tell it, not worrying about what it exposed or how well it fit into the scheme of my present life, hoping that when my tale was done it would mean something to the lives of those who read it. Hoping also that it would clear up, for me, some truths which I needed to absorb more fully, if the miracle of my salvation was to continue to ripen within me.

When I say that we are constructing a global Auschwitz of the future, I am aware it is a metaphor. I do not fear a repetition of the mass murder practiced by Hitler against the Jews and other "inferior" peoples. Nor do I necessarily foresee a thermonuclear holocaust that would inevitably incinerate our planet.

The demons that preoccupy me are more immediate, more concrete. They are the anxious edge in people's voices when they speak about the security of their jobs, the erosion of their savings, and the tensions that build in the neighborhood gasoline lines. They are the tragedies reflected in the daily press: the carnage in Cambodia, the unrest in Colombia, the terrorism in Ireland, the rioting in Iran that fans the flames of Islam. They are the deliberate destruction of international law, the seesawing between détente and cold war, the clamor for more arms, the deployment of navies, missiles and tanks, the despair of fleeing refugees. They are the helplessness of politicians in face of disorder, the spreading lack of confidence in the ability of democratic institutions to cope, as things slide from bad to worse.

As I think about the relentless accumulation of calamities, what I fear most is that the same blindness and indifference and abdication of responsibility that brought about the collapse of my parents' world will overtake us once again, in some unintended, unpredictable way. For the death camps were not only the symbols of a brutal war, but also of a slow capitulation of freedom before tyranny, and of a long calvary that followed.

More and more I am pursued by the vision that gripped me when I revisited Auschwitz, shortly after the Yom Kippur War and the Arab oil embargo that demonstrated with such unexpected and dramatic force the economic and political vulnerability of our democracies.

Standing with one foot in that other world and one foot in this, I saw before me rows of victims in striped rags and wooden clogs, lined up at attention at roll call, with their caps off, to be tattooed, counted, selected, and rendered harmless. I saw them as the scapegoats for every age, whenever demagogic leaders had need for alibis to explain away their failures, or to hold on to their power: Jews in front, as always; then the others — religious minorities, racial groups, political dissidents, unionists, intellectuals, artists, all those who think differently, all those who refuse to "follow the leader" blindly and automatically.

For me this vision is not fantasy. I have seen it in real life, in my own past. I know that it exists in certain places today and I believe it to be the natural order of things to come when chaos, fear, impotence, terror, and finally madness, take over.

The contemporary symptoms of danger are all the more palpable because the burning problems of today are not really comparable with those of forty years ago. If our political decision-makers allow themselves to be guided too literally by the experiences of the past, they will commit irrevocable errors.

In the Europe of the 1930s, the principal dangers were clear. An identifiably evil enemy was seeking to subjugate the civilized world. The sense of purpose, the steps that had to be taken to counter that enemy were also clear. The first thing that was needed was courage to stand up and resist, and to do so in time.

Today, the dangers are of a different order — more complicated, more universal, more widespread. Courage in the face of the "enemy" has become a much subtler ingredient, because we can no longer threaten to eliminate a hostile power without, at the same time, threatening to eliminate ourselves. Moreover, the enemies are manifold; they are everywhere and nowhere; they are difficult to locate, difficult to resist, and difficult to contain.

The brutal events that have ushered in this perilous decade point to an unprecedented pattern of crisis after crisis in the years immediately ahead. How we come out of these crises may well determine whether our children and grandchildren will live free or as slaves as we reach the shores of the third millennium.

Before the war, when my mother prayed for our deliverance, she would sigh, "God bless America"; she was expressing an instinctive conviction that even were Europe to collapse, it would be saved by the United States. It turned out to be a well-founded conviction, and I am its living proof. For America was indeed a powerful, generous nation, ready and able to crush the enemies of freedom, wherever they raised their heads.

It was a similar conviction that brought to my office not so long ago the tormented European gentleman who hoped that I could obtain for him and his family a visa to enter the United States "in the event that . . ." For generations of threatened and frightened humanity, America was the symbol of the last ship, the last refuge, the protector of last resort.

The tall, helmeted black, who crossed an ocean and fought his way over half a continent to pull a skeletal kid through the hatch of his tank into the womb of freedom, has neither the will nor the means to do it again. Twice in this century America sent her youth to Europe and thrice to Asia, to make the earth safe for democracy. Today, America can no longer be counted on to save the confused, angry, fratricidal world outside; America is bleeding from deep wounds herself.

The powerful, wealthy United States, whose human courage and generosity seemed to have no limits, whose social, economic, and political institutions had radiated confidence and stability worldwide, is adrift, it is beset, like most other nations, by tremendous internal problems — inflation, unemployment, a humiliatingly weak currency, bankruptcy and violence in its cities.

The America that was guardian to all mankind, ready to help others with a Marshall Plan in time of peace, with a Lend Lease program in time of war, with the blood of its own sons to protect the liberty of others; the America that saved me, adopted me, educated me, and gave me my chance to climb some of the summits of this earth; the America that, once it made up its mind, could do anything, even put man on the moon, is now engulfed by its own self-doubts.

How many peoples continue to call in the darkness: "America, are you still there? America, are you still there . . . ?" A United States that is not healthy in its own fiber, that cannot live up to its moral commitments, leaves an orphaned world unprotected and exposed to camps and to gulags.

We stand at the threshold of a chaotic, turbulent world, which no single power can any longer control economically or politically or militarily, a world in which one crisis piles upon another, like so many ticking bombs. Americans, who have never had a foreign enemy trample their soil, who have never experienced the cruelty of despotism, for whom austerity, scarcity, rationing are words that spell heresy, have no perception what such a world can be like; and woe to the statesman who, for the sake of an election, dissimulates this truth, for he may bring on another collapse, this time without redemption.

On its present course, the world that awaits us is one in which freedom and prosperity will be rare, coveted, fleeing luxuries. It is a world not equipped to accommodate the explosive growth of population; a world where energy, raw materials, and food production will not meet rising demand, where fathers and sons will steal the bread from each other's mouths, where individuals, and peoples, will have to struggle not to become Musulmen, marked for triage by the cold and impersonal criteria of economic selection, where the few remaining democratic countries will be children without mothers, where conventional politicians faced with overpowering problems will look like boys in ill-fitting long pants, where the busiest industries may be those that produce barbed wire, where the friendship of a Ben or a Niko, of an ally, small or big, who shares the same values and interests, will be an irreplaceable source of strength.

I know that sort of world and I think I know what it takes to be redeemed from it. I stood at its gaping doors, and learned, never to forget, that as long as we have not entered the gas chamber, we will have a chance to reinvent a future worthy of free men.

The effort must begin first and foremost with a decision to awaken the instinctive, passionate, animal will to survive — the will that has always been fundamental to life, the will to face the unknown, but which our elitist, aimless, and protective society have almost lost in the relatively short period of their ascendancy. It must begin with a determination to shed all the clichés, all the habits that, appropriate for other times, now hamstring our movements; it can only begin when we develop new muscles to release the powers of ingenuity and creativity necessary for our survival, just as my comrades and I had to invent the know-how of our survival with every fiber of our beings, every single day and every single night.

The struggle for survival cannot be delegated to this or that providential leader. It can no more be left to a political platform or an economic program or diplomatic doctrine than to the expectation of a miracle; that is the road to bondage.

The struggle for survival in freedom must begin with oneself.

It takes a total effort to make every cell, every organism, work creatively to full capacity, in every home, every village, every town, every region; to make the body of a nation function to a common purpose. It takes a state of mind where the government is perceived neither as a magnanimous Santa Claus nor as an armed sentry on the other side of a barbed-wire fence. It takes an ability to understand the tragic and hypocritical and unpredictable dimension of history, to grasp and act upon appearances of mortal danger, however they may be disguised, before one smells the sulfur of exploding bombs or the stench of burning flesh.

It takes an attitude where the mind knows what it wants so it will not gyrate between passivity and overreaction, where every ounce of energy is conserved, not squandered; it takes an immunity to both euphoria and panic; an adaptability in which one is prepared to work as a buttonhole maker and a scholar, to sell prime technology and barter secondhand coffee; a condition whereby every person is eager to learn to fish for himself.

It requires the readiness to get down on one's knees and scrape the floor with one's nails in order to elude the despots who would march you off to oblivion. It requires a degree of social harmony necessary to assure that the miserable piece of gray bread is divided up fairly.

The return to a world of stability and security must begin at the very roots, with faith in the intelligence of man rather than in the dogmas of a party, a church, or a state; rules prescribed by an allegedly infallible authority give way under the first shock of brutality.

We must begin with the establishment of a new kind of relationship between generations, based on reason and respect, not hierarchy; on a realistic, unsentimental assessment of changing, volatile times, rather than on the naïve wish to package ready-made lives for our children; a relationship based on the premise that the young can be entrusted with the responsibility of determining which inherited values to adhere to and which to reject, what flags to salute, whom to consider as a rival and whom as a friend. A relationship, in short, that places the same confidence in young people, when it is time to live and create, as their elders have placed in them when it was time to destroy and die, on the glorious battlefields of history. For a society that cannot conjugate the passion and enthusiasm of its youth with the experience and responsibility of its decision-makers is a society that must go down.

Before the Soviets and the Nazis overran my hometown I was a boy like all the others at my school; I learned the same things and played the same games. Had the cataclysm, which altered the course of history and warped my personal destiny, been prevented, I would, almost surely, be leading a normal, uneventful existence today among my own people, in the kind of world which Isaac Bashevis Singer has so vividly described, and which Hitler and Stalin so thoroughly destroyed.

In a way I was lucky that I had to fight so early my duel with fate. It forced me to develop to the fullest such physical and mental attributes as I had, to use to the utmost my limbs, my lungs, my nerves, my brains; to make my own choices, my own decisions, to leave nothing to chance, to find within me resources I would not have dreamed I possessed.

The lessons I have culled from the crucible of real life, whatever I know about the undoing of nations and the triumph of man, teach me that as long as hope pulsates within us like blood, redemption is possible, like survival itself, for a society, for a people, for an individual, even for a child, even without parents, without means, without education, without health, even in conditions that stagger the mind.

The weak flicker of life that the manchild managed to preserve amid the infernos of this century has grown into a flame that is no longer threatened with extinction. New and happy lives are now gathered around that flame, and resurrect for me, every day, the loved ones who stood with me around the fire my father lit in our family home for the last time — a time so very far away and yet so very near.